Spirit Scopes

Spirit Scopes

Messages For First Names

Lahna Harris

Moonlight Dove Publishing
Clarksville, Indiana
2019

Messages from Spirit speak of:
Individual life purpose
Life gifts to share
and Life lessons
Whatever *your* message, it is life affirming!

Harris, Lahna
Spirit Scopes: Messages for First Names

ISBN: 978-0-578-44134-4

Cover Design:
    Sybil Watts / NewSoft Publishing
Interior Book Design:
    Sybil Watts / NewSoft Publishing
Interior graphics:
    Sybil Watts / NewSoft Publishing

Moonlight Dove Publishing
Clarksville, Indiana

Dedication

How can I make this divinely inspired book available in print without expressing my heart-felt and soul-felt gratitude for the gifts bestowed to me by Spirit?

I want to extend my thanks to God (Creator of the All That Is), Jesus (my master guide), and the Blessed Mother Mary, who is with me at all times. I am so deeply blessed for their love, guidance and protection. This book is dedicated to them, along with all of my other precious angels and guides.

In addition, my gratitude to all the angels and guides who speak for those who request private sessions and for whom I receive individual messages. Thank you for choosing me to be one of your messengers .... to listen and to assist others through your loving words.

Table of Contents

Acknowledgments

My appreciation and love is extended to every member of my spiritual family who has graced me with encouragement... often in ways mostly unaware by them. That's the way friends and family are: helpful and uplifting with no effort or planning.

I would especially like to mention Beverly and Jim McChesney, Cindy and Michael Fess, Robbie Stone, and Phyllis Vaught-Reynolds, for their unconditional love and support. A heart-felt thanks also, to Sybil Watts, for her patience and expertise as my publishing mentor. You each are so good at allowing spirit to speak and act through you, without question and with generosity of time and talent. I am fortunate to be on the receiving end of your light.

Finally, to John Rieber. Thank you for teaching me how to live from a space of love and to abandon fear. I am eternally grateful for the time and the love we had together.

Introduction

A Note from Lahna

First, please know that I did not *actually* write this book. What has happened is that I have been richly blessed with the privilege of representing Spirit through written messages. Here is how **Spirit Scopes** manifested into being:

When Spirit first spoke to me about writing (channeling) messages for first names, I thought it surely must be my own subconscious thinking. After all, I've noticed over the years that—strangely—people with certain first names often seem to share some of the same personality traits. That thought was quickly followed by Spirit speaking right back: "This has nothing to do with your perceptions or analyses...please write the book." So ... I didn't. Not at first. However, I kept being nudged despite my resistance and contemplation about whether anyone would have any interest whatsoever in reading such a book. It seemed like a generic horoscope about names. Who would want to read it? What kind of a wild notion might this be?

The resistance was not to be successful. Early one morning, I woke up with a first name being given to me, followed immediately with a message for that name. Thus, the first message was written. As soon as the last word hit the paper, another came, and another until there were around five or six messages in a short period of time. This was exciting! It was then, of course, that I knew in no uncertain terms that this book had to be written. Well, at least *for that moment*, I knew.

Throughout the first few months of receiving and writing, my doubt about the validity of this work crept in again and again. The response to every moment of doubt was a gentle rebuttal in the form of yet more messages to write.

I had some lingering questions, and the answers were soon disclosed:

"Why does this, at times, sound like my own writing style?"

It was revealed that words come to and through me in a way that messages can be properly ascertained by me, and therefore written.

"There are so many names that could be included. How many will be addressed, and why these certain names?"

The response was that whatever names are included does not indicate these names are more special than the host of other names. They are simply the ones which reached me for now. In fact, when I thought the book was complete, I began to receive more names. Since that time, what began as what I believed to be a book of messages for approximately 200 names evolved into messages for over 700 names.

It should be noted that many first names have shared messages. It is for those intended, yet in some way, this book will bless all who read it. You will notice this as you browse the book for yourself, and for relatives, friends, and associates. When I read the book after it was complete, I found it interesting that many of the shared messages were within the same letter of the alphabet. It is intriguing, because they were not received in any type of order whatsoever. Spirit also showed me over and over again that I was not in charge of the messages. There were too many instances for me to believe anything else. It was obvious, yet astounding, that the direction was through divine guidance. To describe these experiences would encompass another book. Suffice to say, it was an exhilarating and awe-inspiring experience.

In addition, I was told that other messengers are chosen to provide messages for those in other countries and from other cultures. **Also, not every person with a name included in this book will relate. It is for those intended, yet in some way, this book will bless all who read it.** They will know others with whom they can share the messages, and they may better understand their friends and relatives described by the messages.

Finally, Spirit displayed the sense of humor that is so frequently present when I receive messages for individuals who have one-on-one sessions with me. The light-hearted manner in which I described the book to a few select friends—being like a generic horoscope for names—was actually Spirit's way of revealing the title. Yes, I should have known the title would be provided. Yes. *Spirit Scopes*. It was there all along.

It is with a deep sense of honor, humility, gladness, and awe that this book is shared with you. My hope is that you, and anyone with whom you share it, will be richly blessed by the messages.

Messages For First Names

A

AARON

Stones will not break you—they will only help to build up your foundation and add to the solid fortress called your soul. Dismiss, then, all the rocks hurled at you as being damaging. Instead see them as building blocks to construct your true character of being the Guardian of both yourself and anyone along the way who has the need for armor to fend against the world's arrows. Your task is gallant. Your purpose is defined. You are guided and shielded as you continue to build your fortress and to house those in need of their own safe haven. Thank you for your willingness to bounce the stones away, to recognize the strength of your soul, and to share that strength when needed.

ABIGAIL

Translucent your light is, our angel on Earth. You are one who is an Earth Angel, and you have come here with a special mission. The mission is to spread your unconditional love and acceptance to the point that others will begin to emanate your light and your love for all. If you wish, study Thomas Merton, as he was a beautiful example of an Earth Angel. There have been, and still are, others. They are recognizable by their calm nature, and they are not easily shaken, if at all. This is because the true essence of angelic love is within. This essence is shared with all, even if it is through a glance. Yes, your purpose is exceptionally divine, and a well-earned one. You chose to come here and work toward this mission on Earth. We are happy you have reached your chosen destination; be assured you will also be able to repeat it the next time around.

ADAM

Chirp chirp. The challenge you feel is that you want to progress from chirping to singing. You sense a greater purpose, as you feel you may have arrived here to perform mundane tasks and to live an ordinary life. We say to you: Yes, you certainly can advance beyond your "lot in life" because you also came here to learn how to overcome any feelings of insignificance. Common tasks and a common life are merely relative, based on your own perception. Are you a laborer? Jesus was a carpenter of higher consciousness and a great teacher. Are you a servant? Think of all those who serve for a higher purpose, no matter what their label may be. Are you a white collar professional? Think of all the good you're in a position to manifest. You see, it does not matter what you "do" to earn provision. It is your perception of what your heart can create. We see and hear your song, and it is beautiful. Go forth and continue singing.

ADRIAN / ADRIANNA

It's in the wind … it's in the wind. Do not listen to summations that you are as unpredictable as the wind. Your intentions and ideas are truly misunderstood and underestimated at times. Ignore this. Give attention instead to the inspiration we bring to you. It will feel like a breeze of relief to your sometimes heavy mind. Allow these times of inspiration to permeate your soul. Go within and quietly listen to the messages we bring you. You have much to learn and to teach if you are attuned to these moments of gentle, effortless inspiration. You can carry these truths throughout this lifetime and beyond. We hope you use this awareness and follow through with the role we have given to you: To inspire via your own inspirational experiences.

AL / ALLIE

Cowboy/Cowgirl you are not; however, you can ride the horse called LIFE like a pro. You can even stay aboard the rodeo bronco of life no matter how much it bucks. You can tame any wildness of life that does not serve you or your surroundings. Not only do you have flexibility and endurance —you enjoy the ride. Yes, you take life by the reins and steer it in whatever direction is the most enjoyable. You have learned to enjoy this life, and your purpose is to attract those who are pessimists or who view life as lackluster. Your lust for life and the ability to ride its various waves will transform many whose souls are crying to live life more fully. Thank you for your vitality and your ability to handle life's unruly and seemingly ugly moments. We give you a kaleidoscope of color to augment your ability to appreciate multiple dimensions.

ALAN / ALLEN

Strait jackets or other restraints are meant for no one, our dear one. We ask that you release and free yourself from the confines of any chains you may have created for yourself. Break out? Yes, please do! Some of you with these names are reserved and shy. Others with these same names are bold, sometimes brazen, yet don't always jump over the right hurdles. They land confidently...on the wrong track. We want to tell you that your lesson here on Earth is to find the most auspicious direction and move forward with clarity and focus, neither in a withdrawn manner, nor with too bold of a manner. Set your own bar and then jump. We will guide your sprint, or your standing jump, and will clear the track for you. It is not a track for racing or running. It is a long distance track with hurdles to jump. Once you are on it, you will have accomplished this lesson and will move purposefully in the direction of your calling: To awaken others to their own dreams and free themselves from restraints.

ALANA

Strait jackets or other restraints are meant for no one, our dear one. We ask that you release and free yourself from the confines of any chains you may have created for yourself. Break out? Yes, please do! Some of you with these names are reserved and shy. Others with these same names are bold, sometimes brazen, yet don't always jump over the right hurdles. They land confidently...on the wrong track. We want to tell you that your lesson here on Earth is to find the most auspicious direction and move forward with clarity and focus, neither in a withdrawn manner, nor with too bold of a manner. Set your own bar and then jump. We will guide your sprint, or your standing jump, and will clear the track for you. It is not a track for racing or running. It is a long distance track with hurdles to jump. Once you are on it, you will have accomplished this lesson and will move purposefully in the direction of your calling: To awaken others to their own dreams and free themselves from restraints.

ALBERT / ALBERTA

Those who are called Albert/Alberta are not the same as those called Al or Allie. To you, we send comfort and grace, as you are among the deep thinkers of Earth. Because of this, and because of the time you spend alone, you have the potential to create and innovate. Your contributions can be quiet and need not be accompanied by fanfare. You may often be told you are wise beyond your years. This is so, as most Albert's and Alberta's are old souls who chose to return here to contribute wisdom again and again, whether it's through subtle mentoring or through creative endeavors. You are graced by wings of courage, and you are nestled in our love.

ALENE

Delicate you are, and wispy as an embracing breeze. You are here to offer the lightness of air and the refreshment of pure smiles. As you walk (actually, as you glide) along this life's path, we want you to know that wherever you step, you leave behind your lightness and gentleness. Your role here is quite an easy one: To be nothing but yourself, without a thought as to what you may need to do or accomplish. Your accomplishments come through each time that you leave behind a temperate, clear, pleasant moment. These moments are mostly savored at a subconscious level; however, they have a refreshing effect. Thank you for being this simplistic elixir.

ALEX / ALEXIS

Take up your symbolic sword, as your purpose is to protect those you care for who are in your circles. You do this without aggression, of course, yet with authority and assertiveness. If others are intimidated by your quest for justice and protection, it is only because of their own nature and their own unattractive reflection they may see in your sword. For this reason, your second purpose is to help others see that they need to make changes within themselves to become gentler in their actions. A word of caution: Your sword could be turned against you. Do not let it deter you, as you will only see your beautiful, strong reflection in this glistening symbol of strength.

ALEXANDER / ALEXENDRA

Take up your symbolic sword, as your purpose is to protect those you care for who are in your circles. You do this without aggression, of course, but with authority and assertiveness. If others are intimidated by your quest for justice and protection, it is only because of their own nature and their own unattractive reflection they may see in your sword. For this reason, your second purpose is to help others see that they need to make changes within themselves to become gentler in their actions. A word of caution: Your sword could be turned against you. Do not let it deter you, as you will only see your beautiful, strong reflection in this glistening symbol of strength.

ALEXANDRIA

Take up your symbolic sword, as your purpose is to protect those you care for who are in your circles. You do this without aggression, of course, but with authority and assertiveness. If others are intimidated by your quest for justice and protection, it is only because of their own nature and their own unattractive reflection they may see in your sword. For this reason, your second purpose is to help others see that they need to make changes within themselves to become gentler in their actions. A word of caution: Your sword could be turned against you. Do not let it deter you, as you will only see your beautiful, strong reflection in this glistening symbol of strength.

ALICE

Spin no more, our lady. You often feel that you are spinning in circles, getting nowhere fast. Spin no more. Instead, recognize that each step you take is indeed taking you somewhere. It is taking you to self-realization. Stay off your self-built merry-go-round, as you have much to contribute and create. Yes, many pauses for rest will be needed, but your lesson here is to learn the value of goals and moving toward them. We will keep you refreshed. The golden ring is in each cycle of success. Your purpose is to demonstrate how to stop spinning, and to recognize the cycles of success.

ALICIA / ALYSHA

Sturdy is your resolve, as it should be. You were sent here to stand strong in the face of adversity when it presents itself to you and to anyone you love or serve. Your purpose is to work for others in a position of advocacy and healing. We call you our Social Worker for Wounded Souls. You can be compared to social workers because of their commitment to the higher good of those they are called to assist, for their empathy, and for their fierce, lion-like, protective nature. These divinely appointed individuals may be mistaken for having constant bleeding hearts, but they cannot be shaken from their stand to advocate for others' rights to fairness. Yes, they are among the gentle giants in this world. Yes, you too are among the gentle and strong giants. We say to you: There is no need to literally become a "professional" social worker. One can see these accomplished individuals in all walks of this life ... the ones who are firm in their pure intent to help empower those in need. Your lesson here is to accept this role with unwavering passion, pure intent, and total reassurance that we guide you and are committed to YOUR highest good.

ALLEN / ALAN

Strait jackets or other restraints are meant for no one, our dear one. We ask that you release and free yourself from the confines of any chains you may have created for yourself. Break out? Yes, please do! Some of you with these names are reserved and shy. Others with these same names are bold, sometimes brazen, yet don't always jump over the right hurdles. They land confidently...on the wrong track. We want to tell you that your lesson here on Earth is to find the most auspicious direction and move forward with clarity and focus, neither in a withdrawn manner, nor with too bold of a manner. Set your own bar and then jump. We will guide your sprint, or your standing jump, and will clear the track for you. It is not a track for racing or running. It is a long distance track with hurdles to jump. Once you are on it, you will have accomplished this lesson and will move purposefully in the direction of your calling: To awaken others to their own dreams and free themselves from restraints.

ALLISON

Spin no more, our lady. You often feel that you are spinning in circles, getting nowhere fast. Spin no more. Instead, recognize that each step you take is indeed taking you somewhere. It is taking you to self-realization. Stay off your self-built merry-go-round, as you have much to contribute and create. Yes, many pauses for rest will be needed, but your lesson here is to learn the value of goals and moving toward them. We will keep you refreshed. The golden ring is in each cycle of success. Your purpose is to demonstrate how to stop spinning, and to recognize the cycles of success.

AMANDA

Strong yet soft, you are like most refer to as a cuddly bear ... lovable yet protective ... huggable yet able to defend yourself and others. You will walk the extra mile to obtain bounty for your loved ones, you will take rest, and you will not allow your home or your family to be encroached upon or threatened. You do prefer a clan of close friends and relations, as this represents a haven for you and promotes a sense of safe harbor for all. Your purpose and your lesson are obvious: To provide gentle comfort and undisputed protection when necessary. Your animal totem, of course, is the Bear. Be conscious of this energy, for it will assist in sustaining you through all the seasons of your life.

AMBER

Star light, star bright, first star I see tonight ... we ask that you stop "wishing you may or wishing you might." We want to show you how to use your dreams and your star gazing to rise to the degree of manifestation that affords you the blessings you seek, without all the yearning. When you find yourself wishing, accept our reminder: All that is good and all that is purposeful for you will evolve. However, it is helpful to us if you practice the childlike mindset of believing. Yes, children wish upon the stars, as do adults. The ones who truly believe that their angels and guides form a team with them are the ones who amazingly manifest their desires. Meditate on this. Internalize the belief that wishes come true that are meant to come true, according to those dreams you chose before you arrived here. Just believe, and receive what has been destined for you. Regardless of your dreams, we want you to know that you are a blessing to all who are near you. They, too, want reciprocal blessings for you. Thank you for allowing those around you to receive the smiles and hugs you give them, both from within and in the physical form. You are a treasure for all.

AMELIA

A taste of hospitality is what you bring to your world. You embody the essence of refreshing, sweet tea on a sweltering hot day that makes the heat more tolerable. You reflect the elegance of a parasol, twirling whimsically while protecting and welcoming the elements to join the naturally occurring fun. You bring the coziness of cinnamon rolls to welcome the morning. You are the open door, inviting all to partake of wholesome gatherings. Your purpose is to enrich and vitalize family and friends through your warmth, friendliness, and openness. There is a great need in this world for graciousness and pureness of heart. You help to fulfill that need, and your reward is the knowledge that you take the edge off of the oftentimes harsh human existence.

AMY

Acknowledge your strength as well as your humility. We view you as the sweet syrup that can grace a bitter scone and make it tolerable. That is to say, you bring such grace and caring to every situation. If the situation is filled with ugliness, harshness, and other negativity, it can transform simply because you are present with your natural, loving nature. You bring purity to life around you. For this you are greatly rewarded at many levels, especially your personal gratification, knowing you make such a heart-felt difference.

ANDREA

Shuffle the cards and let them fall into place, our magician. You have such a knack at bringing order to chaos and having fun at the same time. If you have not yet realized your purpose, we ask that you pay attention to the frequent times when there is confusion or disarray and lack of common sense solutions. Then see that your input and magical touch turns the situation into a smooth and pleasant undertaking. Your greatest intuitive skill lies in your inner knowing of how to morph scattered energies into grounded ones. So, our Master of Life's Card Tricks, carry on with your input and output. We surround you with indigo light to help your visions along the way.

ANDREW / ANDY

Shuffle the cards and let them fall into place, our magician. You have such a knack at bringing order to chaos and having fun at the same time. If you have not yet realized your purpose, we ask that you pay attention to the frequent times when there is confusion or disarray and lack of common sense solutions. Then see that your input and magical touch turns the situation into a smooth and pleasant undertaking. Your greatest intuitive skill lies in your inner knowing of how to morph scattered energies into grounded ones. So, our Master of Life's Card Tricks, carry on with your input and output. We surround you with indigo light to help your visions along the way.

ANGELA / ANGELINA

Your name is angelic, and we allow you to smile and laugh with high frequencies. When others see and hear your smiles and laughter, it is in and of itself calming in a most refreshing way. We ask you to continue providing the nourishment of laughter to yourself and others, as there are so many who miss this from their souls' daily needs. You indeed bring angelic wings that soar with happiness and joy.

ANITA

Clover attracts the bees, which bring us honey. You, our flower, have great ability to turn what may appear to be menacing circumstances into sweet results. Although you do not attract negativity, certain people and situations may falsely appear to be threatening. Always realize that, if meant to be, the situation will transform to the best result. It may, as with the pollination from bees, take the involvement of more than what appears on the surface. It will, in time, be transmuted as long as it is in divine order. You may ask why you are a conduit for such "change for the better." It is because you are not only the clover that attracts bees; you are also a 4-leaf clover for many, and you seek out good fortune. Be comforted in knowing you are an optimist at heart and a changer of conditions. We will send you 4-leaf clovers to remind you that you are a good luck charm, and that we will provide you with the sometimes unexpected means you need to carry forth your purpose of transforming circumstances.

ANN / ANNA / ANNE

Dear one, do not let the soulful sound of your name fool you. Others are at times surprised, as they have expectations of softness from you. This is not true. You are assertive in every way, and will deflect negative energy in all forms, especially every-day hurtful actions and words. You are actually a hero, which is your chosen path. Steadfast, you are one who others look to for sound answers and frank responses. You are guided and surrounded by many angels for the strength to be a citadel in your home, work, and play. What a gallant role you have chosen. We give you the energy of Garnet for grounding and loyalty to your calling. We respect you so much.

ANNETTE

Slow burn. Don't let this misconception alter your path. You are not a victim of a slow burn. You are not a victim at all. Your graciousness may at times result in unappreciative opportunists gravitating toward you. However, this is in no way a slow burn to your pure and light-filled soul. Continue always on your path of service. You will know how to veer from the misled; and therefore, you will not be misled. We exalt you for your pure heart and your authentic desire to share your time and your gifts to benefit where they may.

ANNIE

Clover attracts the bees, which bring us honey. You, our flower, have great ability to turn what may appear to be menacing circumstances into sweet results. Although you do not attract negativity, certain people and situations may falsely appear to be threatening. Always realize that, if meant to be, the situation will transform to the best result. It may, as with the pollination from bees, take the involvement of more than what appears on the surface. It will, in time, be transmuted as long as it is in divine order. You may ask why you are a conduit for such "change for the better." It is because you are not only the clover that attracts bees; you are also a 4-leaf clover for many, and you seek out good fortune. Be comforted in knowing you are an optimist at heart and a changer of conditions. We will send you 4-leaf clovers to remind you that you are a good luck charm and that we will provide you with the sometimes unexpected means you need to carry forth your purpose of transforming circumstances.

ANTHONY

Shuffle the cards and let them fall into place, our magician. You have such a knack at bringing order to chaos and having fun at the same time. If you have not yet realized your purpose, we ask that you pay attention to the frequent times when there is confusion or disarray and lack of common sense solutions. Then see that your input and magical touch turns the situation into a smooth and pleasant undertaking. Your greatest intuitive skill lies in your inner knowing of how to morph scattered energies into grounded ones. So, our Master of Life's Card Tricks, carry on with your input and output. We surround you with indigo light to help your visions along the way.

APRIL

In addition to the gentle Spring showers that bring new growth, as your name reflects, you are no sitting duck for freeloaders or naysayers. Your soft, cultivating rain can easily change to a thunderstorm should you need to blow away anything or anyone menacing. You realize you do not have time for negativity while you are fulfilling your purpose of being a nourisher. We have provided you with the ability to transmute circumstances toward an evolution of goodness and progress. Carry on your irrigation in promoting the world around you to evolve in the most positive direction. Your calm power will be kept intact by your angels and guides. We surround you with both sky blue and ocean blue to maintain an inner, placid spirit.

ART / ARTHUR

Like a chunk of butter in the warm sun, you melt hearts with your rays of light. You shine forth tenderness with sunbeams that promote growth and awareness of the benefits from allowing the light in. You then provide rain showers for additional growth. It is your purpose to reveal the substance necessary for self-love and self-actualization. Unlike hot and cold, this substance is gentle, yet paradoxical, with the warmth of sun and coolness of raindrops. You are a healer of the heart and teach that growth is possible without harshness. This is indeed something that, if not natural, could not be accomplished by most. This gift for you *is* natural, and fortunate are those who are blessed to receive your presence.

ASHLEY

Quiet boom. Heat lightening. Powerful in a delicate manner is what you are. Without being frightening, you can accomplish change like the parting of the Red Sea. You can admonish wrongdoers without raising your voice or lifting a hand. You are a delicacy for any individual or company by which you are employed, and you are your own best advocate. This type of change-making, which some call authority, (we know it is actually quiet, directed energy) is what you came here to exercise for the purpose of improving communication skills among your circles. We provide you with the gift of diplomacy, and we give you the energy of a mother's nurturing touch. You will feel this maternal energy whenever you are in the slightest distress, and it will carry you forth.

AUDREY

Smile, smile, smile. People look to you for the joy of your smile and how it transfers joy to them. You have no hidden agendas. A refreshing spirit for all to behold, your mission is to remind all that there are genuinely happy people, and that this joy can be captured and nurtured. This brings hope and newly-found attention to the lighter side of life. It also brings meaningful joy from spirit. You know the truth, and you are free!

AUTUMN

Strong yet soft, you are like most refer to as a cuddly bear ... lovable yet protective ... huggable yet able to defend yourself and others. You will walk the extra mile to obtain bounty for your loved ones, you will take rest, and you will not allow your home or your family to be encroached upon or threatened. You do prefer a clan of close friends and relations, as this represents a haven for you and promotes a sense of safe harbor for all. Your purpose and your lesson are obvious: To provide gentle comfort and undisputed protection when necessary. Your animal totem, of course, is the Bear. Be conscious of this energy, for it will assist in sustaining you through all the seasons of your life.

AVA

Sorghum molasses. You may feel that your journey has been sticky, slow, and frustrating. You may feel you have the residual stickiness and messiness of past difficult or preposterous experiences on your life path, making it difficult to step forward freely, without obstruction. We have news for you: Without the mess there would be no sweetness. We say to you that no matter how messy, the sweetness is what holds together your path. The sugar experiences do make things sticky and serve as a reminder that, although the path at times seems like scalding concrete or filled with icy shards, it is seasoned with the sweetness which makes you go "Yum." You must remember the yums. They overpower the sour taste that life sometimes hands you. You must remember that the sweetness of life pours slowly throughout your time here ... so slowly that you may not even notice it. Do remember that messiness is merely a reminder of the sweetness that accompanies it and embellishes your life. We will send you delectable reminders of real molasses and honey along your way. Even better, we always surround you with the innocent energy of the sweetest cherubs of the universe, fluttering and smiling upon you.

BAILEY

Surrogates are fine. However, you prefer the authentic thing. Therefore, do avoid a partner who offers less than the type of relationship you desire. Seek out only that which you really want. Too often, people accept what is available rather than waiting for what may have soon appeared. Your lesson is to seek the gold. Appreciate the steel, copper, nickel, brass and alloys. Commit, though, to the golden wealth and warmth of outcomes which are destined for you. We adorn you with golden hats, to be a reminder of your worth. There is no substitute, no surrogate for your amazing energy. Accept nothing other than a match for your well-being.

BARBARA

Sink your feet deep into the sand. Feel the energy of a million particles that will stabilize you, and at the same time remind you of how many actions it takes to become one with the All That Is. You long for a purpose, and we want to direct you to meditation. If you are unable to stand motionless in the sand, stand on the Earth. Feel its nurturing energy. Feel the millions of vibrations that resonate as one world. You are the same. Your many steps, your countless thoughts and actions—all are manifesting as one. YOU—One with the All That Is.

BARRY

Riding shotgun is not your style. You were born as a leader, and you need to be in the driver's seat. This is not to say that you are power hungry or driven by ego. However, because of your purpose as a leader, you will need to control the occasional spike of human ego. Your lesson, then, is to recognize when you are acting from ego or from purpose. There is a difference, and you will learn that purposeful action makes your heart feel good. Ego actions feel like they manifest from the head and will tighten up the solar plexus. Pay great attention to this, as effective leadership must come from inspired purpose and be heartfelt. We give you a license that never expires to steer life's vehicles in the right directions. This includes rides and trips that your teams occasionally embark upon with lack of direction. Our humble yet gregarious leader, we surround you with wisdom and knowledge to accomplish your purpose.

BART

You are most comfortable flying above the flocks—all the various flocks. You are not one to be a bird of similar feather ... you can and you do relate to and are accepted by many groups, yet you prefer individualism. For these reasons, we send you Eagle energy. Your courage and leadership abilities are connected to your purpose of seeing much, overseeing when necessary, and rising above whatever may interfere with your path.

BEAU / BO

Yes, you are able-bodied and able-minded, as your name in this society often implies. You *are* aware, though, that there is so much more than what your name implies as to level of mind and body strength. You know that you *are* your purpose, you *are* your soul's path, and you *are* your spirit incarnate. Even better ... you know that this is *everyone's* truth. We assist you always in dispelling society's myth associated with the type of strength attached to your name. If your purpose is to be a virulent protector, so be it, and you will fulfill it. If your purpose is to be a meek servant, so be it, and you will fulfill it. In other words, despite what the world in general expects you to be and pressures you to be, we help you to continue BEING unabashedly YOU. Your purpose is to be a reflection of the necessity of being the truth of who you are ... for everyone.

BECKY

Our adventurous one, the saying, "throw caution to the wind" often describes you. When you have a passion toward something (or even an intense interest), you forge forward with no fear. This manner of approaching life does not work for most. Although it backfires for you occasionally, it does help toward serving your purpose: To demonstrate the self-fulfillment that following your bliss can bring, along with the benefits of perseverance when things do not quite work out as envisioned. This will keep you on your destined path (from which you veer at times because of your nature). You have the inner strength to endure the backfires, and you have the gratitude and excitement to celebrate the wild successes. Your lesson here is to know how to distinguish danger from difficulty, and you are doing well. We want you to know that we are a protective presence for you whether you are feeling the utmost confidence or recovering from a bump in the road.

BELINDA

Lavender fields are what you represent ... the soft, subtle, graceful beauty that brings about relaxation and appreciation of the All That Is ... the lullaby for the heart when the heart needs soothing. The contrast needed against the sometimes harsh existence on this plane. Your natural balm to troubled souls is not always present. We provide this for you to grace those in need at the appointed times, just as we provide this harmonious state of being to you when needed. We want you to know that you are here for the sole purpose of being the embrace which elicits a sigh of relief from angst. Your calming elixir is priceless, yet a complimentary gift from the angels through you. Thank you for coming into existence to assist us in providing this valuable level of healing.

BELLA

We liken you to a Ferris Wheel for viewing life. You bring attention to the panoramic view of the world and everyday life in general. On the seat you provide for others, they are able to see beyond the close detail. Detail is important, yes, but there are so many who do not look beyond their nose. The broad spectrum, the vast possibilities, the grand view is often missed. Not only do you assist in providing the big picture ... you assist in allowing others to view life at every level. As the Ferris Wheel rises to various heights, it also descends to various lows, and repeats. So it is with you and the viewing seats you provide. You allow a comprehensive exploration of life ... of life's questions, of life's challenges, of life's solutions, and mostly of life's overall beauty. When looking at the grand scheme of things, the beauty and breathtaking views outweigh all else. Thank you for bringing attention to this; you are serving your purpose well.

BELLE

Soft streamers of starlit chiffon ... this is how we would describe your energy. Your energy rests gently on each and every individual with whom you come into contact. You are what many on this Earth call unforgettable. Your essence remains long after you have physically left a room, and its effects are uplifting, yet in a calming manner. You and your effects are relished, and at times the cause of your effect is not even realized. Being one who does not seek out celebrity, this is of no concern to you. You came here to unobtrusively create a glow ... an everlasting glow. Your lesson is to relax with your natural ability to bring solace to others.

BEN / BENJAMIN

Tough as nails. Tougher than nails. We want you to know that this is not what you are expected to be. In fact, it isn't even what you signed up to be before arriving here. You wanted to be assertive—a leader, yet pliant, not made of steel ... definitive in direction, but not harsh. If you find yourself in a position where you feel you're expected to be aggressive, call on us and we will give you the angelic strength to approach the situation with unbiased and focused kindness, while keeping the reins of dissidence firmly under control. Some will, and some will not respect you for this gentle authority.

Pay no heed to earning respect; it matters not. You are fulfilling your role here to take loving charge where otherwise chaos and squabbles would have resulted. We call you our Orchestrator of Positive Outcomes, and we send continuous blessings to you for assistance. We surround you with the energies of orange and gold for courage, combined with Christ-like love.

BERT

You are most comfortable flying above the flocks—all the various flocks. You are not one to be a bird of similar feather … you can and do relate to and are accepted by many groups; yet you prefer individualism. For these reasons, we send you Eagle energy. Your courage and leadership abilities are connected to your purpose of seeing much, overseeing when necessary, and rising above whatever does not serve you.

BESS / BESSIE

Your name may reflect old school traditions. You have this name for the purpose of breaking through paradigms that do not fit into the current world. We do not speak of virtues; these need to remain intact. In fact, while you are promoting more modern ways of accomplishing things, we want you to know that you will also help remind others that restoration of lost values in this society is vital. While helping seniors keep up with the technological advances necessary to function in this modern world, you will also instill missing and lost pieces of common courtesy and morality. You have been placed here in this time for the dual purpose of which we speak. You arrived with the internal knowledge of modern technology blended with high standards. Your presence is needed. Thank you for being a principled example of goodness within modern society.

BETH

Fail, fail, the gang's all here! Beth, our bringer of confidence, we want you to know how needed you are to those who think they are failures. You have shown many, and will continue to help these troubled souls, to see that the proverbial phrase of, "Failure is not a person; it is simply an event," is true. It is simply an occurrence, a result that can teach about how and what to avoid in order to reach a goal. More important, though, is your role of teaching that these sometimes disconcerting results serve a higher purpose: To discover confidence and self-assuredness. Those whom you touch with this knowledge will learn that each step in this life takes them closer to where they are destined to be. Praise them for all their steps. Remind them of their true divinity within, and help them shine that divinity back to the world, with the confidence that pure love emanates. Thank you for your light and for lifting others.

BETHANY

Fail, fail, the gang's all here! Bethany, our bringer of confidence, we want you to know how needed you are to those who think they are failures. You have shown many, and will continue to help these troubled souls to see that the proverbial phrase of, "Failure is not a person; it is simply an event," is true. It is simply an occurrence, a result that can teach about how and what to avoid in order to reach a goal. More important, though, is your role of teaching that these sometimes disconcerting results serve a higher purpose: To discover confidence and self-assuredness. Those whom you touch with this knowledge will learn that each step in this life takes them closer to where they are destined to be. Praise them for all their steps. Remind them of their true divinity within, and help them shine that divinity back to the world, with the confidence that pure love emanates. Thank you for your light and for lifting others.

BETSY

Surely, you say, *"There must be something good for me."* Lassie, there is and always has been. You can build boulders larger than those that seem to block you. You can traverse rugged paths and clear the way toward progress, paving golden roads for easy ingress to fortunes of love, well-being and peacefulness. Ah, yes, our road paver ... yes, there indeed is something good for you and for all with whom you share the secrets of clearing and paving a path of abundance at all levels. The 'good' that comes to you is through your very purpose of clearing rubble and making room for enlightenment, as the results manifest in the higher energetic frequencies that you came here to experience and to share. You arrived here having learned the lesson of how to fulfill this purpose. Continue to move as you feel directed by us, and we will, of course, direct you on every path.

BETTY

The rising of the dawn is always a reason for celebration, for gratefulness of a new day, for hope of all things good, and for thankfulness about life. It is this we want you to always remember: It is easy to become stifled ... to drift into a mindset so filled with the worries of everyday life that many in their human experience forget the magnificence and the miracle of the dawn. We want you to always be mindful of this grace and to go one step further ... and farther ... to remind those who have become lackadaisical toward life about this generosity of the universe. Thank you for becoming and offering the reminder.

BEV / BEVERLY

Bev / Beverly, you are an Earth Angel who brings kindness, maternal-like nurturing, and beauty to all of life and to those who are around you at any given time. You often become a mentor to others, whether for a few moments or for years. You came here equipped with wisdom of the ages and compassion toward others. You are a great discerner and cautious all the while. With no effort on your part, you touch others in ways they need the most, and you seldom tire in your role, because we have taught you how to care for your own needs as well. Thank you for choosing to carry out this admirable role.

BILL / BILLY

Startling you are at times, our bold one. When others fear taking a stand, you hesitate not. You have the propensity to do so in unconventional ways ... breaking protocol and political correctness. You are needed for your mannerisms when the standard is being accepted, yet change is required for the good of all concerned. So, continue to be the one to upset the proverbial apple cart when it is necessary. We have your back!

BLAINE

Righteous could be your middle name. As with most middle names, you are not called righteous often, yet it is part of your identity. Although you may not think of yourself as righteous, let us say to you: At the core of your being, you are aware of what is right, what is good, what is true, and what is virtuous. When you need reminders to tune in to your innermost knowledge, we will send you a "gut feeling" to symbolize the power of your truth. When you falter, and you will, we will reinforce you and assist you in continuing to rise to your wealth of goodness.

BLAIR

We give you a coat of golden cotton, a coat reinforced with the gentleness of lambs and the power of a Norse god. Your lesson is to discern when your coat needs to be used as armor, used as comfort, or as a basic, all-weather coat. You will learn when and why this coat is used, and you will reach a level of confidence which will take you through all your days. At one point, you will never need the coat, as you will have all the self-assurance you need. This is what you chose to learn before arriving here. Your purpose is to give the symbolic coat to those who also need to learn to free themselves from doubt ... the freedom that results from self-love ... and the courage to step into the world, donned with armor and comfort until such time as they, too, give the coat away.

BO / BEAU

Yes, you are able-bodied and able-minded as your name in this society often implies. You are aware, though, that there is so much more than what your name implies as to level of mind and body strength. You know that you *are* your purpose, you *are* your soul's path, and you *are* your spirit incarnate. Even better ... you know that this is *everyone's* truth. We assist you always in dispelling society's myth associated with the type of strength attached to your name. If your purpose is to be a virulent protector, so be it and you will fulfill it. If your purpose is to be a meek servant, so be it and you will fulfill it. In other words, despite what the world in general expects you to be and pressures you to be, we help you to continue BEING unabashedly YOU. Your purpose is to be a reflection of the necessity of being the truth of who you are for everyone.

BOB / BOBBY

Everyone looks to you for answers. You are a source for knowledge about a myriad of subject matters. You are confident enough that others feel you will provide them with the truth when they listen to you. Your self-assuredness is such that some may see you as arrogant. Ignore that. Those who need your input will receive it; those who do not will find their way through others' input. You chose to show up as an authority on the topics of your choice, and you have been provided with all the gifts required to accomplish this goal. You are the personification of the student and the teacher. We call you The Professor, as the best professors are also the ones who continue to be open to learn.

BRAD / BRADLEY

Carry the weight. You are so capable of taking on burdens with no heaviness wrought upon your body, mind, or soul. You arrived here with the shoulders of Atlas and the mental constitution of a heavyweight. For this, many are thankful that you are able to take part of their personal load away. We wish to alert you, however, to ask in prayer for the logic and guidance you need as to how much load you should bear at any given time. We want you to use your utmost discretion in taking on the weight so that you can continue to endure and bless others with the assistance you so generously give. You will instinctively know when individuals need to carry all of their weight ... the weight which results in their necessary life lessons. You are rare to this Earthly existence.

BRANDI / BRANDY

Until the bell tolls. This is how you view life decisions and life changes. You do not step ahead too soon. You move forward with life, and only in due time ... in other words, not until the bell tolls, not until you know it is time. For this we commend you, as your purpose is to teach others to hesitate from opening the petals of a flower before it is time for it to bloom. You teach emergence, unfoldment, and flow. Not many on Earth learn this lesson at the soul depth. Not many are able to wait—and to recognize—the perfect timing of living life's chapters. You, our wise one, are one such rare spirit in human form, knowing and working with divine timing.

BRANDON / BRENDON

Until the bell tolls. This is how you view life decisions and life changes. You do not step ahead too soon. You move forward with life, and only in due time ... in other words, not until the bell tolls, not until you know it is time. For this we commend you, as your purpose is to teach others to hesitate from opening the petals of a flower before it is time for it to bloom. You teach emergence, unfoldment, and flow. Not many on Earth learn this lesson at the soul depth. Not many are able to wait—and to recognize—the perfect timing of living life's chapters. You, our wise one, are one such rare spirit in human form, knowing and working with divine timing.

BREANNA / BRIANNA / BRIAHNA

We call you our dewdrop. As the sun kisses a morning bloom, you glisten with wonder for each new day. Your silent sheen opens others' eyes and hearts to the true beauty of the universe and to the millions of miracles occurring daily ... every minute. You do not even need to utter a word of wisdom. You reflect all that is magical with your shimmering soul. Your particular influence on the world around you is necessary to the whole—the whole which has become lost in strife, fear, and busy-ness. Thank you, our refreshing dewdrop.

BRENDA

How saucy you can be! Life on this Earth needs spice, and you have the ability to bring it. When you feel the need to temper your blend of spicy, caring nature, call on us and you will be given the means to remain true to your soul self while conducting your Earthly business. It is your sauciness, however, that enhances your world and those in it—even if it is while standing in a checkout lane. The angels thank you for bringing zest to the mundane when most needed.

BRETT

The distant rhythm you hear, and have always heard, is beyond that of the common expression that you are hearing the beat of a different drummer. Your unique rhythm is a personal trademark. It is always there, yet never intrusive. It is always subtle, yet direct and meaningful. It is inner truth in expression. It is accomplishment without "sounding off." Your purpose is to be a reminder that all individuals—if they listen—have their still, subtle rhythm on which to base their life's journey. This brings inner peace to those who recognize their inner truth.

BRIAN / BRYAN

Until the bell tolls. This is how you view life decisions and life changes. You do not step ahead too soon. You move forward with life, and only in due time ... in other words, not until the bell tolls, not until you know it is time. For this we commend you, as your purpose is to teach others to hesitate from opening the petals of a flower before it is time for it to bloom. You teach emergence, unfoldment, and flow. Not many on Earth learn this lesson at the soul depth. Not many are able to wait—and to recognize—the perfect timing of living life's chapters. You, our wise one, are one such rare spirit in human form, knowing and working with divine timing.

BRICE / BRYCE

You are the tungsten, or solid rock, for many. Your chosen purpose to be a rock to which certain friends and loved ones turn may often be a difficult one. Conversely, it provides you with great self-fulfillment. You knew this before making the choice. The shared benefit of holding others up and being their touchstone, combined with the uplifting emotions that result for you, is exactly as it is meant to be. We honor you with a symbolic ring to represent the marriage of mutual blessings.

BRIDGETTE

Bridgette, you wear a symbolic crown of emeralds. The emeralds represent your ability to bring healing to others with your touch...with your smile ... with your heart. These emeralds also represent your love for the healing Mother Earth. We ask you to sink your feet into the ground and connect with this Earth energy. You need this Earth energy because of your healing capacities. It will keep you feeling secure and grounded, and as the healing energies from the Earth rise up and fill you, your heart will be most filled. Your crown of emeralds is not a materialistic thing whatsoever. You are connected more with the richness of the universe, the wealth of the innate knowledge you were born with when you arrived here, and the treasure chest within your heart of your desire to just be. And to do no harm; only to help when you can.

BRITTANY

Slow, rolling waves over motionless rocks create a contrast of strength ... strength of flow and power of stance. The waves learn that they can continue to move despite the resolute stones. The stones learn that when a position is required to maintain balance, the movement around and over them will not adversely affect them in the present moment, yet over time will create polished beauty. Your lesson is to learn how to be the wave and how to be the stone. Bring refreshing, cleansing beauty to the undaunted. Allow yourself to view threats to your convictions as an addition of peace to what must be unwavering in the now moment. You do have an understanding that, over time, the resolute may be altered or transformed by the beauty of a natural course of change. Embrace this understanding while you are being a mainstay of peaceful existence during this lifetime. We support you with the grace of Earth angels who we send to you throughout your time here.

BRUCE

Tend to the garden. By this we mean to not take shortcuts. Avoid leaving out steps, as this will only result in little or no growth. Do not sow until you till; use only rich soil and quality seeds. You have learned, our friend, the proper manner to begin and tend to your life's many gardens. We give you the best tools so that you will not, with one misstep of choices, fail. However, you must heed our messages. Listen and be alert to the sound of the finch as you go about your trail, and feel one with all while you work your gardens. The finch will let you know by its tune when you are in harmony with your purposeful work. Should you ever wonder if you are tending properly to your Earthly life's gardens, remember the finch's congratulatory tune and celebrate your harvests of all that is good, all that is true, and all that is love. We will also be congratulating you with our heavenly hugs which you may feel from time to time by the warmth around your shoulders.

BUD / BUDDY

Little ones love to be in your company. They enjoy being in the flow of goodness, of kindness, and of fun. You are like a favorite teacher, bringing interesting information, rewarding positive behavior, and offering unconditional acceptance. You are a magnet to children who otherwise experience negative living environments. You have a demeanor which provides simple, enjoyable direction. Be the example. Be the teacher. Be the Earth angel. Be the innocent fun. Be the love. We wrap you in the brilliance of sun kissed clouds.

CAILLEY

Sky-lit, you are able to see a vast panorama of possibilities, unlike most on this Earth walk. You carry with you the secrets and the magic of a million stars, the power of the sun, and the stillness of the moon ... not all at once ... but when whichever of these promotes well-being and brings answers that are being sought. Allow others to look to you for inspiration in finding their answers and to realize that some mysteries must remain mysteries. In so doing, they too will embrace the universe's panorama.

CAITLYN

Surrey, surrey. You feel you would love the traveling style of yesteryear. The hustle and bustle of highways pale in comparison to the byways of old. You would prefer to ride in a beautiful surrey or walk down a sidewalk with a parasol, through a quaint town lined with trees and lampposts. Such charm, and not racing to and fro as it seems is the norm at this time. We say to you: Your purpose is to teach others to slow down and look around ... to soak in the natural beauty of truly being alive and acknowledging surroundings. There is always something eloquent to find in the environment if only the current pace is reduced. You know how to embellish the daily humdrum of busy-ness with beholding the quiet beauty among society's noise. Yes, ride your symbolic surrey and carry your symbolic parasol. This elegant energy will help you cope with the world's fast pace and set a good example for those who heed your advice.

CALEB

The rails are what keep the trains on track. Each railroad car is dependent on well-maintained tracks. We say to you: Maintain each track in your life so as to minimize the possibility of being derailed. Do not depend on your powerful engine to get you through to your destinations. Pay attention to the details (rails) of your life to ensure that there are not major mishaps along the way. The rails are your core group of family and friends, and they also include your career path. Your train may jump the track occasionally. This life on Earth cannot be free from being derailed now and then. We want you to know, however, that we are here with you to help mend the track and maintain safety to the degree possible from our realm. Your lesson is to learn that, despite any malfunctioning rails, you are able to reach your intended stations, yet rails that have been unattended will slow you down. Neglect increases the odds for "accidents" and delays. Your purpose is to alert those closest to you to pay attention to their rails, too, as this will result in a smoother ride for all.

CAMERON

Pragmatism is practical. However, pragmatism used too diligently and consistently may take some of the fun out of life that you deserve. You did not come to this Earth to be serious and exercise conservatism in your life on a daily basis. However, we say to you that you may have the tendency to do so. Your lesson is to observe the mundane situations objectively, take the actions you know are proper, and move on to lighter life experiences. You will learn to remove yourself from the rut of the concrete, black-and-white decision making and practical mode. You will learn to remove your blinders and see the panoramic view of the world and its charm. Further, you will learn when to remove the blinders ... when to approach life with prudence and when to simply enjoy yourself. In doing so, you will serve as an example of responsibly living this life to the fullest.

CANDICE

Frilly, frilly, frilly. "Why do some people like frills all the time, every day?" You may ask yourself that question often, as you prefer few or no flashy accessories with almost anything. Our realist, your lesson is to discover and appreciate the confetti, the streamers, and the sequins of life. You chose this lesson so that you can be complete with your experience of life on this plane. Your self-assignment of pragmatism for the sake of progress, as well as assisting your soul family with this type of approach to progress, has been met. You can relax a little now. It has been difficult at times to like the ribbons and the bows of life, yet you are now aware you need to be delighted in these things that elevate the experience of living. Use the lace, plant the flowers, accent with glitter. There are those who will teach you about the frills and the smiles brought forth through a more light-hearted approach. You will learn to incorporate the ribbons with a plain tradition, and you will smile as you continue assisting your circle. This is a completion of sorts for you, and you will have more variety from which to choose when the time comes to incarnate again.

CANDY

Frilly, frilly, frilly. "Why do some people like frills all the time, every day?" You may ask yourself that question often, as you prefer few or no flashy accessories with almost anything. Our realist, your lesson is to discover and appreciate the confetti, the streamers, and the sequins of life. You chose this lesson so that you can be complete with your experience of life on this plane. Your self-assignment of pragmatism for the sake of progress, as well as assisting your soul family with this type of approach to progress, has been met. You can relax a little now. It has been difficult at times to like the ribbons and the bows of life, yet you are now aware you need to be delighted in these things that elevate the experience of living. Use the lace, plant the flowers, accent with glitter. There are those who will teach you about the frills and the smiles brought forth through a more light-hearted approach. You will learn to incorporate the ribbons with a plain tradition, and you will smile as you continue assisting your circle. This is a completion of sorts for you, and you will have more variety from which to choose when the time comes to incarnate again.

CARA

Your lesson is to avoid throwing your pearls to the swine. Not that there is anything bad about swine—all creatures are valuable. We refer to the symbolism to which the word 'swine' is known. There are those who will muddy up your pure and clear intentions ... as well as your talents. Be cautious with whom you share. "Sign up" with only those who have your best interests at heart. We will assist with decisions along your path. When in doubt, ask and we will provide you with guidance. Resist any person or situation that does not represent what is in your best interest as well as their own. Remember, we will help and send the guidance for your direction. You will realize that your pearls are gifts from the angels, and you will treasure them, not allowing them to go to waste.

CAREY / CARY

Hoist your sails! You're in for quite a journey. The course may be rough and treacherous; however, you are a natural navigator who can assess the winds, the storms, the still waters, the sun and the moon as though you were born with a barometer on your forehead and a compass in your heart. Along the way, you will rescue occupants of other ships that have become lost in the sea of confusion, or even have been shipwrecked. You are brave and noble, finding your way always to safe shores and rewarding ports of call. Your angels are constantly guiding you and providing strength.

CARL / CARLA

Stringing things, or people, along is not your style. You have the gift of Directness with a Smile, even if the news is not desirable. You deliver with grace and have an uncanny ability to make an undesirable situation tolerable with your charming nature. We say charming as with an innocent manner, not a deceiving manner. This authentic, caring charm is so helpful to lift others up at times when no one else could do the same. We caution you to take this responsibility seriously, as some with this gift fall into a temptation to use it for their benefit, even when they are not being deceitful. Hang on to the trustworthy charm you came here to share. It will bring smiles and uplift spirits.

Intensity is a trait you also possess. Know when it is necessary and when you must temper it, else you stand the risk of your purpose backfiring on you. Hence, you would need to work on learning this lesson in your next life. You have learned much on your journeys; we do not want to see you take any steps backward. We place a garland of lilies around your heart to keep it pure and to allow you to feel our unconditional love.

CARLY

Stringing things, or people, along is not your style. You have the gift of Directness with a Smile, even if the news is not desirable. You deliver with grace and have an uncanny ability to make an undesirable situation tolerable with your charming nature. We say charming as with an innocent manner, not a deceiving manner. This authentic, caring charm is so helpful to lift others up at times when no one else could do the same. We caution you to take this responsibility seriously, as some with this gift fall into a temptation to use it for their benefit, even when they are not being deceitful. Hang on to the trustworthy charm you came here to share. It will bring smiles and uplift spirits.

Intensity is a trait you also possess. Know when it is necessary and when you must temper it, else you stand the risk of your purpose backfiring on you. Hence, you would need to work on learning this lesson in your next life. You have learned much on your journeys; we do not want to see you take any steps backward. We place a garland of lilies around your heart to keep it pure and to allow you to feel our unconditional love.

CARMELITA

It's in the wind – it's in the wind. Do not listen to summations that you are as unpredictable as the wind. Your intentions and ideas are truly misunderstood and underestimated at times. Ignore this. Give attention instead to the inspiration we bring to you. It will feel like a breeze of relief to your sometimes heavy mind. Allow these times of inspiration to permeate your soul. Go within and quietly listen to the messages we bring you. You have much to offer and to teach if you are attuned to these moments of gentle, effortless inspiration, and you can carry these truths throughout this lifetime and beyond. We hope you use this awareness and follow through with the role we have given to you: To inspire via your own inspirational experiences.

CARMEN

Start it up! You have a knack for igniting and setting things in motion. We call you our Initiator and Accelerator, as you are among the ones who are sent here to put things in motion and then move them forward. We caution you, too, that there are times to put on the brakes, and this is the lesson you are here to learn. We may add that you have been doing well with both this life's purpose and this life's lesson. You have arrived here with the knowledge instilled within your soul that, once something is ablaze, you are aware of exactly when to stoke the fire. Conversely, you know when to let the coals dim and fade out, because some blazes are not for the common good. Carmen, we have provided you with our gift of Cedarwood and Spruce energy for your need to stay both heightened and grounded; you have such a high calling. Visit Cedarwood and Spruce when you feel the need to elevate your consciousness and when you feel the need to get "back to Earth." Share this message with others who you will know require it. Thank you for your response to the call to step out, step up, and ignite! We cherish you.

CAROL

Carol, there are many names that seem delicate, yet carry with them much strength. Your name is one such name. Commitment, with sureness in your actions, are the gifts we give you. Accept nothing less than the deepest truth, as you are loyal to what is true. Always be mindful of faithfulness—to yourself and others—for without this you will feel unfulfilled. We provide you with the discernment to recognize truth at all times, and the graciousness of fidelity to all aspects of your life on Earth.

CAROLINE

Your name is among the delicacies of names. Soft, yet durable. Cooperative, yet not vulnerable. Gifted, yet humble. A leader, yet a team player. Delicacies are looked upon in the human experience as an expensive luxury. We say to you: There is a potential for most to be such a delicacy; there simply needs to be more evolved learning, which in turn will lead to these innate traits which you demonstrate. Your purpose is to merely be present. Those who are here to learn to tap into the higher consciousness you possess will cross your path in various ways. They will learn through osmosis, as we will bring them into your path and will move them on. Thank you for being the catalyst for creating enlightenment.

CAROLYN

Carolyn, there are many names that seem delicate, yet carry with them much strength. Your name is one such name. Commitment, with sureness in your actions, are the gifts we give you. Accept nothing less than the deepest truth, as you are loyal to what is true. Always be mindful of faithfulness—to yourself and others—for without this you will feel unfulfilled. We provide you with the discernment to recognize truth at all times, and the graciousness of fidelity to all aspects of your life on Earth.

CARRIE

Hoist your sails! You're in for quite a journey. The course may be rough and treacherous; however, you are a natural navigator who can assess the winds, the storms, the still waters, the sun and the moon as though you were born with a barometer on your forehead and a compass in your heart. Along the way, you will rescue occupants of other ships that have become lost in the sea of confusion, or even have been shipwrecked. You are brave and noble, finding your way always to safe shores and rewarding ports of call. Your angels are constantly guiding you and providing strength.

CARSON

The green, green grass of home calls you at every turn. You are indeed a homebody at heart, although you have also an urge to venture out to other areas. Do not hesitate to expand your geographical experiences, as these will only accentuate your contributions to your "home." So, our dear Carson, continue to explore wherever you are led, knowing that you are always able to return to your home base with enhanced knowledge and abilities to be used for the betterment of your core family.

CARTER

Sober as you may appear at times, you do have a sense of humor that lifts people and situations out of their doldrums. More than this, when you instinctively know that your lighthearted approach is needed, you bring resolution to conflicts more easily than had you not been present. Your natural ability to use humor without being offensive ... and to apply your words to be relevant to the situation ... is indeed a gift. Your purpose is to use this gift when you have a knowing that through your happy, diplomatic approach, peaceful outcomes will be realized. In turn, you will have great joy in knowing you have made a difference that many could not have accomplished alone.

CASEY

Descending on you daily are angels of consequence. They bring you blessings for all the good things and the care that you bring to people on a regular basis. You cannot help but have good consequences, as you came here for the express purpose of bringing happiness and contentment to those around you, and you are able to do this in many ways, at many levels. You are versatile, and this versatility and adaptability will benefit you as well, all through the times of this life. Your chameleon-like demeanor is rare and priceless, as you have the foresight and ability to adapt when needed. This is a gift we have given you to help with your work here.

CASSIDY

Bring it to reality, our objective one. You will find yourself among idealists. We love idealists so much. You are among them because you ARE one, with a special exception. Although idealists do have the capacity to step back and look at the whole picture—and frequently must as a result of living this human existence—you achieve this more readily. You also are diplomatic, which brings the inclusion of objectivity with idealism to a successful outcome most often. Your purpose is to act as a mediator, a negotiator, a diplomat. Whichever you choose, this world needs you to help with balance between a sometimes overabundance of loftiness and a feasible, viable solution.

CASSIE

Descending on you daily are angels of consequence. They bring you blessings for all the good things and the care that you bring to people on a regular basis. You cannot help but have good consequences, as you came here for the express purpose of bringing happiness and contentment to those around you, and you are able to do this in many ways, at many levels. You are versatile, and this versatility and adaptability will benefit you as well, all through the times of this life. Your chameleon-like demeanor is rare and priceless, as you have the foresight and ability to adapt when needed. This is a gift we have given you to help with your work here.

CATHERINE

Never fear the wrath from those you may perceive to be your enemies. Your genuine kindness and the pure light that emanates from your being will almost always divert anyone who has ill intentions. Your light is so bright that it deflects negative energies and attracts all things positive. Your purpose is manifested through your nurturing mannerisms that convert hard-shelled souls into baby-like souls wishing to be held in pure light. Should you be confronted by wrong doers despite your demeanor, please know that you are protected when you call on us, your angels.

CATHY

Never fear the wrath from those you may perceive to be your enemies. Your genuine kindness and the pure light that emanates from your being will almost always divert anyone who has ill intentions. Your light is so bright that it deflects negative energies and attracts all things positive. Your purpose is manifested through your nurturing mannerisms that convert hard-shelled souls into baby-like souls wishing to be held in pure light. Should you be confronted by wrong doers despite your demeanor, please know that you are protected when you call on us, your angels.

CHANDLER

Bring on the confetti! You know how to celebrate. You are looked upon as the one who sees the rainbow in the storm, believes the pie in the sky can be reached, and focuses on the brilliance of stars rather than the darkness between them. You are the one who can turn what seems to be a dismal situation into a bright lesson that can have lasting, positive effects. Despite this, we know you experience doubt, and at times become weary of being the one looked to for a cheerful attitude. Of course you do. You are in human form. We have eternally surrounded you with a gleaming garland, and during these times we make it even brighter. Your role requires a great deal of energy; we assist you with this while you acknowledge the balance and move forward. Yes, we also give you space to rest so that you can regenerate. Thank you for having chosen to serve this life purpose repeatedly.

CHARLES

Tell us your dreams, and we will help you follow them. You must tell us your dreams. You confuse us by asking us for one thing and then another. If you want two dreams, tell us. If you want three or four dreams, tell us. If you want one dream, tell us. We're here and ready to help you. Open up your heart and open up your soul. It will tell your mind and your thoughts what your dream is or what your dreams are. Then, with the vision, tell us about your dream or dreams. We will always support you.

Those with this name are dreamers, and they have respectable dreams with purpose. They will succeed in following their dreams, but they need to be focused on what really IS the dream. We see you writing your dreams across the sky. When you do so, we will know, and we will guide you with a beam of light moving forward in front of you ... you will not falter. Again, we encourage you and want to remind you that we are here. Your path is clear as long as you are clear. Thank you for being a dreamer. The universe needs dreamers, and we love you.

CHARLIE

Tell us your dreams, and we will help you follow them. You must tell us your dreams. You confuse us by asking us for one thing and then another. If you want two dreams, tell us. If you want three or four dreams, tell us. If you want one dream, tell us. We're here and ready to help you. Open up your heart and open up your soul. It will tell your mind and your thoughts what your dream is or what your dreams are. Then, with the vision, tell us about your dream or dreams. We will always support you.

Those with this name are dreamers, and they have respectable dreams with purpose. They will succeed in following their dreams, however, they need to be focused on what really IS the dream. We see you writing your dreams across the sky. When you do so, we will know, and we will guide you with a beam of light moving forward in front of you … you will not falter. Again, we encourage you and want to remind you that we are here. Your path is clear as long as you are clear. Thank you for being a dreamer. The universe needs dreamers, and we love you.

CHARLOTTE

Take a bow, Charlotte, for you are a star in so many eyes. You rise above the daily routine to heights that are uncommon to ordinary days. You have a charismatic countenance which is uplifting and motivating. When you are around, everything becomes more exciting about life. You are capable of celebrity status, yet you tend to place your attention on your immediate locality to share your progressive words. This is a gift to others, as your optimism is contagious. We applaud you.

CHELSEA

Sky-lit, you are able to see a vast panorama of possibilities, unlike most on this Earth walk. You carry with you the secrets and the magic of a million stars, the power of the sun, and the stillness of the moon … not all at once … but when whichever of these promotes well-being and brings answers that are being sought. Allow others to look to you for inspiration in finding their answers and to realize that some mysteries must remain mysteries. In so doing, they too will embrace the universe's panorama.

CHERI

Cheri, we call you our level-headed joy bringer. Logical, yet always cheerful, you bring a combination which is much needed in this world. You never seem to lose sight of the balance needed to achieve results in any situation or any relationship. You are the scales of temperament that evenly weigh all the possibilities and arrive with a quick result. Not many are willing to take on this position; we are grateful for those of your name who do so.

CHERYL

A Blast from the Past. All the things taught by those who are wise about not holding on to the past are correct. However, at another level, you possess the ability, which so many do not, to glean happy thoughts and memories, and to hold the lessons—both good and not-so-good—in your soul. You can visit the past briefly and move on without interruption of your present moment. You are also gifted at creating good memories for yourself and your loved ones ... memories which bring joy to the moment being experienced. Congratulations on being so adept with this purpose.

CHEYENNE

Don't worry about a thing. Why do you ponder so? Know that you and the world are at peace, regardless of events. That's the way it has been designed despite the way things appear externally. You need movement to stabilize your depth. Be wary of becoming stagnant in a cesspool of woe. There are vast possibilities of movement to bring you to balance. Creativity, body/mind/spirit work, or simply walking can be just a few. Find your movement and rise to new heights while remaining securely grounded. Your pensiveness, then, will be productive. You will have the depth of the soul's universal longing for truth at hand, and you will have the ability to share in a positive manner.

CHRIS

"To each his own." This is a common saying. However, it reflects one of the major lessons you are here to learn. Your lesson is to acknowledge that your differences and others' differences are simply the necessary parts which make the whole. How would the world look if it were all one color, or all black and white, all flat, all rolling terrain, all dry, or all covered with foliage? How could it even survive? You are not only here to learn how important diversity is, but to be a constant reminder about the importance of the macrocosm ... the big picture of life on this Earth. The planet will only be sustained

by nurturing it all. Teach this, please. It may feel like a daunting task you have been charged with, and we want you to know that whatever influence you create will not be like a job for you ... in fact, it will come naturally because we constantly guide you. If you doubt your actions and words (and you will), know that the doubt is not coming from the pure source. Just relax with this lifetime; the rest will fall into place.

CHRISTINA

"To each his own." This is a common saying. However, it reflects one of the major lessons you are here to learn. Your lesson is to acknowledge that your differences and others' differences are simply the necessary parts which make the whole. How would the world look if it were all one color, or all black and white, all flat, all rolling terrain, all dry, or all covered with foliage? How could it even survive? You are not only here to learn how important diversity is, but to be a constant reminder about the importance of the macrocosm ... the big picture of life on this Earth. The planet will only be sustained by nurturing it all. Teach this, please. It may feel like a daunting task you have been charged with, and we want you to know that whatever influence you create will not be like a job for you ... in fact, it will come naturally because we constantly guide you. If you doubt your actions and words (and you will), know that the doubt is not coming from the pure source. Just relax with this lifetime; the rest will fall into place.

CHRISTINE

"To each his own." This is a common saying. However, it reflects one of the major lessons you are here to learn. Your lesson is to acknowledge that your differences and others' differences are simply the necessary parts which make the whole. How would the world look if it were all one color, or all black and white, all flat, all rolling terrain, all dry, or all covered with foliage? How could it even survive? You are not only here to learn how important diversity is, but to be a constant reminder about the importance of the macrocosm ... the big picture of life on this Earth. The planet will only

be sustained by nurturing it all. Teach this, please. It may feel like a daunting task you have been charged with, and we want you to know that whatever influence you create will not be like a job for you ... in fact, it will come naturally because we constantly guide you. If you doubt your actions and words (and you will), know that the doubt is not coming from the pure source. Just relax with this lifetime; the rest will fall into place.

CHRISTOPHER

"To each his own." This is a common saying. However, it reflects one of the major lessons you are here to learn. Your lesson is to acknowledge that your differences and others' differences are simply the necessary parts which make the whole. How would the world look if it were all one color, or all black and white, all flat, all rolling terrain, all dry, or all covered with foliage? How could it even survive? You are not only here to learn how important diversity is, you are also here to be a constant reminder about the importance of the macrocosm ... the big picture of life on this Earth. The planet will only be sustained by nurturing it all. Teach this, please. It may feel like a daunting task you have been charged with, and we want you to know that whatever influence you create will not be like a job for you ... in fact, it will come naturally because we constantly guide you. If you doubt your actions and words (and you will), know that the doubt is not coming from the pure source. Just relax with this lifetime; the rest will fall into place.

CHUCK

Tell us your dreams, and we will help you follow them. You must tell us your dreams. You confuse us by asking us for one thing and then another. If you want two dreams, tell us. If you want three or four dreams, tell us. If you want one dream, tell us. We're here and ready to help you. Open up your heart and open up your soul. It will tell your mind and your thoughts what your dream is or what your dreams are. Then, with the vision, tell us about your dream or dreams. We will always support you.

Those with this name are dreamers, and they have respectable dreams with purpose. They will succeed in following their dreams, yet they need to be focused on what really IS the dream. We see you writing your dreams across the sky. When you do so, we will know, and we will guide you with a beam of light moving forward in front of you. You will not falter. Again, we encourage you and want to remind you that we are here. Your path is clear as long as you are clear. Thank you for being a dreamer. The universe needs dreamers, and we love you.

CINDY / CINDI

As an easy rain caresses the Earth, your gentle nature embraces all you encounter. You bring pure caring to your family, your friends, your associates, your pets, others' pets, and to the very essence of life ... to the vegetation, the animals, the sky and yes, to the Earth. Your deep appreciation and gratitude are reciprocal to the All That Is. You serve your purpose by reflecting this gratefulness. Hark, do not be dismayed when you are surrounded by what is seemingly much less than the beauty of the All That Is. Always remember that the universe will achieve balance —balance which you may not understand. And always remember that we will refresh and restore your thankfulness. We mostly want you to always remember that your special touch on all you do, say, and think will never change. You are eternally caring and will eternally bring comfort to all.

CLAIRE

Icy mountains begin to warm when you stand at the foothills. You must ask yourself if the melting ice is a result of heat from your wrath and anger or if it is melting because of the warmth from your heart center. When you ask yourself this question, you will automatically know. If the meltdown is from a space inside you which reflects anger, you can transmute that heat to the heart warmth. We will tell you how: Just ask us for assistance to go to your center of love, and in an instant your heart will remember why you are here. You are here to transform cold personalities with your display of the inner knowledge that, when coming from a space of love, LOVE will always prevail. The icy ones will recognize your gift of shifting from anger to softness and will consequently learn the same lesson you have internalized. This is a tough calling, and we send you support from cherubs to constantly soften the hard shell in which you feel you may have arrived here, and to remind you of the sweetness of youthful innocence. We will carry you through.

CLARENCE

Icy mountains begin to warm when you stand at the foothills. You must ask yourself if the melting ice is a result of heat from your wrath and anger or if it is melting because of the warmth from your heart center. When you ask yourself this question, you will automatically know. If the meltdown is from a space inside you which reflects anger, you can transmute that heat to the heart warmth. We will tell you how: Just ask us for assistance to go to your center of love, and in an instant your heart will remember why you are here. You are here to transform cold personalities with your display of the inner knowledge that, when coming from a space of love, LOVE will always prevail. The icy ones will recognize your gift of shifting from anger to softness and will consequently learn the same lesson you have internalized. This is a tough calling, and we send you support from cherubs to constantly soften the hard shell in which you feel you may have arrived here, and to remind you of the sweetness of youthful innocence. We will carry you through.

CLARISE

Icy mountains begin to warm when you stand at the foothills. You must ask yourself if the melting ice is a result of heat from your wrath and anger or if it is melting because of the warmth from your heart center. When you ask yourself this question, you will automatically know. If the meltdown is from a space inside you which reflects anger, you can transmute that heat to the heart warmth. We will tell you how: Just ask us for assistance to go to your center of love, and in an instant your heart will remember why you are here. You are here to transform cold personalities with your display of the inner knowledge that, when coming from a space of love, LOVE will always prevail. The icy ones will recognize your gift of shifting from anger to softness and will consequently learn the same lesson you have internalized. This is a tough calling, and we send you support from cherubs to constantly soften the hard shell in which you feel you may have arrived here, and to remind you of the sweetness of youthful innocence. We will carry you through.

CLARISSA

Icy mountains begin to warm when you stand at the foothills. You must ask yourself if the melting ice is a result of heat from your wrath and anger or if it is melting because of the warmth from your heart center. When you ask yourself this question, you will automatically know. If the meltdown is from a space inside you which reflects anger, you can transmute that heat to the heart warmth. We will tell you how: Just ask us for assistance to go to your center of love, and in an instant your heart will remember why you are here. You are here to transform cold personalities with your display of the inner knowledge that, when coming from a space of love, LOVE will always prevail. The icy ones will recognize your gift of shifting from anger to softness and will consequently learn the same lesson you have internalized. This is a tough calling, and we send you support from cherubs to constantly soften the hard shell in which you feel you may have arrived here, and to remind you of the sweetness of youthful innocence. We will carry you through.

CLARK

Behold the newness in all things...in the past, the present, and later. Like a work of art, knowledge is perceived for the learners' perceptions, which is either assimilated or ignored. You will know what applies to you and what to ignore. You are divinely guided to the precise knowledge you need that will add to your already deeply-rooted wisdom. Yes, you have learned in many lifetimes and we bid you success, as now you have acquired enough to propel others into the endless sea of wise currents and waves. It is your time to enjoy ... to observe the newness arise in those who derive benefits from your natural way of directing them to the knowledge they most need.

CLAUDE

Utensils are a necessary part of this life on Earth. Your lesson is to make use of the resources which are made available to you in order to implement your purpose, which is to provide instruction on how to ask for, search for, and find the "utensils" which will create progress, harmony, and success in whatever endeavors are at hand. It can be from making a meal, re-inventing the wheel, organizing a space, or creating a blueprint for a goal. You will learn and know where to find the utensils, or resources, and will share the knowledge throughout this lifetime. In past lives, you were scattered and blew with the wind in whatever direction the moment held. For this reason, you have chosen to return and become more centered and resourceful for yourself and your vast array of friends, acquaintances, and of course, family. Do not doubt that you will learn this ability. We are guiding you and presenting our "utensils" to you; you will know.

CLAUDETTE

Clear all the decks, Claudette. It gets too crowded. Too many interests dilute your richness. Clear the decks and give your attention to a few. You will know which one or which ones to devote your loyalty. They are the interests which are not merely interests; they are the ones that fire such a passion that you cannot clear them from any decks. Let the ones go that are intriguing, yet do not ignite that fire. This goes for people in your life as well. Your striking presence makes people gravitate toward you. Crowds do not serve you well. Limit the seating at your personal stadium. Allow all to visit, and allow only a limited number of back stage passes. Those with passes are those who will share with you mutually enriching experiences. Your life lesson is to achieve clarity. We say to you: Learn what is extraneous and what is pertinent to your life's purpose. Your purpose is to pass along this ability.

CLAUDIA

Utensils are a necessary part of this life on Earth. Your lesson is to make use of the resources which are made available to you in order to implement your purpose, which is to provide instruction on how to ask for, search for, and find the "utensils" which will create progress, harmony, and success in whatever endeavors are at hand. It can be from making a meal, re-inventing the wheel, organizing a space, or creating a blueprint for a goal. You will learn and know where to find the utensils, or resources, and will share the knowledge throughout this lifetime. In past lives, you were scattered and blew with the wind in whatever direction the moment held. For this reason, you have chosen to return and become more centered and resourceful for yourself and your vast array of friends, acquaintances, and of course, family. Do not doubt that you will learn this ability. We are guiding you and presenting our "utensils" to you; you will know.

CLINT / CLINTON

Strong yet soft, you are like most refer to as a cuddly bear ... lovable yet protective ... huggable yet able to defend yourself and others. You will walk the extra mile to obtain bounty for your loved ones, you will take rest, and you will not allow your home or your family to be encroached upon or threatened. You do prefer a clan of close friends and relations, as this represents a haven for you and promotes a sense of safe harbor for all. Your purpose and your lesson are obvious: To provide gentle comfort and undisputed protection when necessary. Your animal totem, of course, is the Bear. Be conscious of this energy, for it will assist in sustaining you through all the seasons of your life.

COLE

Soulful you appear, Cole, and soulful you are. You are among the deep thinkers and empaths of this world. Your serious and compassionate approach does not equate with sullenness or sadness regarding life. You are also among those who celebrate life, who laugh, and who can bring joy. You are actually a portrait of duality ... the duality of somberness and gladness. The most important role you play ... your purpose ... is that of a joyful and caring soul. Your touching demeanor softens hearts and alleviates callousness that may surround others' auras. You bring about suppleness of spirits in need of awakening. We ask that you surround yourself with the color pink for the love you deserve to receive in return for the empathy you give.

COLLEEN

Start it up! You have a knack for igniting and setting things in motion. We call you our Initiator and Accelerator, as you are among the ones who are sent here to put things in motion and then move them forward. We caution you, too, that there are times to put on the brakes, and this is the lesson you are here to learn. We may add that you have been doing well with both this life's purpose and this life's lesson. You have arrived here with the knowledge instilled within your soul that, once something is ablaze, you are aware of exactly when to stoke the fire. Conversely, you know when to let the coals dim and fade out, because some blazes are not for the common good. Colleen, we have provided you with our gift of Cedarwood and Spruce energy for your need to stay both heightened and grounded; you have such a high calling. Visit Cedarwood and Spruce when you feel the need to elevate your consciousness and when you feel the need to get "back to Earth." Share this message with others who you will know require it. Thank you for your response to the call to step out, step up, and ignite! We cherish you.

COLLETE

Start it up! You have a knack for igniting and setting things in motion. We call you our Initiator and Accelerator, as you are among the ones who are sent here to put things in motion and then move them forward. We caution you, too, that there are times to put on the brakes, and this is the lesson you are here to learn. We may add that you have been doing well with both this life's purpose and this life's lesson. You have arrived here with the knowledge instilled within your soul that, once something is ablaze, you are aware of exactly when to stoke the fire. Conversely, you know when to let the coals dim and fade out, because some blazes are not for the common good. Colleen, we have provided you with our gift of Cedarwood and Spruce energy for your need to stay both heightened and grounded; you have such a high calling. Visit Cedarwood and Spruce when you feel the need to elevate your consciousness and when you feel the need to get "back to Earth." Share this message with others who you will know require it. Thank you for your response to the call to step out, step up, and ignite! We cherish you.

CONNIE

Hoist your sails! Your life here will be quite a journey. The course may be rough and treacherous; however, you are a natural navigator who can assess the winds, the storms, the still waters, the sun, and the moon as though you were born with a barometer on your forehead and a compass in your heart. Along the way, you will rescue occupants of other ships that have become lost in the sea of confusion, or even have been shipwrecked. You are brave and noble, finding your way always to safe shores and rewarding ports of call. Your angels are constantly guiding you and providing strength.

CONSTANCE

Hoist your sails! Your life here will be quite a journey. The course may be rough and treacherous; however, you are a natural navigator who can assess the winds, the storms, the still waters, the sun and the moon as though you were born with a barometer on your forehead and a compass in your heart. Along the way, you will rescue occupants of other ships that have become lost in the sea of confusion, or even have been shipwrecked. You are brave and noble, finding your way always to safe shores and rewarding ports of call. Your angels are constantly guiding you and providing strength.

COREY / CORY

Hoist your sails! You're in for quite a journey. The course may be rough and treacherous; however, you are a natural navigator who can assess the winds, the storms, the still waters, the sun and the moon as though you were born with a barometer on your forehead and a compass in your heart. Along the way, you will rescue occupants of other ships that have become lost in the sea of confusion, or even have been shipwrecked. You are brave and noble, finding your way always to safe shores and rewarding ports of call. Your angels are constantly guiding you and providing strength.

COURTNEY

Simplicity and Simplistic are not just words to you; they are verbs and adjectives. They represent a way of living. You take this manner of talking about keeping things simple to an authentic level. You help to organize without a great deal of hullabaloo, you cook without making a big project of it (even 3-course meals), and you provide guidance toward the KISS (keep it simple, sweetie) philosophy. In so doing, Courtney, you serve your purpose. You create a calm environment, which is sought after by so many. We help you with constant, peaceful energy so that you can manifest these simplistic, vital outcomes. We also send you the energy of Celestite to fill your physical space with tranquil energy. Thank you for bringing to this lifetime an important aspect from which others benefit both directly and indirectly.

CRYSTAL / KRYSTAL

Crystal / Krystal, you are as the evergreen, always exhibiting beauty throughout the seasons of your life. Your lesson is to learn how to be consistent. This will help with your ability to count on yourself to always "BE" when you feel you may be less than your true value. Your purpose is to demonstrate this consistency. Too many plant themselves in a comfortable spot. They do grow; however, they do not always reach their full potential of enjoying the constant beauty of life. They go through the seasons and often allow the winter seasons to freeze their glamour and their goals. So, our splendid evergreen, stand tall, display your eternal beauty, and provide nurturing to others who can also be evergreen, with your nudge.

CURT / CURTIS

Tough as nails. Tougher than nails. We want you to know that this is not what you are expected to be. In fact, it isn't even what you signed up to be before arriving here. You wanted to be assertive—a leader, yet pliant, not made of steel ... definitive in direction, yet not harsh. If you find yourself in a position where you feel you're expected to be aggressive, call on us and we will give you the angelic strength to approach the situation with unbiased and focused kindness, while keeping the reins of dissidence firmly under control. Some will, and some will not respect you for this gentle authority. Pay no heed to earning respect; it matters not. You are fulfilling your role here to take loving charge where otherwise chaos and squabbles would have resulted. We call you our Orchestrator of Positive Outcomes, and we send continuous blessings to you for assistance. We surround you with the energies of orange and gold for courage, combined with Christ-like love.

CYNDI

As an easy rain caresses the Earth, your gentle nature embraces all you encounter. You bring pure caring to your family, your friends, your associates, your pets, others' pets, and to the very essence of life ... to the vegetation, the animals, the sky and yes, to the Earth. Your deep appreciation and gratitude are reciprocal to the All That Is. You serve your purpose by reflecting this gratefulness. Hark, do not be dismayed when you are surrounded by what is seemingly much less than the beauty of the All That Is. Always remember that the universe will achieve balance—balance which you may not understand. And always remember that we will refresh and restore your thankfulness. We mostly want you to always remember that your special touch on all you do, say, and think will never change. You are eternally caring and will eternally bring comfort to all.

CYNTHIA

As an easy rain caresses the Earth, your gentle nature embraces all you encounter. You bring pure caring to your family, your friends, your associates, your pets, others' pets, and to the very essence of life ... to the vegetation, the animals, the sky and yes, to the Earth. Your deep appreciation and gratitude are reciprocal to the All That Is. You serve your purpose by reflecting this gratefulness. Hark, do not be dismayed when you are surrounded by what is seemingly much less than the beauty of the All That Is. Always remember that the universe will achieve balance— balance which you may not understand. And always remember that we will refresh and restore your thankfulness. We mostly want you to always remember that your special touch on all you do, say, and think will never change. You are eternally caring and will eternally bring comfort to all.

DAKOTA

Diamonds in the sand. Yes, your lesson during this lifetime is to not only realize that there are diamonds among the trillions of grains of sand ... you will learn to recognize those sparkling individuals who are precious, yet possess an indestructible spirit. Your purpose is to bring to attention their worth and help them to shine, as only they can. There are an endless number of diamonds in the sand, and most are unaware of their value. They are easily found. In fact, all grains are gleaming gems. However, some are just not ready to glisten with impenetrable endurance. They are here to learn different lessons. You are one such diamond who is aware of your value, and you will recognize those who are unaware or feel cracked. They are not marred, and you will know exactly how to transform their inferior self-image to that of gleaming intention for the benefit of the planet. We will help transport you to the many beaches where these dear jewels are waiting to be discovered.

DALE

Instill what you can, when you can, where you can ... because you are a teacher and ah, you have been a master before. Whether you teach love, patience, academics or spiritual truth, you impart the perfect words to resonate within and to be internalized for the recipients' use toward their benefit. We in turn instill all you need to be directed as the humble master you are. And yes, you are a 5-star student on our honor roll. You do have such honor, and we are pleased.

DAMIEN

You are the buck that stands ground in defense of winning a mate at all costs. We want to advise you, though, our brave one, that vying for a mate is not the way in which you discover the truth in deep companionship. Unlike the buck, you need not be the strongest or the most intimidating male in order to capture the prize of a mate. You arrived here in order to learn the lesson of heart attraction and soul attraction being paramount, and we must say, you either already have discovered this lesson or most definitely will internalize this lesson during your current lifetime. Those incarnations which may follow will find you grounded in the true attraction of choosing a mate. This in turn will also help you with all of your choices. What attracts your heart and your soul, versus winning at all costs, will enrich your journey.

DAMON

You are the buck that stands ground in defense of winning a mate at all costs. We want to advise you, though, our brave one, that vying for a mate is not the way in which you discover the truth in deep companionship. Unlike the buck, you need not be the strongest or the most intimidating male in order to capture the prize of a mate. You arrived here in order to learn the lesson of heart attraction and soul attraction being paramount, and we must say, you either already have discovered this lesson or most definitely will internalize it during your current lifetime. Those incarnations which may follow will find you grounded in the true attraction of choosing a mate. This in turn will also help you with all of your choices. What attracts your heart and your soul, versus winning at all costs, will enrich your journey.

DAN

Find the golden morsels in everyday life. Avoid the tendency to look above or below the daily golden nuggets. They're all around you, each and every day. Avoid the tendency to get stuck in worry and fear. You do have the tendency to mull over things that don't really matter in the big picture. Do what you must; do not fret over it, and please do look for those morsels of wonder. They're all around you. Every day you will see them, and you may need to be more alert. Increase your awareness; that's why you came here ... to increase your awareness of the wonder and the glory and the miracles that are all around you, constantly. You will learn this lesson during your current lifetime. When you do, you will be able to share with others who are unable to see. You will be able to help them open their eyes and awaken to those morsels that are all around them, all the time, every day. They will thank you for the examples you set ... for the little things you say to them that help them awaken and see the glory, and to see that they do not have to fret needlessly. They do not have to dwell on what appear to be problems that are in the long run unimportant. They will see the importance of their day-to-day life being equally important as the grand picture of their life. You will teach them to take each moment and make it glorious in some way.

We thank you for taking on this seemingly heavy duty, and remind you that you have chosen this, and you will rise above your mulling. You will rise above it, and you will be so filled ... so filled with laughter and smiles. We give you Clear Quartz crystal to enhance every positive thought and observation. You are programmed to not increase negative thoughts and observations. They will not be enhanced ... only the positive will be augmented. We also give you Gold Quartz to enhance your happiness and your self-confidence. Go now, do your job; you chose it. You have all the capabilities to see, to feel, and to hear the glorious.

DANA

Fear not, Dana, as you are equipped with all you need for this lifetime to succeed in any endeavor and to have successful relationships. You are family oriented, yet able to pull off a career. We say fear not, although you actually harbor no fear. It is natural for you to take on any aspect of life with self-assuredness. The purpose you have chosen is to be a rock, a foundation on which others stand and build. Be certain to have your own sturdy foundation, as no one else will provide it ... they perceive you as quite strong already. You are seen as independent in your strength. It all comes easily to you, and we say to keep your foundation strong, and stand strong for your own needs.

DANEEN

You may ask yourself, "Whatever happened to this thing called love?" You, our tender soul, seek the best in others and in every situation. You are often disappointed in the lack of genuine caring and compassion from individuals and from the world as a whole. We want to tell you to cling to that which is true, for you shall find much that is true. We want to tell you never to fear that you will succumb to so many worldly ways which you find unnatural to your kind soul. You are the essence of love, truth, and compassion. Yes, you will have times when you may not feel or act as such. You are in human form—it will happen. Always know, despite these times, that your core kindness will prevail, and all will be well.

DANIEL

Find the golden morsels in everyday life. Avoid the tendency to look above or below the daily golden nuggets. They're all around you, each and every day. Avoid the tendency to get stuck in worry and fear. You do have the tendency to mull over things that don't really matter in the big picture. Do what you must; do not fret over it, and please do look for those morsels of wonder. They're all around you. Every day you will see them, and you may need to be more alert. Increase your awareness; that's why you came here ... to increase your awareness of the wonder and the glory and the miracles that are all around you, constantly. You will learn this lesson during your current lifetime. When you do, you will be able to share with others who are unable to see. You will be able to help them open their eyes and awaken to those morsels that are all around them, all the time, every day. They will thank you for the examples you set ... for the little things you say to them that help them awaken and see the glory, and to see that they do not have to fret needlessly. They do not have to dwell on what appear to be problems that are in the long run unimportant. They will see the importance of their day-to-day life being equally important as the grand picture of their life. You will teach them to take each moment and make it glorious in some way.

We thank you for taking on this seemingly heavy duty, and remind you that you have chosen this, and you will rise above your mulling. You will rise above it, and you will be so filled ... so filled with laughter and smiles. We give you Clear Quartz Crystal to enhance every positive thought and observation. You are programmed to not increase negative thoughts and observations. They will not be enhanced ... only the positive will be augmented. We also give you Gold Quartz to enhance your happiness and your self-confidence. Go now, do your job; you chose it. You have all the capabilities to see, to feel, and to hear the glorious.

DANIELLE

Unlike so many, you are not one who has ever needed to ponder your purpose. You have many passions, yet you have always known which of those passions is your primary calling. You may feel you have not yet forged ahead to carry your torch toward victory in meeting your purpose and shining with joy. We want you to know at a deep level that this is not a task for you. Simply acknowledge and move forward with it. Your actions will all be in perfect timing, and we will create the opportunities for you to move easily and gleefully along your destined path. We provide you with confirmations repeatedly and give you the consciousness of the violet-white light. You will always be connected with us. In any moments of doubt, move your focus to the violet-white light, and the doubt will be removed.

DANNA

Find the golden morsels in everyday life. Avoid the tendency to look above or below the daily golden nuggets. They're all around you, each and every day. Avoid the tendency to get stuck in worry and fear. You do have the tendency to mull over things that don't really matter in the big picture. Do what you must; do not fret over it, and please do look for those morsels of wonder. They're all around you. Every day you will see them, and you may need to be more alert. Increase your awareness; that's why you came here ... to increase your awareness of the wonder and the glory and the miracles that are all around you, constantly. You will learn this lesson during your current lifetime. When you do, you will be able to share with others who are unable to see. You will be able to help them open their eyes and awaken to those morsels that are all around them, all the time, every day. They will thank you for the examples you set ... for the little things you say to them that help them awaken and see the glory, and to see that they do not have to fret needlessly. They do not have to dwell on what appear to be problems that are in the long run unimportant. They will see the importance of their day-to-day life being equally important as the grand picture of their life. You will teach them to take each moment and make it glorious in some way.

We thank you for taking on this seemingly heavy duty, and remind you that you have chosen this, and you will rise above your mulling. You will rise above it, and you will be so filled ... so filled with laughter and smiles. We give you Clear Quartz crystal to enhance every positive thought and observation. You are programmed to not increase negative thoughts and observations. They will not be enhanced ... only the positive will be augmented. We also give you Gold Quartz to enhance your happiness and your self-confidence. Go now, do your job; you chose it. You have all the capabilities to see, to feel, and to hear the glorious.

DANNY

Find the golden morsels in everyday life. Avoid the tendency to look above or below the daily golden nuggets. They're all around you, each and every day. Avoid the tendency to get stuck in worry and fear. You do have the tendency to mull over things that don't really matter in the big picture. Do what you must; do not fret over it, and please do look for those morsels of wonder. They're all around you. Every day you will see them, and you may need to be more alert. Increase your awareness; that's why you came here ... to increase your awareness of the wonder and the glory and the miracles that are all around you, constantly. You will learn this lesson during your current lifetime. When you do, you will be able to share with others who are unable to see. You will be able to help them open their eyes and awaken to those morsels that are all around them, all the time, every day. They will thank you for the examples you set ... for the little things you say to them that help them awaken and see the glory, and to see that they do not have to fret needlessly. They do not have to dwell on what appear to be problems that are in the long run unimportant. They will see the importance of their day-to-day life being equally important as the grand picture of their life. You will teach them to take each moment and make it glorious in some way.

We thank you for taking on this seemingly heavy duty, and remind you that you have chosen this, and you will rise above your mulling. You will rise above it, and you will be so filled ... so filled with laughter and smiles. We give you Clear Quartz crystal to enhance every positive thought and observation. You are programmed to not increase negative thoughts and observations. They will not be enhanced ... only the positive will be augmented. We also give you Gold Quartz to enhance your happiness and your self-confidence. Go now, do your job; you chose it. You have all the capabilities to see, to feel, and to hear the glorious.

DARCY

Lay it on the line, our candid one. Your gifts are the ability to speak your truth without harshness, and to analyze situations, events, and individuals with concise precision. Because you are known for your consistent frankness and accurate perceptions, you are honored by most as a voice of reason. We say to you: Take care to avoid getting lost in a world that is so full of opportunities to step in and summarize. Pay attention also to your own life path on a daily basis to ensure you are living your own truth. This is your lesson: To share your gifts, yet shower yourself with the same love of truth.

DARLENE

Look to the sunset. Look to it for the calming colors. Look to it for nature's art. Look to it to remind you that endings can be beautiful and that there are promises for new beginnings. Look to it to remind yourself that this day is done and how beautiful it was! Look to it to relax, with a knowing that you have done your best and are tucking the day in with warmth and acceptance ... also knowing that you yourself bring comfort, warmth, beauty, acceptance, and hope along your chosen path. Well done, our reflection of sunset colors.

DARREL / DARRYL / DARYL

Our adventurous one, the saying, "throw caution to the wind" often describes you. When you have a passion toward something (or even an intense interest), you forge forward with no fear. This manner of approaching life does not work for most. Although it backfires for you occasionally, it does help toward serving your purpose, which is to demonstrate the self-fulfillment that following your bliss can bring, along with the benefits of perseverance when things do not quite work out as envisioned. This will keep you on your destined path (from which you veer occasionally because of your nature). You have the inner strength to endure the backfires, and you have the gratitude and excitement to celebrate the wild successes. Your lesson here is to know how to distinguish danger from difficulty, and you are doing well. We want you to know that we are a protective presence for you whether you are feeling the utmost confidence or recovering from a bump in the road.

DAVE

Do not be dismayed should you be called the silent one. You will be referred to as such out of respect and because you have a certain mystique about you that makes your words valuable. Your calm demeanor attracts both outgoing and shy individuals. You are the calm in most storms, the "go to" individual for sound advice, and the shoulder sought out by many. Not to say you are boring ... quite the contrary. Your inner light and your sense of humor is also appreciated, and you know exactly when to show your outgoing side in order to prevent awkward communication.

DAVID

Do not be dismayed should you be called the silent one. You will be referred to as such out of respect and because you have a certain mystique about you that makes your words valuable. Your calm demeanor attracts both outgoing and shy individuals. You are the calm in most storms, the "go to" individual for sound advice, and the shoulder sought out by many. Not to say you are boring ... quite the contrary. Your inner light and your sense of humor is also appreciated, and you know exactly when to show your outgoing side in order to prevent awkward communication.

DAWN

Slowly, we say to you ... slowly. You have a tendency to move a little too quickly through things that need more time in order to best perform the task at hand, and to more thoroughly derive joy from your work. Your lesson here is to learn to savor every action you take as though it is of importance to your soul's development of peace within yourself. This particular life lesson is learned through appreciation of your moments.

We also want you to know that "rattling the cage" gets you nowhere, plus it can agitate the very people who would love you most. Your other lesson is to find the ability to tame your restlessness, which leads to your purpose. Once achieved, you will be of great help to those who also need to be in touch with a milder approach. Call on us when you need respite from your head-on tendencies. We will bring you tolerance and comfort.

DEAN

"Who goes there?" "Can I trust you?" These are questions similar to your approach to many life situations. Your lesson for this lifetime is Trust. You have been learning, and will continue to learn, whom to trust. More important, you are learning *how* to trust, and even *more* important, you are

learning to trust *yourself.* You have classic beauty of the soul, and those like you who are living here in these times attract those who will take advantage of kindness. Fret not, for the element of trust and the discernment of such will help you coast through this lifetime with golden sails. Your angels will direct you toward this higher understanding. Your kindness will result in no offense to those from whom you turn away when you realize their presence is not for your higher good. You will actually serve your purpose as a catalyst for the self-serving lost ones to realize an elevated frequency and get in touch with the source of right intention. We adorn you with a symbolic, indigo blue scarf that projects the big picture and gives you clarity of vision.

DEANA

"Who goes there?" *"Can I trust you?"* These are questions similar to your approach to many life situations. Your lesson for this lifetime is Trust. You have been learning and will continue to learn whom to trust. More important, you are learning *how* to trust, and even *more* important, you are learning to trust *yourself.* You have classic beauty of the soul, and those like you who are living here in these times attract those who will take advantage of kindness. Fret not, for the element of trust and the discernment of such will help you coast through this lifetime with golden sails. Your angels will direct you toward this higher understanding. Your kindness will result in no offense to those from whom you turn away when you realize their presence is not for your higher good. You will actually serve your purpose as a catalyst for the self-serving lost ones to realize an elevated frequency and get in touch with the source of right intention. We adorn you with a symbolic, indigo blue scarf that projects the big picture and gives you clarity of vision.

DEBBIE / DEBI

All's well that ends well. This is, or could be, your motto. You are focused on the end result. No matter what happens between point A and point Z, your ultimate goal is to bring the objective to fruition. The world needs you, as you are the one who gets things done, who achieves the task at hand and the projects which may take a while. You are the glue that holds together what may at times seem to be intricacies. You are a leader who takes on your role with pleasure. Your example is seen and acted upon, although you may not realize this.

We are grateful that you have come here to be such a helper ... a valued facilitator. Your rewards are great, as they are received by realizing your intended results. We honor you always and provide you the fortitude to continue your focus on good and beneficial endings to all you do here on Earth.

DEBORAH / DEBRA

All's well that ends well. This is, or could be, your motto. You are focused on the end result. No matter what happens between point A and point Z, your ultimate goal is to bring the objective to fruition. The world needs you, as you are the one who gets things done, who achieves the task at hand and the projects which may take a while. You are the glue that holds together what may at times seem to be intricacies. You are a leader who takes on your role with pleasure. Your example is seen and acted upon, although you may not realize this.

We are grateful that you have come here to be such a helper ... a valued facilitator. Your rewards are great, as they are received by realizing your intended results. We honor you always and provide you the fortitude to continue your focus on good and beneficial endings to all you do here on Earth.

DELORIS

Chains will never bind you. Chains from relationships, chains from career, and even chains from your own choices. Take heed to realize when you are vulnerable to being bound. When you feel this, move in another direction. You may at times be uncertain if you are indeed at risk of being chained or if this is simply fear and doubt. We say to you: Just ask. We will show you yellow to signify that you need to proceed. No yellow signifies no action from you, which will keep you in freedom mode. Your lesson is to learn to celebrate freedom at all levels. We especially refer to the freedom to be You. Never hesitate to resist straying away from who you are, despite external circumstances. This will keep freedom ringing within your soul. The bells of self-actualization sound sweet. Enjoy their music.

DENISE

Flowing from the stream to the pond to the lake and to the ocean ... allowing yourself to be carried through the tributaries of life without question is quite difficult. However, your lesson is to learn to float to your destinations and to your destiny during this life without resistance or question. Indeed, this is seemingly impossible to the human experience. However, you will learn and you will feel the freedom and exhilaration of going with the flow, as the saying goes. You will reach both small and great goals along the way, and you will swim easily in all types of currents with ease, once you simply allow your river of life to unfold. We send you invisible, weightless life jackets of courage and rafts of comfort to help you along the way.

DENNIS

You wear it well. Whether it be a tuxedo or work jeans, you exude elegance. Whether it be a smile or a sad face, you radiate love. There is nothing paradoxical about you. It may be said about you that what you see is what you get. What the world gets from you is authenticity regardless of where you are, who you are with, or what you are doing. You are true to your ideals, your goals, your beliefs, and your relationships. Your lesson for this lifetime is to simply accept those who have not reached the spiritual truths with which you arrived. Your purpose, no matter how unintentional on your part, is to be a shining example of living your own truth. We honor you, especially for your genuine smiles.

DESIREE

Do not throw your treasures away. Your treasures, of course, are not material items. Your treasures are the individuals who have come into your lifetime here to teach you and to learn from you. Your lesson is to hone the quality of unconditional acceptance ... especially to your immediate family. There will be those with challenges and who make less than honorable choices. It is your role to love them, anyway, despite the fact that you may wholly disagree with them. Your demonstration of tolerance will help create a shift in not only those who are on a path which does not serve them; your acceptance will also create a shift in the entire family unit. Yes, this will have a rippling effect and will bring your people to a higher state of cooperating as a whole. We ask you, when you are tempted to walk away, to remember that the individuals closest to you are in your lifetime as gems to be held close to your heart.

DEVON

You are the buck that stands ground in defense of winning a mate at all costs. We want to advise you, though, our brave one, that vying for a mate is not the way in which you discover the truth in deep companionship. Unlike the buck, you need not be the strongest or the most intimidating male in order to capture the prize of a mate. You arrived here in order to learn the lesson of heart attraction and soul attraction being paramount, and we must say, you either already have discovered this lesson or most definitely will internalize it during this lifetime Those incarnations which may follow will find you grounded in the true attraction of choosing a mate. This in turn will also help you with all of your choices. What attracts your heart and your soul, versus winning at all costs, will enrich your journey.

DIANE

"Who goes there?" *"Can I trust you?"* These are questions similar to your approach to many life situations. Your lesson for this lifetime is Trust. You have been learning, and will continue to learn, whom to trust. More important, you are learning *how* to trust, and even *more* important, you are learning to trust *yourself.* You have classic beauty of the soul, and those like you who are living here in these times attract those who will take advantage of kindness. Fret not, for the element of trust and the discernment of such will help you coast through this lifetime with golden sails. Your angels will

direct you toward this higher understanding. Your kindness will result in no offense to those from whom you turn away when you realize their presence is not for your higher good. You will actually serve your purpose as a catalyst for the self-serving lost ones to realize an elevated frequency and get in touch with the source of right intention. We adorn you with a symbolic, indigo blue scarf that projects the big picture and gives you clarity of vision.

DICK

To be you is to want for nothing. You will reach this fulfillment … this gratitude for whatever is surrounding you, during this lifetime. Your lesson (which you chose) is to be aware of the richness of life regardless of possessions and yes, even comfort levels. You may experience feast and you may experience famine this time around—your choice. You may be surrounded with fine embellishments and accessories or with only bare necessities. We extend to you our congratulations for choosing the lesson of gratitude. This is a big step in the process of loving, giving, receiving, and most of all—acceptance.

DIXIE

Don't let your name fool you or the world around you. All who know you will quickly learn that your name and your substance are different matters. Yes, you are outgoing and friendly as your name seems to reflect. However, you have the determination, whenever needed, to attend to both ordinary tasks and larger projects. Cheerful you are, a bringer of gladness to others, and you simultaneously provide the trust they have that you will follow through with any task or project in which you choose to participate and contribute. A depth of joy is what you bring. Flourish you will, our joyful worker.

DON

Don, the truth is all you need, so where shall you find it? You've been looking here, there, to and fro. Why do you seek in the wrong places? Why have you not looked into your own soul? This is where truth resides. It's where the truth resides for everyone. Many have found it. However, you have not, or so you feel you haven't. Not yet. It is good that you study many topics. It's good that you listen to many things; it will help you teach others. However, you look for the truth and you wonder why you have not discovered whatever it is you are seeking. You feel that there's such a void. You have vast knowledge because of your interests, because you thirst for so much understanding. You suffer so, because you have not found that little piece of whatever it is you're looking for. We say to you: That piece is the truth, and the truth lies in your soul. You can see the truth, feel the truth, and hear the truth on levels you have never experienced if you only look within. Be still. Trust. Trust that the truth will reveal itself. You won't have to put any effort into it, not like all the effort you've put into all the learning you've already done. Relax. Believe. Trust. The truth will come.

And what is the truth about? It's about who you are, who you have been, and who you will be. It's about your purpose. You must discover this yourself. It is your quest for this lifetime. You will discover, and you will carry forward your purpose so that when you arrive the next time, you will be clear about your purpose beforehand. You will not have to seek the truth in the manner you have this time. You will return with vast knowledge.

For now, be aware. Be aware of who you are. You will know. You will have such peace, and it will be soon so that you can carry on. You'll be here for much longer with that truth of who you are. We embrace you with comfort; we embrace you with the light you so need. We embrace you and we reinforce you with faith.

DONALD

Don, the truth is all you need, so where shall you find it? You've been looking here, there, to and fro. Why do you seek in the wrong places? Why have you not looked into your own soul? This is where truth resides. It's where the truth resides for everyone. Many have found it. However, you have not, or so you feel you haven't. Not yet. It is good that you study many topics. It's good that you listen to many things; it will help you teach others. However, you look for the truth and you wonder why you have not discovered whatever it is you are seeking. You feel that there's such a void. You have vast knowledge because of your interests, because you thirst for so much understanding. You suffer so, because you have not found that little piece of whatever it is you're looking for.

We say to you: That piece is the truth, and the truth lies in your soul. You can see the truth, feel the truth, and hear the truth on levels you have never experienced if you only look within. Be still. Trust. Trust that the truth will reveal itself. You won't have to put any effort into it, not like all the effort you've put into all the learning you've already done. Relax. Believe. Trust. The truth will come.

And what is the truth about? It's about who you are, who you have been, and who you will be. It's about your purpose. You must discover this yourself. It is your quest for this lifetime. You will discover, and you will carry forward your purpose so that when you arrive the next time, you will be clear about your purpose beforehand. You will not have to seek the truth in the manner you have this time. You will return with vast knowledge.

For now, be aware. Be aware of who you are. You will know. You will have such peace, and it will be soon so that you can carry on. You'll be here for much longer with that truth of who you are. We embrace you with comfort; we embrace you with the light you so need. We embrace you and we reinforce you with faith.

DONNA

You may ask yourself, "*Whatever happened to this thing called love?*" You, our tender soul, seek the best in others and in every situation. You are often disappointed in the lack of genuine caring and compassion from individuals and from the world as a whole. We want to tell you to cling to that which is true, for you shall find much that is true. We want to tell you never to fear that you will succumb to so many worldly ways that you find unnatural to your kind soul. You are the essence of love, truth, and compassion. Yes, you will have times when you may not feel or act as such. You are in human form—it will happen. Always know, despite these times, that your core kindness will prevail, and all will be well.

DONOVAN

Stand alone or don't stand at all. This is your personal "stance." We wish to tell you to reassess. You have heard the old and popular saying *"No Man is an Island."* This is true, especially for you. Your island is rich with character and creativity. However, without the support and cooperation from those members of your circle, who are willing to stand with you, your island will sink, and you will drown with your stubbornness. We beseech you to explore and accept your vulnerabilities. Then, with sureness and humility, accept the fact that you, as with all, can succeed—in general—much better with supporters. This is not to say you need to give up your independence—that is a different, wonderful trait and asset. Just accept the encouragement and support. It is healthy!

DOREEN

Stalwart as you may be, there is a cuddly side of you that few see, yet sense that it is there. You are excellent at choosing who will see this soft side, and you are just as keen at maintaining your strong stance on any subject you feel needs an unrelenting position. Quiet as you may at times be, when you speak, others want to know what you have to say, as they become aware that you do not over-use words nor do you speak idly. Your task here is to teach the art of discrimination when speaking.

DORIS

To each his own – this is a common saying. However, it reflects one of the major lessons you are here to learn. Your lesson is to acknowledge that your differences and others' differences are simply the necessary parts which make the whole. How would the world look if it were all one color, or all black and white, all flat, all rolling terrain, all dry, or all covered with foliage? How could it even survive? You are not only here to learn how important diversity is, you are also here to be a constant reminder about the importance of the macrocosm ... the big picture of life on this Earth. The planet will only be sustained by nurturing it all. Teach this, please. It may feel like a daunting task you have been charged with, and we want you to know that whatever influence you create will not be like a job for you ... in fact, it will come naturally because we constantly guide you. If you doubt your actions and words (and you will), know that the doubt is not coming from the pure source. Just relax with this lifetime; the rest will fall into place.

DOROTHY

Trip the light fantastic! *"Easy Does It"* is your motto. You go about this life on Earth in a confident manner with the innate knowledge that worry is counterproductive, and you know how to incorporate fun into your job. You delight in all you do, as you find purpose and excitement in all your endeavors. Starlight and fireflies are magic to your eyes, and you in turn reflect light amid darkness for others to see. You can lead the way because your "light" attitude negates worry about outcomes. Stay amazed with this life. It is your destiny to be shining with happiness.

DOUG

Air flow. Yes, it is a critical thing! And Doug, with no effort on your part, you create an air flow around you and everywhere you walk that is cleansing and healing. Your natural gift of changing the flow for the enhancement of people, places, and circumstances was provided to you when you chose this role. We constantly stoke your consciousness almost as though it levitates into the realm of an awareness that is not always experienced by those who are—and those who are not—seeking to discover such serenity. Because of this, you are able to naturally bring this awareness wherever you may be. We delight in your ability and in your own joy of sharing this gift of manifesting an elevated air flow in all your surroundings, in all you do, and for all who walk this Earth plane who come into your energy, or air flow field.

DOUGLAS

Air flow. Yes, it is a critical thing! And Doug, with no effort on your part, you create an air flow around you and everywhere you walk that is cleansing and healing. Your natural gift of changing the flow for the enhancement of people, places, and circumstances was provided to you when you chose this role. We constantly stoke your consciousness almost as though it levitates into the realm of an awareness that is not always experienced by those who are—and those who are not—seeking to discover such serenity. Because of this, you are able to naturally bring this awareness wherever you may be. We delight in your ability and in your own joy of sharing this gift of manifesting an elevated air flow in all your surroundings, in all you do, and for all who walk this Earth plane who come into your energy, or air flow field.

DREW

You may feel that you work and work and work, yet get more and more and more in debt. The lesson you chose to learn here is to recognize that debt is more than financial bills, and work is more than a vocation or a profession. You will learn during this lifetime that debt can encompass many things, including debt to yourself when it concerns ignoring, or not seeking, your passion. You will learn how to release yourself from self-debt, and you will learn to recognize where your true passion lies ... yet only if you wish. If you do wish, we will guide you to the areas where you will find passion. Your purpose will then be to fulfill the passion. Whatever that passion is, you will share it excitedly and graciously. We send you prayer beads for enhancing your ability to rise and meet your passion. These beads will direct you to your work and free yourself from self-doubt.

DUSTIN

Two for one. Three for two. YOU, Dustin, bring the extra bonus to all you give and to all you are asked to do. Your commitment to give your all, and your generosity, are what contribute to your purpose of teaching excellence through example. Your unselfishness may only be learned by few; however, your influence will be felt by those who enter your energy field and experience your kindness. This will be internalized by those who are meant to progress with altruistic characteristics and actions. We behold you for your benevolent work and for your ability to approach all activity and thought with quality. We provide you with the energy of white and gold to reflect your spiritual abundance toward all you encounter.

ED

Ed, our high jumper, you seek to reach the heights of any and every endeavor of which you are a part, or which you choose to pursue. For some, reaching for the stars and having their heads in the clouds does not work, because this mindset is often unrealistic and causes disappointment. However, you are among the high jumpers who know exactly how to use the pole to elevate and project yourself over the top even after you have missed the bar, knocked it down, and have taken falls ... sometimes resulting in emblematic injuries. You view the injuries as non-serious and certainly non-life threatening. Your unquestioned beliefs take you to your desired heights and beyond ... to higher goals. Ed, your gift is unwavering belief. Your purpose is to serve as an influence. Your lesson is to acquire the wisdom to know just how high to set the bar in order to understand that, while there are no limits, you have accomplished your personal best. You are indeed a track star of your self-competition, and we grace you with the ability to be content with this life. We often send you grounding energy so that you can maintain the balance you need and appreciate this lifetime, whether on the track or walking among nature, soaking up this Earth's beauty.

EDDIE

The challenge is yours to accept or not. We helped you arrive here with more than one purpose from which to choose. The reason for this challenge is the learning of best choices for the sake of your soul's development. You have experienced this difficulty in past lives, and you may wish to achieve the lesson now. This is not easy without our guidance. Therefore, if you do choose to meet this challenge, we will guide you. Should you feel you are not yet ready, we will also guide you to a divine purpose and ask that you act on the signs we give you that you will feel in the energy center just beneath your heart. Either way, you will meet a divine purpose. We send you the energy of yellow Topaz to bring additional personal strength.

EDWARD

Edward, our high jumper, you seek to reach the heights of any and every endeavor of which you are a part, or which you choose to pursue. For some, reaching for the stars and having their heads in the clouds does not work, because this mindset often is unrealistic and causes disappointment. However, you are among the high jumpers who know exactly how to use the pole to elevate and project yourself over the top even after you have missed the bar, knocked it down, and have taken falls ... sometimes resulting in emblematic injuries. You view the injuries as non-serious and certainly non-life threatening. Your unquestioned beliefs take you to your desired heights and beyond ... to higher goals. Edward, your gift is unwavering belief. Your purpose is to serve as an influence. Your lesson is to acquire the wisdom to know just how high to set the bar in order to understand that, while there are no limits, you have accomplished your personal best. You are indeed a track star of your self-competition, and we grace you with the ability to be content with this life. We often send you grounding energy so that you can maintain the balance you need and appreciate this lifetime whether on the track or walking among nature, soaking up this Earth's beauty.

EDGAR

Falling like thunder is how we see you ... the kind of soft thunder which is so welcomed by those who desire the tranquility experienced by nature sounds. Your calming yet distant presence is just what is needed by your friends and loved ones. Your quiet thunder, your comforting and safe presence, calms and helps stress surrender to serenity. This soft thunder also is a reminder that a cleansing rain may be nigh. How refreshing and nurturing you are to those who will savor your gentleness and the hope for a cleansing of stress.

EDWIN

Falling like thunder is how we see you ... the kind of soft thunder which is so welcomed by those who desire the tranquility experienced by nature sounds. Your calming yet distant presence is just what is needed by your friends and loved ones. Your quiet thunder and your comforting, safe presence helps stress surrender to serenity. This soft thunder also is a reminder that a cleansing rain may be nigh. How refreshing and nurturing you are to those who will savor your gentleness and the hope for a cleansing of stress.

ELAINE

Turnstiles, turnstiles, everywhere are turnstiles—which one will you use? You arrived here with multiple opportunities to experience a vastness of journeys, as well as portals to areas of service. One of the most important lessons you came here to learn is how to trust your inner knowing about these gateways. You may make decisions you regret, and you may even regret decisions you have dismissed ... the ones you did not make at all.

We want you to know of something you must delve into in order to reach your life's goal of achieving discernment. We want you to delve into the stillness. By this we do not mean to become a monk. We mean to make silence an ally. We mean to immerse yourself into the directions that the silence will take you ... like a soft, quilted turnstile that will take you from what seems to be a merry-go-round into a meadow of welcomed insights. These epiphanies will come from us, and you will recognize them by the feeling you get when you behold the beauty of a butterfly in the breeze.

We say to you: Be cautious not to stay on turnstiles, as they take you in circles. The oneness circle does not exist in this manner. Place your intent, instead, on the "from and to" objective of the turnstiles with the function of transporting you from doubt to certainty about the inherent goodness of the destination. We are pleased to assist you in choosing these entrances into discernment and the resulting blessings.

ELENA

Turnstiles, turnstiles, everywhere are turnstiles—which one will you use? You arrived here with multiple opportunities to experience a vastness of journeys, as well as portals to areas of service. One of the most important lessons you came here to learn is how to trust your inner knowing about these gateways. You may make decisions you regret, and you may even regret decisions you have dismissed ... the ones you did not make at all.

We want you to know of something you must delve into in order to reach your life's goal of achieving discernment. We want you to delve into the stillness. By this we do not mean to become a monk. We mean to make silence an ally. We mean to immerse yourself into the directions that the silence will take you ... like a soft, quilted turnstile that will take you from what seems to be a merry-go-round into a meadow of welcomed insights. These epiphanies will come from us, and you will recognize them by the feeling you get when you behold the beauty of a butterfly in the breeze.

We say to you: Be cautious not to stay on turnstiles, as they take you in circles. The oneness circle does not exist in this manner. Place your intent, instead, on the "from and to" objective of the turnstiles with the function of transporting you from doubt to certainty about the inherent goodness of the destination. We are pleased to assist you in choosing these entrances into discernment and the resulting blessings.

ELI / ELIJAH

You are not one for false bravado. You wear your shield of confidence as a banner announcing that you have overcome fear-based beliefs. Your courage is not as a bandy rooster, puffed up. It is as a solid mountain, unmoved by turmoil. We give you the strength of mountains, treed with oaks, to sustain your valor. You are aware at a level beyond your consciousness of this space of strength within. Your internal dialog is not moved or disturbed by the external events of this worldly existence. Your purpose is to provide courage and confidence to those who are in most need. Some of them will receive your help on a temporary basis; others will present themselves as family members and close friends. Do not worry about who, when, where, how, or for how long. We will take care of that part, and your inner knowledge will guide you.

ELISE

Soft streamers of starlit chiffon ... this is how we would describe your energy. Your energy rests gently on each and every individual with whom you come into contact. You are what many on this Earth call "unforgettable." Your essence remains long after you have physically left a room, and its effects are uplifting, in a calming manner. You and your effects are relished, and at times the cause of your effect is not even realized. Being one who does not seek out celebrity, this is of no concern to you. You came here to unobtrusively create a glow ... an everlasting glow. Your lesson is to relax with your natural ability to bring solace to others.

ELIZABETH

The albatross you feel you carry is for a noble reason, *and* you need not feel this weight. Align yourself with angelic lightness, and this burden you have taken on will feel feathery. Release the serious nature you may have attached to your purpose of lifting the lost from their self-created despair. Acknowledge the valuable direction and tenderness you willingly give. Treat your purpose as a welcomed spiritual gift and enjoy the manifestations of healing the darkened hearts that need your light. Once you do this, we will be much more able to help you soar with no feelings of heavy, Earth angel wings. Being willing is the secret that you need to make this happen.

ELLA

Turnstiles, turnstiles, everywhere are turnstiles—which one will you use? You arrived here with multiple opportunities to experience a vastness of journeys, as well as portals to areas of service. One of the most important lessons you came here to learn is how to trust your inner knowing about these gateways. You may make decisions you regret, and you may even regret decisions you have dismissed … the ones you did not make at all.

We want you to know of something you must delve into in order to reach your life's goal of achieving discernment. We want you to delve into the stillness. By this we do not mean to become a monk. We mean to make silence an ally. We mean to immerse yourself into the directions that the silence will take you … like a soft, quilted turnstile that will take you from what seems to be a merry-go-round into a meadow of welcomed insights. These epiphanies will come from us, and you will recognize them by the feeling you get when you behold the beauty of a butterfly in the breeze.

We say to you: Be cautious not to stay on turnstiles, as they take you in circles. The oneness circle does not exist in this manner. Place your intent, instead, on the "from and to" objective of the turnstiles with the function of transporting you from doubt to certainty about the inherent goodness of the destination. We are pleased to assist you in choosing these entrances into discernment and the resulting blessings.

ELLEN

Fail, fail, the gang's all here! Ellen, our bringer of confidence, we want you to know how needed you are to those who think they are failures. You have shown many, and will continue to help these troubled souls to see that the proverbial phrase of, "Failure is not a person; it is simply an event," is true. It is simply an occurrence, a result that can teach about how and what to avoid in order to reach a goal. More important, though, is your role of teaching that these sometimes disconcerting results serve a higher purpose: To discover confidence and self-assuredness. Those whom you touch with this knowledge will learn that each step in this life takes them closer to where they are destined to be. Praise them for all their steps. Remind them of their true divinity within, and help them shine that divinity back to the world, with the confidence that pure love emanates. Thank you for your light and for lifting others.

ELLIOTT

Open your eyes, Elliott. You must pay attention, open your eyes, and open all your spiritual senses to experience the light. You are surrounded by beams of brightness that others are able to see, if only you can acknowledge your power. Your lesson for this lifetime is to be aware of the great light, and to BE the illumination for yourself. When you arrive at this height of a light being, you will then have the essence needed to accomplish whatever you wish. Remember, whatever you accomplish, and no matter how many things you achieve, your soul purpose can only be met once you have acknowledged and accepted the light that you are.

EMILE

Hark! Uplift your brethren, our kind one. You are here to support your brothers and sisters of both your biological family and otherwise. Know that without your edification, some would fail. You bring attention to and praise for talents and skills, thus promoting the direction of dreams. Coaches and talent scouts are necessary, and you will enjoy self-fulfillment through your advancing of others' destinies. Thank you.

EMILY

Hark! Lift up your brethren, our sweet Emily. You are here to support your brothers and sisters of both your biological family and otherwise. Know that without your edification, some would fail. You bring attention to and praise for talents and skills, thus promoting the direction of dreams. Coaches and talent scouts are necessary, and you will enjoy self-fulfillment through your advancing of others' destinies. Thank you.

EMMA

Soft streamers of starlit chiffon ... this is how we would describe your energy. Your energy rests gently on each and every individual with whom you come into contact. You are what many on this Earth call "unforgettable." Your essence remains long after you have physically left a room, and its effects are uplifting, yet in a calming manner. You and your effects are relished, and at times the cause of your effect is not even realized. Being one who does not seek out celebrity, this is of no concern to you. You came here to unobtrusively create a glow ... an everlasting glow. Your lesson is to relax with your natural ability to bring solace to others.

EMMETT

Hark! Lift up your brethren, our kind one. You are here to support your brothers and sisters of both your biological family and otherwise. Know that without your edification, some would fail. You bring attention to and praise for talents and skills, thus promoting the direction of dreams. Coaches and talent scouts are necessary, and you will enjoy self-fulfillment through your advancing of others' destinies. Thank you.

ERIC

We liken you to a Ferris Wheel for viewing life. You bring attention to the panoramic view of the world and everyday life in general. On the seat you provide for others, they are able to see beyond the close detail. Detail is important, yes, and yet, there are so many who do not look beyond their nose. The broad spectrum, the vast possibilities, the grand view is often missed. Not only do you assist in providing the big picture ... you assist in allowing others to view life at every level. As the Ferris Wheel rises to various heights, it also descends to various heights, and repeats. So it is with you and the viewing seats you provide. You allow a comprehensive exploration of life ... of life's questions, of life's challenges, of life's solutions, and mostly of life's overall beauty. When looking at the grand scheme of things, the beauty and breathtaking views outweigh all else. Thank you for bringing attention to this; you are serving your purpose well.

ERICA / ERIKA

We liken you to a Ferris Wheel for viewing life. You bring attention to the panoramic view of the world and everyday life in general. On the seat you provide for others, they are able to see beyond the close detail. Detail is important, yes, and yet there are so many who do not look beyond their nose. The broad spectrum, the vast possibilities, the grand view is often missed. Not only do you assist in providing the big picture ... you assist in allowing others to view life at every level. As the Ferris Wheel rises to various heights, it also descends to various heights, and repeats. So it is with you and the viewing seats you provide. You allow a comprehensive exploration of life ... of life's questions, of life's challenges, of life's solutions, and mostly of life's overall beauty. When looking at the grand scheme of things, the beauty and breathtaking views outweigh all else. Thank you for bringing attention to this; you are serving your purpose well.

ERIN

Stones will not break you—they will only help to build up your foundation and add to the solid fortress called your soul. Dismiss, then, all the rocks hurled at you as being damaging. Instead, see them as building blocks to construct your true character of being the Guardian of both yourself and anyone along the way who has the need for armor to fend against the world's arrows. Your task is gallant. Your purpose is defined. You are guided and shielded as you continue to build your fortress and to house those in need of their own safe haven. Thank you for your willingness to bounce the stones away, to recognize the strength of your soul, and to share that strength when needed.

ESTELLE

Soulful you appear, Estelle, and soulful you are. You are among the deep thinkers and empaths of this world. Your serious and compassionate approach does not equate with sullenness or sadness regarding life. You are also among those who celebrate life, who laugh, and who can bring joy. You are actually a portrait of duality ... the duality of somberness and gladness. The most important role you play ... your purpose ... is that of a joyful and caring soul. Your touching demeanor softens hearts and alleviates callousness that may surround others' auras. You bring about suppleness of spirits in need of awakening. We ask that you surround yourself with the color pink for the love you deserve in return for the empathy you give.

ESTHER

Soulful you appear, Esther, and soulful you are. You are among the deep thinkers and empaths of this world. Your serious and compassionate approach does not equate with sullenness or sadness regarding life. You are also among those who celebrate life, who laugh, and who can bring joy. You are actually a portrait of duality ... the duality of somberness and gladness. The most important role you play ... your purpose ... is that of a joyful and caring soul. Your touching demeanor softens hearts and alleviates callousness that may surround others' auras. You bring about suppleness of spirits in need of awakening. We ask that you surround yourself with the color pink for the love you deserve in return for the empathy you give.

ETHAN

Search and Rescue. Search for the love inside your heart and rescue yourself. Search for the knowledge lying deep within your soul, and know yourself. Redeem the gifts you have been given to love and to be loved. You have suppressed love, omitted the inner knowledge, and the miracles of your spiritual gifts in past life times. You are destined to rise above the worldly chains to realize your full spiritual influence upon your own soul. Consequently, you will spread this love into the vast universe. Your immediate purpose, however, is to spread the love during this lifetime, on this Earth plane, to the souls here who are impoverished from love. We will shower them with the energy of Rose Quartz and open their heart centers as you reveal the pure love you were sent to teach. You, as well, are nourished and supported by us with this pure, loving energy.

EUGENE

You may feel that you work and work and work, yet get more and more and more in debt. The lesson you chose to learn here is to recognize that debt is more than financial bills, and work is more than a vocation or profession. You will learn during this lifetime that debt can encompass many things, including debt to yourself when it concerns ignoring, or not seeking, your passion. You will learn how to release yourself from self-debt, and you will learn to recognize where your true passion lies ... and only if you wish. If you do wish, we will guide you to the areas where you will find passion. Your purpose will then be to feed the passion. Whatever that passion is, you will share it excitedly and graciously. We send you prayer beads for enhancing your ability to rise and meet your passion. These beads will direct you to your work and free yourself from self-debt.

EULA

Sometimes the dice just do not fall in place. Keep tossing the dice, anyway. Your lesson is to realize that risks are necessary in this particular world in which you find yourself. You simply cannot turn away just because one throw of the dice is scattered and without the desired result. Your highest and best good is achieved through perseverance and the belief that, with effort and continued visualization, the dice will fall to serve your purpose. Life is not a game; it is a learning journey that has peaks and valleys. Behold all of it, for without both, it is simply monotone. Accomplishments are not realized through playing one note or rolling the same dice. Practice the whole scale and have scores of dice in your pocket. You will learn the excitement that comes from uncertainty combined with persistence.

EUNICE / UNICE

Like a loaf of freshly-baked bread, you draw family, friends, and other visitors to your welcoming, cozy home and remind them of the nurturing they crave through connection with the home base. Star light, star bright, all's well and good tonight ... this is the peaceful countenance you exude. You will always be surrounded with people who gravitate toward and embrace the energy of a home with the welcome mat always available. This Earth on which you live is in grave need of wholesome connections. Thank you for serving this purpose.

EVA

The moon holds mysteries, and so do you. You gaze at the moon and wonder. We say to you: Gaze within to discover the wondrous mystery of You. You are looked upon by the world around you as curious and mysterious. In others' eyes, you gracefully waltz through your days and glide across your personal dance floor. For this, you are sometimes admired and are sometimes perplexing. Your philosophical nature compels and repels, depending on the individuals who notice your enigmatic presence. Your lesson is to understand that, despite what you may see as a larger mystery of the moon, or the universe in general, it is the realization that you hold the universe within. Revel in your truth. Celebrate the ancient truths that you hold. Let the moonlight of your very soul softly shine within, and outward. For this you will be doubly blessed.

EVAN

We call you The Heart and the Moon. Both the heart and the moon emanate soft, subtle, calming energy. You are one such individual who strives to live from the heart, and you do put forth the soft energy of a peaceful evening, which brings about solace. When combined, the heart and the moon create a lullaby of nurturing, and a sense of harmony with the Earth, the stars ... the universe itself ... the ease of harmony with the All. How precious this energy is that you share. We shower you with pastel rays so that you, too, can feel the blessing of the same energy others feel from you.

EVE

The moon holds mysteries, and so do you. You gaze at the moon and wonder. We say to you: Gaze within to discover the wondrous mystery of You. You are looked upon by the world around you as curious and mysterious. In others' eyes, you gracefully waltz through your days and glide across your personal dance floor. For this, you are sometimes admired and are sometimes perplexing. Your philosophical nature compels and repels, depending on the individuals who notice your enigmatic presence. Your lesson is to understand that, despite what you may see as a larger mystery of the moon, or the universe in general, it is the realization that you hold the universe within. Revel in your truth. Celebrate the ancient truths that you hold. Let the moonlight of your very soul softly shine within, and outward. For this you will be doubly blessed.

EVEYLN

Our dear one, some may say you are a martyr for a cause, for your career, or for those you love, and that you make sacrifices with no regard for your own well-being. Some may even imply that your unselfish actions may be to gain love and attention from others. We say to you: Do not allow how others may perceive your quest toward service to influence how you approach this lifetime. There are those who simply will not understand your calling to serve through using your gift of patience and through sharing universal love from your heart center. This purpose actually is fulfilling to you and brings the joy to this life on Earth that so many seek. We surround you with many shades of blue to infuse you with placidity and to reciprocate the serenity you bring to the world in which you are living.

FAY / FAYE

Our loyal one, you cherish those you love, and you do not betray for a moment ... not even if they wrong you. Your devotion surpasses anything that would tarnish your faithfulness. This abiding loyalty is the same for your principles, your work, and anything to which you commit. Those whom call you their friend are blessed, as the friendship will be enduring. Consequently, you are richly blessed by the reciprocal love you naturally create. You have graced this Earth many times. During these lifetimes you have learned the value and wisdom of commitment and respect. This wisdom has culminated for you and has crowned you with grace, dignity, and love.

FAITH

It is an honor for us that you have this name. You chose the lesson of dodging the slings and arrows that come from times when you do not demonstrate the word that your name seems to demand. Yes, you are aware that the word "demand" is not necessary as to actions which are synonymous with the nature of your name. You chose to demonstrate that faith is a personal matter and that showboating faith is more for the human ego than it is for spiritual growth. Yes, our faithful one, we acknowledge your inner faith. Yes, we know of your quiet belief in destined outcomes. You have the wisdom to know with whom you can share genuine love, belief, and faith. This is enough, and you cherish the opportunities to exhibit authentic faith. There are many on your path who appreciate and understand this truth. We are with you, assisting you when you are ridiculed or taunted regarding your name. We give you golden light to caress you at all times.

FELICIA

There are two sets of Felicia's. One is unassuming and would always rather be in the background, diligently performing her career task and quietly taking care of business at home. These Felicia's are humble, yet firm when approaching a stubborn individual. The fact that they are no more than ordinary by nature by no means equates to weakness when confronted with difficult situations or people. These Felicia's are here for the purpose of exhibiting strength despite appearing weak, and in so doing, rising above any self-effacing habits. They will step into their power despite their humility.

The other set of Felicia's are alluring and may have many romantic relationships before they settle for "the one." By the time "the one" is discovered, these Felicia's will have learned a valuable lesson in choices. They will know that just because there are many choices, there is no reason to try each one. They will learn the great value of connectedness and they will not depend on their magnetic attractiveness; they will honor the soul. This allure will also be present in all of their pursuits; it will not be difficult to gain employment, friends, or inclusion. The wonderful part of this is that, as with romance, these Felicia's chose the lesson of right choice and achieving the ability to easily discern the path for the highest and best good.

FERN

"One more for the road and one more for old time's sake." Fern, you instinctively know when to walk away with grace. You also are able to revisit "old times" without melancholy setting in. Nostalgia, yes, not sadness. This balance of cherishing memories, and even revisiting "old times" without becoming wistful is something that many wish they possessed. Your purpose is to teach those who cling to the past that it is healthy to hold the past fondly in the heart, yet to also take the lessons needed in order to progress on their soul path. You recognize the imitations among the glitter which is not gold, and you do not linger. You cherish those that are golden. You value it all, as it all contributes to evolvement. We give you the energy of snowflake obsidian to help you maintain this balance you exude.

FIONA

Stand alone or don't stand at all. This is your personal stance. We wish to tell you to reassess. You have heard the old and popular saying *"No man, or woman, is an island."* This is true, especially for you. Your island is rich with character and creativity. However, without the support and cooperation from those members of your circle, who are willing to stand with you, your island will sink, and you will drown with your stubbornness. We beseech you to explore and accept your vulnerabilities. Then, with sureness and humility, accept the fact that you, as with all, can succeed—in general—much better with supporters. This is not to say you need to give up your independence—that is a different, wonderful trait and asset. Just accept the encouragement and support. It is healthy!

FLO

Like a loaf of freshly-baked bread, you draw family, friends, and other visitors to your welcoming, cozy home and remind them of the nurturing they crave through connection with the home base. Star light, star bright, all's well and good tonight ... this is the peaceful countenance you exude. You will always be surrounded with people who gravitate toward and embrace the energy of a home with the welcome mat always available. This Earth on which you live is in grave need of wholesome connections. Thank you for serving this purpose.

FLORENCE

Stately you are at times. At other times, you are a roll-up-your-sleeves-and-get-your-hands-dirty kind of girl. Your lesson is to understand that there is no delineation between those born with the proverbial silver spoon and those born to humble, plebeianistic circumstances. You are learning this equality-consciousness role well, which is critical for the Earth. It may still take a long while before no differences are noticed, and you are among those who have been, are now, and will be establishing the mentality of fairness for all. Keep up the duality of your appearance; for in the world's recognition of contrast will come acceptance that all are significant and essential.

FLOYD

Much has been said about those with your name. Those with this name rise above any preconceptions of others about who they really are. Independence and self-love are the lessons you are here to learn, and you arrived here with the scenarios in place which will help you attain these traits. You are able, or will be able, to dismiss negative feedback about anything to do with YOU, because you know deep at your core who you are, and this is what you will or already have learned ... to cope with this world as it is. The journey is not an easy one, yet you have all you need to realize your value. Once this is achieved, you will know self-actualization, move along your path more easily, and more thoroughly treasure the ALL.

FRAN

"*To thine own self be true.*" Ah, our beloved, we see that you struggle to please others. This is, in one regard, honorable. However, it is usually only good for others, while you minimize your own self-worth. Your lesson here is one of the most difficult to achieve and internalize: It is to stand on, act on, and speak your truth. It is to respect all that you are, all that you stand for, and all that you do ... even when you feel you err. Each error is simply a stepping stone toward accepting your SELF and loving the amazing individual known as YOU. Our love for you is deep, and we constantly embrace you, accept you, and protect you. We send ascended masters for strength, courage, and the ability to love others without compromising your core being.

FRANCES / FRANCIS

"To thine own self be true." Ah, our beloved, we see that you struggle to please others. This is, in one regard, honorable. However, it is usually only good for others, while you minimize your own self-worth. Your lesson here is one of the most difficult to achieve and internalize: It is to stand on, act on, and speak your truth. It is to respect all that you are, all that you stand for, and all that you do ... even when you feel you err. Each error is simply a stepping stone toward accepting your SELF and loving the amazing individual known as YOU. Our love for you is deep, and we constantly embrace you, accept you, and protect you. We send ascended masters for strength, courage, and the ability to love others without compromising your core being.

FRANCESCA

"To thine own self be true.". Ah, our beloved, we see that you struggle to please others. This is, in one regard, honorable. However, it is usually only good for others, while you minimize your own self-worth. Your lesson here is one of the most difficult to achieve and internalize: It is to stand on, act on, and speak your truth. It is to respect all that you are, all that you stand for, and all that you do ... even when you feel you err. Each error is simply a stepping stone toward accepting your SELF and loving the amazing individual known as YOU. Our love for you is deep, and we constantly embrace you, accept you, and protect you. We send ascended masters for strength, courage, and the ability to love others without compromising your core being.

FRANCIE / FRANCINE

"To thine own self be true." Ah, our beloved, we see that you struggle to please others. This is, in one regard, honorable. However, it is usually only good for others, while you minimize your own self-worth. Your lesson here is one of

the most difficult to achieve and internalize: It is to stand on, act on, and speak your truth. It is to respect all that you are, all that you stand for, and all that you do ... even when you feel you err. Each error is simply a stepping stone toward accepting your SELF and loving the amazing individual known as YOU. Our love for you is deep, and we constantly embrace you, accept you, and protect you. We send ascended masters for strength, courage, and the ability to love others without compromising your core being.

FRANK

Much has been said about those with your name. Those with this name rise above any preconceptions of others about who they really are. Independence and self-love are the lessons you are here to learn, and you arrived here with the scenarios in place which will help you attain these traits. You are able, or will be able, to dismiss negative feedback about anything to do with YOU, because you know deep at your core who you are, and this is what you will or already have learned ... to cope with this world as it is. The journey is not an easy one, yet you have all you need to realize your value. Once this is achieved, you will know self-actualization, move along your path more easily, and more thoroughly treasure the ALL.

FRANKIE

Much has been said about those with your name. Those with this name rise above any preconceptions of others about who they really are. Independence and self-love are the lessons you are here to learn, and you arrived here with the scenarios in place which will help you attain these traits. You are able, or will be able, to dismiss negative feedback about anything to do with YOU, because you know deep at your core who you are, and this is what you will or already have learned ... to cope with this world as it is. The journey is not an easy one, yet you have all you need to realize your value. Once this is achieved, you will know self-actualization, move along your path more easily, and more thoroughly treasure the ALL.

FRANKLIN

Much has been said about those with your name. Those with this name rise above any preconceptions of others about who they really are. Independence and self-love are the lessons you are here to learn, and you arrived here with the scenarios in place which will help you attain these traits. You are able, or will be able, to dismiss negative feedback about anything to do with YOU, because you know deep at your core who you are, and this is what you will or already have learned … to cope with this world as it is. The journey is not an easy one, yet you have all you need to realize your value. Once this is achieved, you will know self-actualization, move along your path more easily, and more thoroughly treasure the ALL.

FRED

"How soon we part," you often think concerning others. Not surprisingly, others frequently think the same regarding you. Your lesson here is to have staying power and patience. Wait it out, whether it be a grocery line, a traffic snarl, or more important, a relationship. When you feel impatient with life—with things, with people, with work—remember to wait it out. We give you this secret formula so that you can learn the significance of improved outcomes through staying power. Once you begin the journey of patience, you will feel all the blessings of serenity and acceptance which have evaded you. We send you the color blue to bathe you in calmness during this learning process.

FREDA

The challenge is yours to accept or not. We helped you arrive here with more than one purpose from which to choose. The reason for this challenge is the learning of best choices for the sake of your soul's development. You have experienced this difficulty in past lives, and you may wish to achieve the lesson now. This is not easy without our guidance. Therefore, if you do choose to meet this challenge, we will guide you.

Should you feel you are not yet ready, we will also guide you to a divine purpose and ask that you act on the signs we give you that you will feel in your energy center just beneath your heart. Either way, you will meet a divine purpose. We send you the energy of Yellow Topaz to bring additional personal strength.

FREDDIE

The challenge is yours to accept or not. We helped you arrive here with more than one purpose from which to choose. The reason for this challenge is the learning of best choices for the sake of your soul's development. You have experienced this difficulty in past lives, and you may wish to achieve the lesson now. This is not easy without our guidance. Therefore, if you do choose to meet this challenge, we will guide you. Should you feel you are not yet ready, we will also guide you to a divine purpose and ask that you act on the signs we give you that you will feel in your energy center just beneath your heart. Either way, you will meet a divine purpose. We send you the energy of Yellow Topaz to bring additional personal strength.

FREDERICK

"How soon we part," you often think concerning others. Not surprisingly, others frequently think the same regarding you. Your lesson here is to have staying power and patience. Wait it out, whether it be a grocery line, a traffic snarl, or more important, a relationship. When you feel impatient with life—with things, with people, with work—remember to wait it out. We give you this secret formula so that you can learn the significance of improved outcomes through staying power. Once you begin the journey of patience, you will feel all the blessings of serenity and acceptance which have evaded you. We send you the color blue to bathe you in calmness during this learning process.

FOREST / FORREST

We are serious about this when we say to you that you are sometimes too serious. You may often hear others ask you why you are so serious. While you frequently mask your deep thoughts and depth of feeling with surface humor, it is difficult for you to stay light (internally) for long. Therefore, we reveal your lesson: To have the ability to remain serious about your desires and longing for the world to rise above difficulties, yet allow yourself time to enjoy its wonders. Permit yourself to enjoy your time here more often. This will raise your vibration and consequently assist the environment around you. Actually, it will send higher frequency waves farther than you may realize. Our dear, concerned one, we in turn lift you and bring happenchances that will make you smile, elicit laughter from your caring soul, and imprint those smiles. These imprinted smiles are there for you to revisit when you feel you are sinking into an extended period of worried reflection. We encourage you to continue your work for the better good of all, and to be mindful of the ALL THAT IS. This awareness will transform your soul to approach your chosen work to that of more joy.

FORRESTER

We are serious about this when we say to you that you are sometimes too serious. You may often hear others ask you why you are so serious. While you frequently mask your deep thoughts and depth of feeling with surface humor, it is difficult for you to stay light (internally) for long. Therefore, we reveal your lesson: To have the ability to remain serious about your desires and longing for the world to rise above difficulties, yet allow yourself time to enjoy its wonders. Permit yourself to enjoy your time here more often. This will raise your vibration and consequently assist the environment around you. Actually, it will send higher frequency waves farther than you may realize. Our dear, concerned one, we in turn lift you and bring happen-chances that will make you smile, elicit laughter from your caring soul, and imprint those smiles. These imprinted smiles are there for you to revisit when you feel you are sinking into an extended period of worried reflection. We encourage you to continue your work for the better good of all, and to be mindful of the ALL THAT IS. This awareness will transform your soul to approach your chosen work to that of more joy.

GABRIEL / GABRIELLE

Cast iron skillets are what you prefer when you're cookin'. You bring weight and substance to any project or undertaking where you are involved ... large or small. Yes, this also literally includes cooking. What it does not include is any conflict or other type of disagreement. In these times, you prefer the softness of a subtle breeze, floating past it and away from it with no weighty words or actions. We provide you with the endurance of cast iron in all your endeavors and a compass to guide and divert the winds of dissonance when necessary. Cast iron provisions and delicate diplomacy are much needed, and it is your purpose to provide both. You have the strength to carry out such a paradoxical role.

GAIL

Translucent your light is, our angel on Earth. You are one who is an Earth Angel, and you have come here with a special mission. The mission is to spread your unconditional love and acceptance to the point that others will begin to emanate your light and your love for all. If you wish, study Thomas Merton, as he was a beautiful example of an Earth Angel. There have been, and still are, others. They are recognizable by their calm nature, and they are not easily shaken, if at all. This is because the true essence of angelic love is within. This essence is shared with all, even if it is through a glance. Yes, your purpose is exceptionally divine, and a well-earned one. You chose to come here and work toward this mission on Earth. We are happy you have reached your chosen destination; be assured you will also be able to repeat it the next time around.

GARRETT

Spin the wheel and see what comes up for you! You are a risk taker, and that is how you fuel your soul. Your lesson is to learn when to take a risk and when to walk away ... what is a reasonable and good risk and what is a poor risk. This may apply to every aspect of life and to every situation. You have been learning about risks that have not been worth taking, and you have realized the positive outcomes of worthy risks. An important part of your lesson is to learn to take no action when in doubt. Ask for guidance when unsure if to proceed one way or another. Your soul will still continue to soar with every opportunity you have to venture, and your good outcomes will increase. We send you our gift of discernment to support you with this life's lesson. Surround yourself with indigo blue and gold for further inspiration and wisdom.

GARRY / GARY

Spin the wheel and see what comes up for you! You are a risk taker, and that is how you fuel your soul. Your lesson is to learn when to take a risk and when to walk away ... what is a reasonable and good risk and what is a poor risk. This may apply to every aspect of life and to every situation. You have been learning about risks that have not been worth taking, and you have realized the positive outcomes of worthy risks. An important part of your lesson is to learn to take no action when in doubt. Ask for guidance when unsure if to proceed one way or another. Your soul will still continue to soar with every opportunity you have to venture, and your good outcomes will increase. We send you our gifts of discernment to support you with this life's lesson. Surround yourself with indigo blue and gold for further inspiration and wisdom.

GENE

You may feel that you work and work and work, yet get more and more and more in debt. The lesson you chose to learn here is to recognize that debt is more than financial bills and work is more than a vocation or profession. You will learn during this lifetime that debt can encompass many things, including debt to yourself when it concerns ignoring, or not seeking, your passion. You will learn how to release yourself from self-debt and you will learn to recognize where your true passion lies ... yet only if you wish. If you do wish, we will guide you to the areas where you will find passion. Your purpose will then be to feed the passion. Whatever that passion is, you will share it excitedly and graciously. We send you prayer beads to enhance your ability to rise to your passion. These beads will direct you to your work and free yourself from self-debt.

GEOFF

You arrived here with the desire for peace and with the reluctance for anything to do with bombs. You are saddened with any type of conflict, and you avoid confrontations at every turn. This is not to say you are what is called thin skinned. Quite the contrary. It takes courage to express this deep-rooted sensitivity to anything contradictory to peace. We are standing so close behind you that you will appear to have wings to those who can "see" or perceive us. We are protecting you from the discomfort of conflict.

GEOFFREY

You arrived here with the desire for peace and with the reluctance for anything to do with bombs. You are saddened with any type of conflict, and you avoid confrontations at every turn. This is not to say you are what is called thin skinned. Quite the contrary. It takes courage to express this deep-rooted sensitivity to anything contradictory to peace. We are standing so close behind you that you will appear to have wings to those who can "see" or perceive us. We are protecting you from the discomfort of conflict.

GEORGE

You are a life-long charmer and have no trouble beginning relationships. You attract romantic partners into your life like a magnet. We wish to advise you to prevent illusory expectations from those who are bowled over by you. Use diligence in selecting a mate with whom you feel you are able to devote your charm toward, as you will be tempted to stray until you find the one who wins your pure intentions and love. Use your charm in order to increase your career status, and reserve your romantic charm to avoid disappointing those who wish to be your partner but who are not the ones you would choose. Your lesson is authenticity. This will be easy to attain, as you are genuine in your heart with almost everything. However, practicing this authenticity in all arenas is the quest we give you to achieve. This will prepare you for all future lifetimes so that you will be equipped to choose new lessons and intentions of purpose.

GEORGIA

In the beehives of life, you perform the role of Queen Bee the best. Those with your name have usually been team players and played each role of a bee family ... especially the worker bee ... and have come to the realization that the queen's work is performed with the most efficiency. The queen is in a position to realize the completion of the goal. Therefore, you have likely chosen to return to this present lifetime to plan, direct, and see the results of your guidance. You are respected – not feared. You are not one to control, yet are followed. Be cautious, our soft ruler, to maintain benevolence and understanding. A step into a quest for power will be a step that destroys the hive you so love. We don you with capes of our guidance, for even the queen needs advice and direction. We also include capes of protection to help you survive and endure ... to ensure you are sustained until your Earthly hive has reached its potential.

GEORGEANNA

In the beehives of life, you perform the role of Queen Bee the best. Those with your name have usually been team players and played each role of a bee family ... especially the worker bee – and have come to the realization that the queen's work is performed with the most efficiency. The queen is in a position to realize the completion of the goal. Therefore, you have likely chosen to return to this present lifetime to plan, direct, and see the results of your guidance. You are respected, not feared. You are not one to control, yet are followed. Be cautious, our soft ruler, to maintain benevolence and understanding. A step into a quest for power will be a step that destroys the hive you so love. We don you with capes of our guidance, for even the queen needs advice and direction. We also include capes of protection to help you survive and endure ... to ensure you are sustained until your Earthly hive has reached its potential.

GERALD

"*Who goes there?*" "*Can I trust you?*" These are questions similar to your approach to many life situations. Your lesson for this lifetime is Trust. You have been learning and will continue to learn whom to trust. More important, you are learning *how* to trust, and even *more* important, you are learning to trust *yourself.* You have classic beauty of the soul, and those like you who are living here in these times attract those who will take advantage of kindness. Fret not, for the element of trust and the discernment of such will help you coast through this lifetime with golden sails. Your angels will direct you toward this higher understanding. Your kindness will result in no offense to those from whom you turn away when you realize their presence is not for your higher good. You will actually serve your purpose as a catalyst for the self-serving, lost ones to realize an elevated frequency and get in touch with the source of right intention. We adorn you with a symbolic, indigo blue scarf that projects the big picture and gives you clarity of vision.

GERRI

We hope you never tire or feel offended by being what some refer to as a Class Clown. That is merely a convenient label. Refreshing moments and reminders to stray away from too much seriousness are greatly needed on the Earth plane. What a gift you have chosen to bring to this lifetime: To elicit the healing properties of laughter. When you are referred to as the comic relief or comedian or jokester, it is in essence a gratitude phrase from those who derive uplifting moments from your positive presence. Notice the energy shift when you contribute your gift. You are frequently present when most needed. Your lesson is to follow your instincts about when your purpose to elevate is queued by us. This is how you will bring much healing. Yes, laughter is truly good medicine, and you are endowed with thousands of prescriptions. We say to you: Those who have chosen this purpose may often feel pressure to sustain their healing amusement. We want you to know that we realize this difficulty and will pave a restful road from the possible feeling of being responsible for glee on a constant basis. These will be respites from what you may feel to be a demanding role, and they will be plentiful. We guarantee this, and we assure you that we will assist in bringing you balance.

GINA

"How dare you?!" Yes, you may hear this often throughout your time here. Why? You may be well aware by now that you rock the boat with your risk taking, with your direct approach, and with your free-spirited mannerisms. Your approach is filled with zest and fervor, something which is not always welcomed in conditions of social, professional, political, and yes—even day-to-day restraints. You do not always understand these restraints, and we say to you: Cherish your boldness. It may not be endearing to some ... do not let these different energies thwart you. Your boldness is necessary for you to carry out your purpose of discovering the freedom you so desire to be your authentic self.

GINNY

"How dare you?!" Yes, you may hear this often throughout your time here. Why? You may be well aware by now that you rock the boat with your risk taking, with your direct approach, and with your free-spirited mannerisms. Your approach is filled with zest and fervor, something which is not always welcomed in conditions of social,

professional, political, and yes—even day-to-day restraints. You do not always understand these restraints, and we say to you: Cherish your boldness. Although it may not be endearing to some, do not let these different energies thwart you. Your boldness is necessary for you to carry out your purpose of discovering the freedom you so desire to be your authentic self.

GLEN

"How dare you?!" Yes, you may hear this often throughout your time here. Why? You may be well aware by now that you rock the boat with your risk taking, with your direct approach, and with your free-spirited mannerisms. Your approach is filled with zest and fervor, something which is not always welcomed in conditions of social, professional, political, and yes—even day-to-day restraints. You do not always understand these restraints, and we say to you: Cherish your boldness. Although it may not be endearing to some, do not let these lower energies thwart you. Your boldness is necessary for you to carry out your purpose of discovering the freedom you so desire to be your authentic self.

GLENDA

"How dare you?!" Yes, you may hear this often throughout your time here. Why? You may be well aware by now that you rock the boat with your risk taking, with your direct approach, and with your free-spirited mannerisms. Your approach is filled with zest and fervor, something which is not always welcomed in conditions of social, professional, political, and yes—even day-to-day restraints. You do not always understand these restraints, and we say to you: Cherish your boldness. Although it may not be endearing to some, do not let these lower energies thwart you. Your boldness is necessary for you to carry out your purpose of discovering the freedom you so desire to be your authentic self.

GLORIA

Do not stand in the shadows of others. Your lesson is to realize your worth and to step out with your gifts, for you bring such light to where it is needed. You can also brighten what is already filled with light. Your presence is so welcomed and needed here. You carry with you a halo of unconditional love which many seek. This light is for you, as well as to share ... simply by being present. It is rare for one to carry such illuminating energy of love. We have gifted this to you. Be radiant, our Gloria, for you are after all, glorious!

GRACE / GRACIE

Thoughts float through your consciousness as feathers float through the air. They at times that move slowly and at times suddenly leap or fall. However, like your name, they always travel gracefully until they lightly touch down to remind you that your thoughts can be received with delight ... by both yourself and those who listen to your spoken words. You love experiencing thought for its intrinsic value as well as contemplative and entertaining values. It is notoriously said that all actions begin with a thought. Well, of course that is accurate. You, our graceful thinker, take thinking to new heights. You relish your "thinking" time and are able to easily bring novel ideas to whatever the occasion may be. You are a Designer of Thought—gracefully shaping ideas into actions and assisting those who have a need for creative processes. Your purpose is to consult those who are not "graced" with this particular ability. We ask you to meditate on a regular basis, and we will infuse your "thoughts" with the sacred violet flame to assist you at all levels.

GUY

Strong yet soft, you are like most refer to as a cuddly bear ... lovable yet protective ... huggable yet able to defend yourself and others. You will walk the extra mile to obtain bounty for your loved ones, you will take rest, and you will not allow your home or your family to be encroached upon or threatened. You do prefer a clan of close friends and relations, as this represents a haven for you and promotes a sense of safe harbor for all. Your purpose and your lesson are obvious: To provide gentle comfort and undisputed protection when necessary. Your animal totem, of course, is the Bear. Be conscious of this energy, for it will assist in sustaining you through all the seasons of your life.

GWEN

Pragmatic, yet fun loving. You present as quite puzzling to most of the world. You are paradoxical, as an accountant wearing a party hat. Embrace the rarity of having a level head and a mature approach to life that leads to solutions of all kinds. You also have the ability to cut a rug, sing karaoke, throw a wildly successful (yet safe) celebration, and to initiate spontaneous trips and cookouts. You get our point. We say to you: Make the best use of your logical and practical methods of everyday concerns, whether they be mundane or dramatic developments. The fact that you are also fun-loving and lighthearted will cause those around you to pay much more attention to what you say when things are of a serious or routine nature. This gift is something you chose to bring to this lifetime, so that others who would normally resist guidance, will accept it when it comes from you. We rejoice in the amazingly well-balanced YOU. This role can be both difficult and enjoyable. We are aware you thrive with your dual purpose, and that you have chosen this role throughout many lifetimes. You bring people together at all levels ... whichever level is required at any given moment.

GWENDOLYN

Pragmatic, yet fun loving. You present as quite puzzling to most of the world. You are paradoxical, as an accountant wearing a party hat. Embrace the rarity of having a level head and a mature approach to life that leads to solutions of all kinds. You also have the ability to cut a rug, sing karaoke, throw a wildly successful (yet safe) celebration, and to initiate spontaneous trips and cookouts. You get our point. We say to you: Make the best use of your logical and practical methods of everyday concerns, whether they be mundane or dramatic developments. The fact that you are also fun-loving and lighthearted will cause those around you to pay much more attention to what you say when things are of a serious or routine nature. This gift is something you chose to bring to this lifetime so that others, who would normally resist guidance, will accept it, when it comes from you. We rejoice in the amazingly well-balanced YOU. This role can be both difficult and enjoyable. We are aware you thrive with your dual purpose, and that you have chosen this role throughout many lifetimes. You bring people together at all levels ... whichever level is required at any given moment.

HAILEY / HALEY / HAYLEY

Grab your partner, 'round you go ... you are a master of dancing with life. You not only have an innate ability to choreograph and orchestrate ... you are gifted in choosing partners and teams that will mutually benefit one another. Your dance involves cooperation blended with fun. What a joyful planner you are! Your purpose is to turn chaos into cheerful order, and you do it in an easy, simple manner. The steps you outline are interesting, yet stress-free. You will apply this gift in all walks of life, and the benefits to yourself and all with whom you work will elevate the experience of life on this Earth. We bring to you wholesome songs within your heart to fuel your vitality and leadership role.

HAL

Grab your partner, 'round you go ... you are a master of dancing with life. You not only have an innate ability to choreograph and orchestrate ... you are gifted in choosing partners and teams which will mutually benefit one another. Your dance involves cooperation blended with fun. What a joyful planner you are! Your purpose is to turn chaos into cheerful order, and you do it in an easy, simple manner. The steps you outline are interesting yet stress-free. You will apply this gift in all walks of life, and the benefits to yourself and all with whom you work will elevate the experience of life on this Earth. We bring to you wholesome songs within your heart to fuel your vitality and leadership role.

HALLIE

Grab your partner, 'round you go ... you are a master of dancing with life. You not only have an innate ability to choreograph and orchestrate ... you are gifted in choosing partners and teams which will mutually benefit one another. Your dance involves cooperation blended with fun. What a joyful planner you are! Your purpose is to turn chaos into cheerful order, and you do it in an easy, simple manner. The steps you outline are interesting yet stress-free. You will apply this gift in all walks of life, and the benefits to yourself and all with whom you work will elevate the experience of life on this Earth. We bring to you wholesome songs within your heart to fuel your vitality and leadership role.

HANNAH

Hannah and the deep blue sea. Your depth of philosophy sinks much of your thought to parts of your consciousness that can only be understood by few. We know you struggle to communicate on a level which is looked upon to be "normal", or the level from which the majority understands. We ask that you do not permanently adjust your thoughts in order to be accepted. This would be a tragedy, as you came here to share your profound insights and discover new approaches to problem solving. We are helping you achieve a balance between depth and surface. Your thoughts will be clear regardless of if you are problem solving or attending a casual get-together. You will never have to remain with a surface level of communication, nor will you be submerged to the point that you feel you are drowning in weighty reflection. We will be your float on the sea of clouds, mountains, deserts, and Earth.

HAROLD

Solo. You are comfortable with being what is called a loner. However, we use the word "solo" because you excel at accomplishing projects, tasks, and assignments without assistance. You are a one-man band when it comes to the job at hand. Although you are perfectly fine with being alone, you have social skills that carry you through life, and you do enjoy a balance of people time and alone time. You can sing a solo or you can sing in a chorus ... whichever suits you at any given moment. This versatility is what will prevent you from becoming hermit-like and will help you live a well-rounded existence. Your purpose is to teach independence and autonomy. Your lesson is to internalize the truth that people can rely on one another and achieve a community-like spirit. Take your solo flights; you are gifted in this regard. Take your community flights as well. We have always been and always will be your parachute, whichever way you are traveling at any given time.

HARRIETT

Crystalline caves surround you when you feel your energy waning. You receive their strength, wisdom, and ancient truths. However, we say to you: Be aware when we send you these timeless healers, and be quiet with them. Honor this honor—allow the cleansing, balancing, knowledge, and healing to be immersed within, and experience transformation after transformation. Yes, the particular journey you have chosen is indeed a superb one, as you will learn more than you have ever learned before to prepare for your next big adventure (a most important one).

HARRY

Solo. You are comfortable with being what is called a loner. However, we use the word "solo" because you excel at accomplishing projects, tasks, and assignments without any assistance. You are a one-man band when it comes to the job at hand. Although you are perfectly fine with being alone, you have social skills that carry you through life, and you do enjoy a balance of people time and alone time. You can sing a solo or you can sing in a chorus ... whichever suits you at any given moment. This versatility is what will prevent you from becoming hermit-like and will help you live a well-rounded existence. Your purpose is to teach independence and autonomy. Your lesson is to internalize the truth that people can rely on one another and achieve a community-like spirit. Take your solo flights; you are gifted in this regard. Take your community flights as well. We have always been and always will be your parachute, whichever way you are traveling at any given time.

HART

Bring it to reality, our objective one. You will find yourself among idealists. We love idealists so much. You are among them because you ARE one, with a special exception. Although idealists do have the capacity to step back and look at the whole picture—and frequently must do so as a result of living this human existence—you achieve this more readily. You also are diplomatic, which brings the inclusion of objectivity with idealism to a successful outcome most often. Your purpose is to act as a mediator, a negotiator, and/or a diplomat. Whichever you choose, this world needs you to help with balance between a sometimes overabundance of loftiness and a feasible, viable solution.

HEATHER

A band of gold is what you are to family, friends, and associates. You are the unifying factor who brings forth the wealth that cooperation creates: wealth of community, wealth of progress, wealth of comradery. The cohesiveness of the band of gold that you represent always manifests oneness of goals and actions. Each action is separate, yet fused by a non-ending circle of agreement. We will help weld together any pieces that fall apart, or help you find a replacement for any individuals who create a gap in this circle. We ask that you remember who you are, unselfishly uniting and creating continuity.

HEIDI

The warmth of a campfire is what you bring to this world. Shared stories, laughter, and dancing flames that reach for the sky. The recollection of this bright warmth against a night sky brings memories forth at times when a smile may be needed ... memories that may feel like a soul hug. Yes, your warmth is both memorable and healing in the now and in the then. The blaze is never threatening. It provides direction from the smoke, as a signal to return to the safe solace of community. You, Heidi, are a bringer of relief to weathered hearts.

HELEN

Starry, starry night—as you gaze upward with awe, know that we have graced you with the same expansive wonder that you feel from this universe's brilliant night sky. Yes, our twinkling star, you are larger than life when it comes to the vastness of your potential, of your giving, of all your actions. We revere you as a constellation filled with talents, which are in turn spilled freely on the inhabitants of Earth. Thank you for shining forth your brilliance. We surround you with glistening stardust of enchantment.

HENRY

Little ones love to be in your company. They enjoy being in the flow of goodness, of kindness, and of fun. You are like a favorite teacher, bringing interesting information, rewarding positive behavior, and offering unconditional acceptance. You are a magnet to children who otherwise experience negative living environments. You have a demeanor which provides simple, enjoyable direction. Be the example. Be the teacher. Be the Earth angel. Be the innocent fun. Be the love. We wrap you in the brilliance of sun kissed clouds.

HILLARY

Your quest is your own, *and* that of others. You advocate for yourself and those who need assistance. For this reason you may tire from time to time, as there are and will be a multitude of others to aid. You must also defend and uphold yourself, as many will not understand your determination toward your work here. We provide you with angelic pillars of strength. We provide you with the energy you need to withstand the seemingly endless work of your multidimensional quest. We provide you with all you need to achieve these goals.

HOLLY / HOLLIE

Grab your partner, 'round you go ... you are a master of dancing with life. You not only have an innate ability to choreograph and orchestrate ... you are gifted in choosing partners and teams which will mutually benefit one another. Your square dance involves cooperation blended with fun. What a joyful planner you are! Your purpose is to turn chaos into cheerful order, and you do it in an easy, simple manner. The steps you outline are interesting yet stress-free. You will apply this gift in all walks of life, and the benefits to yourself and all with whom you work will elevate the experience of life on this Earth. We bring to you wholesome songs within your heart to fuel your vitality and leadership role.

HOMER

Sticking to the basics is something you have never liked to do, and never will. You have a knack of transforming the ordinary to unusual and boredom to excitement. Because of this, children flock to you to stimulate their minds. Adults who are jaded from the conventional gravitate toward you to experience a bigger picture. You may be viewed as eccentric; however, you are simply using the full gamut of availability ... availability of color, sound, texture, and data ... the vastness of possibilities. You realize that this life can be a work of art at every turn. You are among the creative geniuses who see life as a series of canvases and musical instruments. You relish all genres, and you make each work distinctive. Your purpose is to bring zest to the oftentimes blandness of life.

HOPE

In addition to the gentle Spring showers that bring new growth, as your name reflects, you are no sitting duck for freeloaders or naysayers. Your soft, cultivating rain can easily change to a thunderstorm should you need to blow away anything or anyone menacing. You realize you do not have time for negativity while you are fulfilling your purpose of being a nourisher. We have provided you with the ability to transmute circumstances toward an evolution of goodness and progress. Carry on your irrigation in promoting the world around you to evolve in the most positive direction. Your calm power will be kept intact by your angels and guides. We surround you with both sky blue and ocean blue to maintain an inner, placid spirit.

HOWARD

Solo. You are comfortable with being what is called a loner. However, we use the word "solo" because you excel at accomplishing projects, tasks, and assignments without any assistance. You are a one-man band when it comes to the job at hand. Although you are perfectly fine with being alone, you have social skills that carry you through life, and you do enjoy a balance of people time and alone time. You can sing a solo or you can sing in a chorus ... whichever suits you at any given moment. This versatility is what will prevent you from becoming hermit-like and will help you live a well-rounded existence. Your purpose is to teach independence and autonomy. Your lesson is to internalize the truth that people can rely on one another and achieve a community-like spirit. Take your solo flights; you are gifted in this regard. Take your community flights as well. We have always been and always will be your parachute, whichever way you are traveling at any given time.

HUGH

Tough as nails. Tougher than nails. We want you to know that this is not what you are expected to be. In fact, it isn't even what you signed up to be before arriving here. You wanted to be assertive—a leader, yet pliant, not made of steel ... definitive in direction, yet not harsh. If you find yourself in a position where you feel you're expected to be aggressive, call on us and we will give you the angelic strength to approach the situation with unbiased and focused kindness, while keeping the reins of dissidence firmly under control. Some will, and some will not, respect you for this gentle authority. Pay no heed to earning respect; it matters not. You are fulfilling your role here to take loving charge where otherwise chaos and squabbles would have resulted. We call you our Orchestrator of Positive Outcomes, and we send continuous blessings to you for assistance. We surround you with the energies of orange and gold for courage, combined with Christ-like love.

HUNTER

Your lesson here, our sensitive one, is not to succumb to possible expectations because of implications of your name or of your appearance (whatever those may be). Yes, you are a hunter as in a seeker of truth. Yes, you are strong, as in standing on your own solid ground. As you hunt, your catches will be morsels of truth that you have no desire to display; these truths will reside within and be assimilated into your being. Your purpose, then, is to be the reflection of those internalized truths. The natural manner in which these universal lessons of the spirit are conveyed from you will in turn serve as an invisible and silent classroom for the souls who listen. Hunter, you arrived here knowing you need no weapons to gain such deep knowledge. All you need to do is simply be open, and what you seek will manifest within.

IAN

Stacking one stick on top of another will eventually result in all of them falling. We want you to know that your lesson here is to choose substance, and with that substance, to use balance. Each truth you learn is as a stone. The manner in which you stack each stone, as a mason would, will assist you greatly in building your house of inner knowledge. We do not speak of intellectual knowledge; we speak of knowledge that brings great wisdom. We say to you: Treat even the slightest of twigs or sticks as if they were strong stones. Convert them; you can. Build with them your library within. Share each truth as you are led, and you can become a sage who offers valuable truths.

ILENE

Delicate you are, and wispy as an embracing breeze. You are here to offer the lightness of air and the refreshment of pure smiles. As you walk (actually, you glide) along this life's path, we want you to know that wherever you step, you leave behind your lightness and gentleness. Your role here is quite an easy one: To be nothing other than yourself, without a thought as to what you may need to do or accomplish. Your accomplishments come through each time that you leave behind a temperate, clear, pleasant moment. These moments are mostly savored at a subconscious level; however, they have a refreshing effect. Thank you for being this simplistic elixir.

IMOGENE

Being a stickler for detail is both a positive and a negative trait. Your lesson is to learn when to deem the details to be important enough to spend time with versus knowing when insisting that detail be included would be counterproductive. If you persist with the details when it is not necessary, the result could be resistance or resentment from those involved. Therefore, we say to you: There is a delicate balance between being detail oriented toward efficiency and correctness and beating a dead horse, so to speak. You are the first to be chosen for positions that require close attention. You bring value to those types of positions, both at home and at your job environment. The secondary lesson we wish to speak of is that you arrived here to also learn to relax. There is a time and place for details, and there are equally times when you need to realize that it is okay to let go and surrender to tranquility. We send to you boats on placid water. There are many from which to choose so that you will always be able to climb aboard serenity.

IRA

You are among the rather rare, paradoxical ones. Pragmatic and practical, yet with a sense of humor that can bring comic relief at the drop of a hat. Further, your humor is of an intelligent type, which keeps others thinking while chuckling. Those of you with this name make stellar educators. If you are not a teacher or professor, you likely are (and should be) teaching through seminars, presentations, or workshops. Of course, friends and family (especially the children in your family) are included in your teaching mannerisms. You make learning fun. This world is in much need of necessary, yet light-hearted information that can be assimilated, and thus internalized for present and future reference. To help you with your purpose, we surround you with the wisdom of ancient philosophers and the comedic genius of a laugh-a-teer.

IRENE

Delicate you are, and wispy as an embracing breeze. You are here to offer the lightness of air and the refreshment of pure smiles. As you walk (actually, you glide) along this life's path, we want you to know that wherever you step, you leave behind your lightness and gentleness. Your role here is quite an easy one: To be nothing other than yourself, without a thought as to what you may need to do or accomplish. Your accomplishments come through each time that you leave behind a temperate, clear, pleasant moment. These moments are mostly savored at a subconscious level; however, they have a refreshing effect. Thank you for being this simplistic elixir.

IRIS

In addition to the gentle Spring showers that bring new growth, as your name reflects, you are no sitting duck for freeloaders or naysayers. Your soft, cultivating rain can easily change to a thunderstorm should you need to blow away anything or anyone menacing. You realize you do not have time for disharmony while you are fulfilling your purpose of being a nourisher. We have provided you with the ability to transmute circumstances toward an evolution of goodness and progress. Carry on your irrigation in promoting the world around you to evolve in the most positive direction. Your calm power will be kept intact by your angels and guides. We surround you with both sky blue and ocean blue to maintain an inner, placid spirit.

ISAAC

Sink your feet deep into the sand. Feel the energy of a million particles that will stabilize you, and at the same time remind you of how many actions it takes to become one with the All That Is. You long for a purpose, and we want to direct you to meditation. If you are unable to stand motionless in the sand, stand on the Earth. Feel its nurturing energy. Feel the millions of vibrations that resonate as one world. You are the same. Your many steps, your countless thoughts and actions—all are manifesting as one. YOU—One with the All That Is.

ISABELLA / ISABELLE

We liken you to a Ferris Wheel for viewing life. You bring attention to the panoramic view of the world and everyday life in general. On the seat you provide for others, they are able to see beyond the close detail. Detail is important, yes, and yet there are so many who do not look beyond their nose. The broad spectrum, the vast possibilities, the grand view is often missed. Not only do you assist in providing the big picture ... you assist in allowing others to view life at every level. As the Ferris Wheel rises to various heights, it also descends to various heights, and repeats. So it is with you and the viewing seats you provide. You allow a comprehensive exploration of life ... of life's questions, of life's challenges, of life's solutions, and mostly of life's overall beauty. When looking at the grand scheme of things, the beauty and breathtaking views outweigh all else. Thank you for bringing attention to this; you are serving your purpose well.

ISAIAH

Sink your feet deep into the sand. Feel the energy of a million particles that will stabilize you, and at the same time remind you of how many actions it takes to become one with the All That Is. You long for a purpose, and we want to direct you to meditation. If you are unable to stand motionless in the sand, stand on the Earth. Feel its nurturing energy. Feel the millions of vibrations that resonate as one world. You are the same. Your many steps, your countless thoughts and actions—all are manifesting as one. YOU—One with the All That Is.

IVAN

You are among the rather rare, paradoxical ones. Pragmatic and practical, yet with a sense of humor that can bring comic relief at the drop of a hat. Further, your humor is of an intelligent type, which keeps others thinking while chuckling. Those of you with this name make stellar educators. If you are not a teacher or professor, you likely are (and should be) teaching through seminars, presentations, or workshops. Of course, friends and family (especially the children in your family) are included in your teaching mannerisms. You make learning fun. This world is in much need of necessary, yet light-hearted information that can be assimilated, and thus internalized for present and future reference. To help you with your purpose, we surround you with the wisdom of ancient philosophers and the comedic genius of a laugh-a-teer.

IVONNE / YVONNE

Dolphin energy is what we send you, our unique communicator. You communicate at a higher level. Without uttering a native language, and sometimes with only gestures and nods—even with silence—you have an unworldly ability to communicate. We ask that you tune in to this gift for the benefit of all. We surround you with the energies of blue and green to support your message center and your heart center, from where your communication is imparted with love. If ever in doubt about how to interconnect, call on Archangel Gabriel, as there is always guidance available. Some Ivonne's / Yvonne's also can communicate with animal friends. We urge you to heed this call. You have so incredibly much to offer.

IVORY

Delicate you are, and wispy as an embracing breeze. You are here to offer the lightness of air and the refreshment of pure smiles. As you walk (actually, you glide) along this life's path, we want you to know that wherever you step, you leave behind your lightness and gentleness. Your role here is quite an easy one: To be nothing other than yourself, without a thought as to what you may need to do or accomplish. Your accomplishments come through each time that you leave behind a temperate, clear, pleasant moment. These moments are mostly savored at a subconscious level; however, they have a refreshing effect. Thank you for being this simplistic elixir.

IVY

Delicate you are, and wispy as an embracing breeze. You are here to offer the lightness of air and the refreshment of pure smiles. As you walk (actually, you glide) along this life's path, we want you to know that wherever you step, you leave behind your lightness and gentleness. Your role here is quite an easy one: To be nothing other than yourself, without a thought as to what you may need to do or accomplish. Your accomplishments come through each time that you leave behind a temperate, clear, pleasant moment. These moments are mostly savored at a subconscious level; however, they have a refreshing effect. Thank you for being this simplistic elixir.

JACK / JACKIE

Always outgoing, you are looked upon as a bright spot in the day and as an optimist at heart. Your sense of humor is outstanding and anticipated by your "fans" – just about everyone who knows you. Your ability to discuss many topics makes you a sought-after inclusion at gatherings. Your purpose is to lighten up people's day and to share your vast knowledge about numerous topics. You also arrived here to learn the lesson of introspection. Lurking beneath your positive actions is a soul with great depth, with appreciation of nature, with love of the arts, and with a spiritual connection. We wish to remind you to take the time to feed your soul. You do have such a grateful soul; nourish it to the utmost. In this manner, your spirit will soar. The combination of your gregariousness and your spiritual fullness will bless many. And we, our multi-dimensional one, will be by your side to assist with your amazing versatility.

JACOB

Traversing along your life path has caused you to experience callouses and cuts from rough and jagged rocks. Have you seen any streams? Have you noticed the songbirds? Have you witnessed squirrels and other wildlife at play? If not, this could be a result of stubbornly following a choice which does not serve you well. Your lesson is to open your mind to possibilities that will catapult you into a new dimension, to a new route, and to self-actualization. Ask, and you will be guided to the path that is your destiny. Ask and listen. The answer will appear. This change in direction may occur

---

subtly, without an epiphany. You may simply realize at some point that you indeed have been placed where you belong. You will have gained the insight you came here to learn: To allow your purpose to naturally unfold rather than force or continue a choice that does not bring peace.

JADA

Until the bell tolls. This is how you view life decisions and life changes. You do not step ahead too soon. You move forward with life, and only in due time ... in other words, not until the bell tolls, not until you know it is time. For this we commend you, as your purpose is to teach others to hesitate from opening the petals of a flower before it is time for it to bloom. You teach emergence, unfoldment, and flow. Not many on Earth learn this lesson at the soul depth. Not many are able to wait—and to recognize—the perfect timing of living life's chapters. You, our wise one, are one such rare spirit in human form, knowing and working with divine timing.

JADE

Until the bell tolls. This is how you view life decisions and life changes. You do not step ahead too soon. You move forward with life, and only in due time ... in other words, not until the bell tolls, not until you know it is time. For this we commend you, as your purpose is to teach others to hesitate from opening the petals of a flower before it is time for it to bloom. You teach emergence, unfoldment, and flow. Not many on Earth learn this lesson at the soul depth. Not many are able to wait—and to recognize—the perfect timing of living life's chapters. You, our wise one, are one such rare spirit in human form, knowing and working with divine timing.

JAKE

Traversing along your life path has caused you to experience callouses and cuts from rough and jagged rocks. Have you seen any streams? Have you noticed the songbirds? Have you witnessed squirrels and other wildlife at play? If not, this could be a result of stubbornly following a choice which does not serve you well. Your lesson is to open your mind to possibilities that will catapult you into a new dimension, to a new route, and to self-actualization. Ask, and you will be guided to the path that is your destiny. Ask and listen. The answer will appear. This change in direction may occur subtly, without an epiphany. You may simply realize at some point that you indeed have been placed where you belong. You will have gained the insight you came here to learn: To allow your purpose to naturally unfold rather than force or continue a choice that does not bring peace.

JAMES

"*How dare you?!*" Yes, you may hear this often throughout your time here. Why? You may be well aware by now that you rock the boat with your risk taking, with your direct approach, and with your free-spirited mannerisms. Your approach is filled with zest and fervor, something which is not always welcomed in conditions of social, professional, political, and yes—even day-to-day restraints. You do not always understand these restraints, and we say to you: Cherish your boldness. Although it may not be endearing to some, do not let these types of energies thwart you. Your boldness is necessary for you to carry out your purpose of discovering the freedom you so desire to be your authentic self.

JAMIE

Sow the seed and wait. One of your greatest lessons for your life as Jamie is patience, yet it is also one of your greatest gifts. You have had difficult times with waiting, yet we must remind you that the resulting temperament has molded you into a pliable, flexible rock. Strong, resilient, and at times appearing to be unmoved by delays and obstacles, you manifest results through your patience. You actually appear to be complex and even a little mischievous; however, in the end you are respected for your thought-filled approach. We respect you as well for receiving and achieving patience. We surround you with a galaxy of brilliance to help you shine during darkness. Should you feel the light of patience dimming, simply call on us; we are here.

JANE

You may feel that you work and work and work, yet get more and more and more in debt. The lesson you chose to learn here is to recognize that debt is more than financial bills, and work is more than a vocation or profession. You will learn during this lifetime that debt can encompass many things, including debt to yourself when it concerns ignoring, or not seeking, your passion. You will learn how to release yourself from self-debt, and you will learn to recognize where your true passion lies … and only if you wish. If you do wish, we will guide you to the areas where you will find passion. Your purpose will then be to fulfill the passion. Whatever that passion is, you will share it excitedly and graciously. We send you prayer beads for enhancing your ability to rise and meet your passion. These beads will direct you to your work and free you from self-debt.

JANEEN

You may feel that you work and work and work, yet get more and more and more in debt. The lesson you chose to learn here is to recognize that debt is more than financial bills, and work is more than a vocation or profession. You will learn during this lifetime that debt can encompass many things, including debt to yourself when it concerns ignoring, or not seeking, your passion. You will learn how to release yourself from self-debt, and you will learn to recognize where your true passion lies … and only if you wish. If you do wish, we will guide you to the areas where you will find passion. Your purpose will then be to fulfill the passion. Whatever that passion is, you will share it excitedly and graciously. We send you prayer beads for enhancing your ability to rise and meet your passion. These beads will direct you to your work and free you from self-debt.

JANET

Love becomes you. You reflect love at your lowest low and your highest high and all points in between. Rare it is that a human portrays the personification of love in all aspects of life on the Earth plane. You are aware that life is absent of living without embodying love in all you do. It is what you chose to do during this life, and you have achieved it well. Your purpose is to excavate lackluster, revealing the shining essence of love in all elements. We give you our energy of pure intent and ask you to share it accordingly. Adorn yourself with Rose Quartz and Watermelon Tourmaline to remind yourself of your loving heart.

JANICE

Love becomes you. You reflect love at your lowest low and your highest high and all points in between. Rare it is that a human portrays the personification of love in all aspects of life on the Earth plane. You are aware that life is absent of living without embodying love in all you do. It is what you chose to do during this life, and you have achieved it well. Your purpose is to excavate lackluster, revealing the shining essence of love in all elements. We give you our energy of pure intent and ask you to share it accordingly. Adorn yourself with Rose Quartz and Watermelon Tourmaline to remind yourself of your loving heart.

JARED

Stacking one stick on top of another will eventually result in all of them falling. We want you to know that your lesson here is to choose substance, and with that substance, to use balance. Each truth you learn is as a stone. The manner in which you stack each stone, as a mason would, will assist you greatly in building your house of inner knowledge. We do not speak of intellectual knowledge; we speak of knowledge that brings great wisdom. We say to you: Treat even the slightest of twigs or sticks as if they were strong stones. Convert them; you can. Build with them your library within. Share each truth as you are led, and you can become a sage who offers valuable truths.

JASMINE

Burn unit. Scars. You heal the burns and scars that others sustain from abuse of one kind or another. You are the miracle salve to soothe and nurture. Not only do you offer healing energy—you perform corrective surgery for the soul. The invisible stitches you provide also pull together torn hearts and merge the pieces into a whole. Being a nurse for injured souls does not come without its difficulties. Some will not welcome your care. Some will expect more than you can give. But, ah, many will both want and need your "treatments." Do not concern yourself with those who do not welcome or appreciate your care. Simply live your life as the surgeon you chose to be before you arrived here. The patients will come. There will never be too many so as to overwhelm you. This purpose will be served easily by you. We honor you for this service to humankind.

JAY

You are the colorful hot air balloon that helps people realize they can rise to new heights, and have an adventure in doing so. You provide the moral support and the feeling of safety as they lift off, trusting the process while they learn the ropes, so to speak. Who says it's a self-defeating mindset to have one's head in the clouds? Not according to you. Liftoff is not only possible, but exhilarating and productive. You are the epitome of rising above and breaking through the paradigm of limited goals. Fortunate are those who have the presence of mind and the fortitude to follow your lead.

JEAN

You may feel that you work and work and work, yet get more and more and more in debt. The lesson you chose to learn here is to recognize that debt is more than financial bills, and work is more than a vocation or profession. You will learn during this lifetime that debt can encompass many things, including debt to yourself when it concerns ignoring, or not seeking, your passion. You will learn how to release yourself from self-debt, and you will learn to recognize where your true passion lies ... yet only if you wish. If you do wish, we will guide you to the areas where you will find passion. Your purpose will then be to fulfill the passion. Whatever that passion is, you will share it excitedly and graciously. We send you prayer beads for enhancing your ability to rise and meet your passion. These beads will direct you to your work and free you from self-debt.

JEFF

Bombs are not necessary. This is, of course, not literal. You may be quick to anger and set in place bombs. We honor your assertiveness and we are here to quell your aggression, as this will only hamper your soul's growth. We ask that you heed our advice and pause when you feel anger set in. We ask you to wait, process, and choose a different approach. We ask you to pause and remember that we are helping you to be direct without being aggressive, and to be firm yet not harmful in your actions. We are on constant call to help you choose the appropriate response, yet only if you choose to allow us to assist in calming your spirit and replacing it with an approach that will be most beneficial to all. Your soul yearns for our intervention; we are here to help you overcome what is necessary so that you can move forward with your self-actualization. Your gift of demonstrating peaceful means of resolution will surface, and this will fulfill your purpose.

JEFFREY

You arrived here with the desire for peace and with the reluctance for anything to do with bombs. You are saddened with any type of conflict, and you avoid confrontations at every turn. This is not to say you are what is called thin skinned. Quite the contrary. It takes courage to express this deep-rooted sensitivity to anything contradictory to peace. We are standing so close behind you that you will appear to have wings to those who can "see" or perceive us. We are protecting you from the discomfort of conflict.

JENNIFER

Clothe yourself with kindness, for that is what you are. Discard any garb which is unsuitable to your calling. Do not adorn yourself with worldly threads. Don yourself instead with the uniforms of service, each costume unique, yet to clothe the same freely-giving spirit. We treasure you for this unconditional and spontaneous, loving, giving spirit. You are the embodiment of all these, which you chose just before arriving here. You almost chose to come here as a taker ... a hedonist ... instead you made the decision to serve in this glorious way.

We must add that there is another message for another set of Jennifers ... those who are the can-doers. These Jennifer's are never tiring, and others look to them for their confidence in getting the job done. We ask you to heed our words of caution: Some will interpret you as a stubborn know-it-all, too independent and unrelenting in your stance. We advise you to ease up and allow others to do it themselves, as you could possibly thwart their own independence. Otherwise, you are invaluable to those who need assistance with accomplishing tasks at hand.

JENNY

We hope you never tire or feel offended by being what some refer to as a Class Clown. That is merely a convenient label. Refreshing moments and reminders to stray away from too much seriousness are greatly needed on the Earth plane. What a gift you have chosen to bring to this lifetime: To elicit the healing properties of laughter. When you are referred to as the comic relief or comedian or jokester, it is in essence a gratitude phrase from those who derive uplifting moments from your positive presence. Notice the energy shift when you contribute your gift. You are frequently present when most needed. Your lesson is to follow your instincts about when your purpose to elevate is queued by us. This is how you will bring much healing. Yes, laughter is truly good medicine, and you are endowed with thousands of prescriptions. We say to you: Those who have chosen this purpose may often feel pressure to sustain their healing amusement. We want you to know that we realize this difficulty and will pave a restful road from the possible feeling of being responsible for glee on a constant basis. These will be respites from what you may feel to be a demanding role, and they will be plentiful. We guarantee this, and we assure you that we will assist in bringing you balance.

JEREMIAH

To each his own. This is a common saying. However, it reflects one of the major lessons you are here to learn. Your lesson is to acknowledge that your differences and others' differences are simply the necessary parts which make the whole. How would the world look if it were all one color, or all black and white, all flat, all rolling terrain, all dry, or all covered with foliage? How could it even survive? You are not only here to learn how important diversity is, you are also here to be a constant reminder about the importance of the macrocosm ... the big picture of life on this Earth. The planet will only be sustained by nurturing it all. Teach this, please. It may feel like a daunting task you have been charged with, and we want you to know that whatever influence you create will not be like a job for you ... in fact, it will come naturally because we constantly guide you. If you doubt your actions and words (and you will), know that the doubt is not coming from the pure source. Just relax with this lifetime; the rest will fall into place.

JEREMY

Jeremy, our man of men, our sword and shield. We call you The Protector. You come to the aid and rescue of so many. Your advocacy for others spans a vast number of reasons and circumstances. You are chosen to fend for others and, ah, you do it well. You are fearless with the innate knowledge that you, too, are protected by angels and are guided in your every move toward justice and lifting up those who need your help. This purpose of yours is your honor, and your reward is to see the immensity of the effects from your efforts.

JEROME

"*Who goes there?*" "*Can I trust you?*" These are questions similar to your approach to many life situations. Your lesson for this lifetime is Trust. You have been learning and will continue to learn whom to trust. More important, you are learning *how* to trust, and even *more* important, you are learning to trust *yourself*. You have classic beauty of the soul, and those like you who are living here in these times attract those who will take advantage of kindness. Fret not, for the element of trust and the discernment of such will help you coast through this lifetime with golden sails. Your angels will direct you toward this higher understanding. Your kindness will result in no offense to those from whom you turn away when you realize their presence is not for your higher good. You will actually serve your purpose as a catalyst for the self-serving, lost ones to realize an elevated frequency and get in touch with the source of right intention. We adorn you with a symbolic, indigo blue scarf that projects the big picture and gives you clarity of vision.

JERRY

We hope you never tire or feel offended by being what some refer to as a Class Clown. That is merely a convenient label. Refreshing moments and reminders to stray away from too much seriousness are greatly needed on the Earth plane. What a gift you have chosen to bring to this lifetime: To elicit the healing properties of laughter. When you are referred to as the comic relief or comedian or jokester, it is in essence a gratitude phrase from those who derive uplifting moments from your positive presence. Notice the energy shift when you contribute your gift. You are frequently present when most needed. Your lesson is to follow your instincts about when your purpose to elevate is queued by us. This is how you will bring much healing. Yes, laughter is truly good medicine, and you are endowed with thousands of prescriptions. We say to you: Those who have chosen this purpose may often feel pressure to sustain their healing amusement. We want you to know that we realize this difficulty and will pave a restful road from the possible feeling of being responsible for glee on a constant basis. These will be respites from what you may feel to be a demanding role, and they will be plentiful. We guarantee this, and we assure you that we will assist in bringing you balance.

JESSICA

Soulful you appear, Jessica, and soulful you are. You are among the deep thinkers and empaths of this world. Your serious and compassionate approach does not equate with sullenness or sadness regarding life. You are also among those who celebrate life, who laugh, and who can bring joy. You are actually a portrait of duality ... the duality of somberness and gladness. The most important role you play ... your purpose ... is that of a joyful and caring soul. Your touching demeanor softens hearts and alleviates callousness that may surround others' auras. You bring about suppleness of spirits in need of awakening. We ask that you surround yourself with the color pink for the love you deserve to receive in return for the empathy you give.

JESSE / JESSIE

Complacency abounds all around you and your environment. You, our dear one, are the fire that ignites movement. Whether the movement is small or grand does not matter—it is always what is necessary at the moment. We call you our firecracker, yet we say this meaning no harm coming from you, rather a spark that commands just enough attention to the matter at hand. Your dynamic moments that generate movement and action from apathy are your gifts and your specific purpose. And don't forget—you will need igniting at times, too. For this reason we send you bolts of angelic light which you will recognize and instantly know it is a reminder from us to be the spark you came here to be.

JEZABEL

Burn unit. Scars. You heal the burns and scars that others sustain from abuse of one kind or another. You are the miracle salve to soothe and nurture. Not only do you offer healing energy—you perform corrective surgery for the soul. The invisible stitches you provide also pull together torn hearts and merge the pieces into a whole. Being a nurse for injured souls does not come without its difficulties. Some will not welcome your care. Some will expect more than you can give. But, ah, many will both want and need your "treatments." Do not concern yourself with those who do not welcome or appreciate your care. Simply live your life as the surgeon you chose to be before you arrived here. The patients will come. There will never be too many so as to overwhelm you. This purpose will be served easily by you. We honor you for this service to humankind.

JILL

Star light, star bright, first star I see tonight ... we ask that you stop "wishing you may or wishing you might." We want to show you how to use your dreams and star gazing to rise to the degree of manifestation that affords you the blessings you seek, without all the yearning. When you find yourself wishing, accept our reminder: All that is good and all that is purposeful for you will evolve. However, it is helpful to us if you practice the childlike mindset of believing. Yes, children wish upon the stars, as do adults. The ones who truly believe that their angels and guides form a team with them are the ones who amazingly manifest their desires. Meditate on this. Internalize the belief that wishes come true that are meant to come true, according to those dreams you chose before you arrived here. Just believe, and receive what has been destined for you. Regardless of your dreams, we want you to know that you are a blessing to all who are near you. They, too, want reciprocal blessings for you. Thank you for allowing those around you to receive the smiles and hugs you give them, both from within and in the physical form. You are a treasure for all.

JIM

"*How dare you?!*" Yes, you may hear this often throughout your time here. Why? You may be well aware by now that you rock the boat with your risk taking, with your direct approach, and with your free-spirited mannerisms. Your approach is filled with zest and fervor, something which is not always welcomed in conditions of social, professional, political, and yes—even day-to-day restraints. You do not always understand these restraints, and we say to you: Cherish your boldness. Although it may not be endearing to some, do not let these types of energies thwart you. Your boldness is necessary for you to carry out your purpose of discovering the freedom you so desire to be your authentic self.

JIMMY

"How dare you?!" Yes, you may hear this often throughout your time here. Why? You may be well aware by now that you rock the boat with your risk taking, with your direct approach, and with your free-spirited mannerisms. Your approach is filled with zest and fervor, something which is not always welcomed in conditions of social, professional, political, and yes—even day-to-day restraints. You do not always understand these restraints, and we say to you: Cherish your boldness. Although it may not be endearing to some, do not let these types of energies thwart you. Your boldness is necessary for you to carry out your purpose of discovering the freedom you so desire to be your authentic self.

JOAN

Stark reality. It hits most with harshness and strife. But our dear one, you welcome reality as a resolution to any question about almost any matter, and as a learning tool. You take reality and fly with it to transform indecisiveness to a plan and to share the truth of matters. Yes, you make the most of reality; however, we say to you: You have another side that elevates you and those whom you inspire. It is the element of wonder. You behold the wonder of it all on a daily basis. For this reason, you cope well with any type of unpleasantries, because you are so keenly aware of the wondrous elements of the universe ... the reality of unsolved mysteries, and it is so grand! Paradoxical? You decide. Let others decide. You are the personification of "the wonder of reality" as you see it.

JOANIE

Stark reality. It hits most with harshness and strife. But our dear one, you welcome reality as a resolution to any question about almost any matter, and as a learning tool. You take reality and fly with it to transform indecisiveness to a plan and to share the truth of matters. Yes, you make the most of reality; however, we say to you: You have another side that elevates you and those whom you inspire. It is the element of wonder. You behold the wonder of it all on a daily basis. For this reason, you cope well with any type of unpleasantries, because you are so keenly aware of the wondrous elements of the universe ... the reality of unsolved mysteries, and it is so grand! Paradoxical? You decide. Let others decide. You are the personification of "the wonder of reality" as you see it.

JOANNE

Stark reality. It hits most with harshness and strife. But our dear one, you welcome reality as a resolution to any question about almost any matter, and as a learning tool. You take reality and fly with it to transform indecisiveness to a plan and to share the truth of matters. Yes, you make the most of reality; however, we say to you: You have another side that elevates you and those whom you inspire. It is the element of wonder. You behold the wonder of it all on a daily basis. For this reason, you cope well with any type of unpleasantries, because you are so keenly aware of the wondrous elements of the universe ... the reality of unsolved mysteries, and it is so grand! Paradoxical? You decide. Let others decide. You are the personification of "the wonder of reality" as you see it.

JOCELYN / JOSLYN

No, it isn't anything in the water. The productivity you create, and the increase therefrom, is contagious. In every situation, with most in your immediate circle, productivity abounds. You chose to arrive here as an enthusiast for enthusiasm, and what a splendid job you are doing in serving this purpose. You and those you affect find self-reward and satisfaction in positive accomplishments. Look around you at any given moment and see the results of the energy you have brought and continue to bring. We call you the Rabbit of Progress. You create and continue to create. To assist with this purpose, we surround you with the energy of Citrine to help you sustain confidence in fulfilling your role and for physical strength at the human level. Your spiritual strength is well intact.

JODI / JODY

We hope you never tire or feel offended by being what some refer to as a Class Clown. That is merely a convenient label. Refreshing moments and reminders to stray away from too much seriousness are greatly needed on the Earth plane. What a gift you have chosen to bring to this lifetime: To elicit the healing properties of laughter. When you are referred to as the comic relief or comedian or jokester, it is in essence a gratitude phrase from those who derive uplifting moments from your positive presence. Notice the energy shift when you contribute your gift. You are frequently present when most needed. Your lesson is to follow your instincts about when your purpose to elevate is queued by us. This is how you will bring much healing. Yes, laughter is truly good medicine, and you are endowed with thousands of prescriptions. We say to you: Those who have chosen this purpose may often feel pressure to sustain their healing amusement. We want you to know that we realize this difficulty and will pave a restful road from the possible feeling of being responsible for glee on a constant basis. These will be respites from what you may feel to be a demanding role, and they will be plentiful. We guarantee this, and we assure you that we will assist in bringing you balance.

JOE

Falling from a ledge is something you will not do. Ah, you are daring and end up on the ledge frequently. However, you have the quickness and the equilibrium to keep from teetering out of control. You are able to stay grounded during unsettling times and even help others from losing the delicate balance between reality and illusion. Your primary purpose is that of a sincere and helpful friend—and that you are—in addition to pulling people from the ledge whose perceptions have been muddled. Thank you for choosing to be the voice of reason to those who would otherwise lose their balance and fall.

JOEL

We liken you to a Ferris Wheel for viewing life. You bring attention to the panoramic view of the world and everyday life in general. On the seat you provide for others, they are able to see beyond the close detail. Detail is important, yes, and yet there are so many who do not look beyond their nose. The broad spectrum, the vast possibilities, the grand view is often missed. Not only do you assist in providing the big picture ... you assist in allowing others to view life at every level. As the Ferris Wheel rises to various heights, it also descends to various heights, and repeats. So it is with you and the viewing seats you provide. You allow a comprehensive exploration of life ... of life's questions, of life's challenges, of life's solutions, and mostly of life's overall beauty. When looking at the grand scheme of things, the beauty and breathtaking views outweigh all else. Thank you for bringing attention to this; you are serving your purpose well.

JOEY

It takes a lot of confidence to be a cheerful friend, leader, and adviser. You want to be a bright spot in others' days, and you have received the spirit-given gift to do so. You are viewed as charismatic. This isn't something you chose; it is simply a secondary feature of your big personality. Embrace it, and always remember that humility is necessary in order to retain the trust of those whose lives you improve by simply being in the same environment. We know you struggle to stay cheerful for your own soul, and we want you to know that we are here to help with that quest. Look to us and ask us when your spirit is in need of uplifting. We will be there and we ARE here. Sunrise, sunset. This is how we see your daily mood. Always acknowledge the beauty of each. We do acknowledge you in all your ways, with gratitude.

JOHN

Step on the pedal or you will get nowhere. You are admired for your easy-going nature most of the time, which is why we remind you that there are times when you must accelerate, even when you feel the nice and easy approach feels best and most comfortable. In other words, John, step out of your comfort zone more often to ensure all of your goals are achieved in order to meet your purpose. Your purpose is to assist others in transcending personal stagnation. The lesson you came here to learn is to overcome reluctance. Call on us when you feel hesitant to initiate action. We will send you energy to soar to the heights you desire. It is then that you will have the impetus and ability to assist others in doing the same.

JOHNNY

Johnny, we call you the dynamo, as you exude full force energy with almost everything you do, if it is something that truly interests you. Conversely, if you have no interest, you disappear or approach with no motivation ... perhaps with sluggishness. However, we want to praise you for the dynamo that you are. Your enthusiasm is contagious, and any group task is accomplished more quickly and efficiently because of the collective energy that you foster. We do caution you with one thing: You may become annoyed with others who are not on the same energy plane as you. It will help if you step back and abandon your expectation of others. Enough will follow your dynamic lead to manifest great outcomes.

JOLENE

Falling from a ledge is something you will not do. Ah, you are daring and end up on the ledge frequently. However, you have the quickness and the equilibrium to keep from teetering out of control. You are able to stay grounded during unsettling times and even help others from losing the delicate balance between reality and illusion. Your primary purpose is that of a sincere and helpful friend—and that you are—in addition to pulling people from the ledge whose perceptions have been muddled. Thank you for choosing to be the voice of reason to those who would otherwise lose their balance and fall.

JON

Stand alone or don't stand at all. This is your personal "stance." And we wish to suggest that you to reassess. You have heard the old and popular saying "No Man is an Island." This is true, especially for you. Without the support and cooperation from those members of your circle who are willing to stand with you, your island will sink, and you will drown with your stubbornness. We beseech you to explore and accept your vulnerabilities. Then, with sureness and humility, accept the fact that you, as with all, can succeed—in general —much better with supporters. Not to say you need to give up your independence—that is a different, wonderful trait and asset. Just accept the encouragement and support. It is healthy!

JONATHAN

Stand alone or don't stand at all. This is your personal "stance." And we wish to tell you to reassess. You have heard the old and popular saying "No Man is an Island." This is true, especially for you. Without the support and cooperation from those members of your circle who are willing to stand with you, your island will sink, and you will drown with your stubbornness. We beseech you to explore and accept your vulnerabilities. Then, with sureness and humility, accept the fact that you, as with all, can succeed—in general—much better with supporters. Not to say you need to give up your independence—that is a different, wonderful trait and asset. Just accept the encouragement and support. It is healthy!

JORDAN

No, it isn't anything in the water. The productivity you create, and the increase therefrom, is contagious. In every situation, with most in your immediate circle, productivity abounds. You chose to arrive here as an enthusiast for enthusiasm, and what a splendid job you are doing in serving this purpose. You and those you affect find self-reward and satisfaction in positive accomplishments. Look around you at any given moment and see the results of the energy you have brought and continue to bring. We call you the Rabbit of

Progress. You create and continue to create. To assist with this purpose, we surround you with the energy of Citrine to help you sustain confidence in fulfilling your role and for physical strength at the human level. Your spiritual strength is well intact.

JOSEPH

Falling from a ledge is something you will not do. Ah, you are daring and end up on the ledge frequently. However, you have the quickness and the equilibrium to keep from teetering out of control. You are able to stay grounded during unsettling times and even help others from losing the delicate balance between reality and illusion. Your primary purpose is that of a sincere and helpful friend—and that you are—in addition to pulling people from the ledge whose perceptions have been muddled. Thank you for choosing to be the voice of reason to those who would otherwise lose their balance and fall.

JOSEPHINA

Delicate you are, and wispy as an embracing breeze. You are here to offer the lightness of air and the refreshment of pure smiles. As you walk (actually, you glide) along this life's path, we want you to know that wherever you step, you leave behind your lightness and gentleness. Your role here is quite an easy one: To be nothing other than yourself, without a thought as to what you may need to do or accomplish. Your accomplishments come through each time that you leave behind a temperate, clear, pleasant moment. These moments are mostly savored at a subconscious level; however, they have a refreshing effect. Thank you for being this simplistic elixir.

JOSEPHINE

Delicate you are, and wispy as an embracing breeze. You are here to offer the lightness of air and the refreshment of pure smiles. As you walk (actually, you glide) along this life's path, we want you to know that wherever you step, you leave behind your lightness and gentleness. Your role here is quite an easy one: To be nothing other than yourself, without a thought as to what you may need to do or accomplish. Your accomplishments come through each time that you leave behind a temperate, clear, pleasant moment. These moments are mostly savored at a subconscious level; however, they have a refreshing effect. Thank you for being this simplistic elixir.

JOSH / JOSHUA

"Don't look now" could be your slogan, because your life is full of surprises. You have been equipped to handle what comes your way, whether it be good, bad, happy, sad, or neutral circumstances. You are a magnet for others because of your innate flair of thinking and acting quickly with the necessary prudence. Forge ahead, Joshua—you can navigate anything this Earthly life hands you, and you have chosen an honorable incarnation, knowing that should you stumble, we will always hoist you back up.

JOSLYN / JOCELYN

No, it isn't anything in the water. The productivity you create, and the increase therefrom, is contagious. In every situation, with most in your immediate circle, productivity abounds. You chose to arrive here as an enthusiast for enthusiasm, and what a splendid job you are doing in serving this purpose. You and those you affect find self-reward and satisfaction in positive accomplishments. Look around you at any given moment and see the results of the energy you have brought and continue to bring. We call you the Rabbit of Progress. You create and continue to create. To assist with this purpose, we surround you with the energy of Citrine to help you sustain confidence in fulfilling your role and for physical strength at the human level. Your spiritual strength is well intact.

JOY

The albatross you feel you carry is for a noble reason, yet you need not feel this weight. Align yourself with angelic lightness, and this burden you have taken on will feel feathery. Release the serious nature you may have attached to your purpose of lifting the lost from their self-created despair. Acknowledge the valuable direction and tenderness you willingly give. Treat your purpose as a welcomed spiritual gift and enjoy the manifestations of healing the darkened hearts that need your light. Once you do this, we will be much more able to help you soar with no feelings of heavy, Earth angel wings. Being willing is the secret that you need to make this happen.

JOYCE

Little ones love to be in your company. They enjoy being in the flow of goodness, of kindness, and of fun. You are like a favorite teacher, bringing interesting information, rewarding positive behavior, and offering unconditional acceptance. You are a magnet to children who otherwise experience negative living environments. You have a demeanor which provides simple, enjoyable direction. Be the example. Be the teacher. Be the Earth angel. Be the innocent fun. Be the love. We wrap you in the brilliance of sun kissed clouds.

JUDE

Stand alone or don't stand at all. This is your personal "stance." And we wish to suggest that you to reassess. You have heard the old and popular saying "No Man is an Island." This is true, especially for you. Without the support and cooperation from those members of your circle who are willing to stand with you, your island will sink and you will drown with your stubbornness. We beseech you to explore and accept your vulnerabilities. Then, with sureness and humility, accept the fact that you, as with all, can succeed —in general—much better with supporters. Not to say you need to give up your independence—that is a different, wonderful trait and asset. Just accept the encouragement and support. It is healthy!

JUDITH

Judith ... our Beauty. We say this because your role here is to show others about inner beauty. Physical appearances may be easy on the eye, or otherwise. Most realize that those living on Earth exhibit various levels of aesthetic value. You are to demonstrate that each is a work of art. Although interpreted differently by each of those observing or viewing, the fact is that there is inner beauty in each one. We urge you to continue to share your spark of inner beauty in order to fulfill your purpose: To show a mirror to those who do not recognize this truth, so they can see that they are a reflection of God's beauty.

JUDY

Judy ... our Beauty. We say this because your role here is to show others about inner beauty. Physical appearances may be easy on the eye, or otherwise. Most realize that those living on Earth exhibit various levels of aesthetic value. You are to demonstrate that each is a work of art. Although interpreted differently by each of those observing or viewing, the fact is that there is inner beauty in each one. We urge you to continue to share your spark of inner beauty in order to fulfill your purpose: To show a mirror to those who do not recognize this truth, so they can see that they are a reflection of God's beauty.

JULIE

You came to Earth to spread your sweetness, because you knew that this special type of kindness is so needed by its inhabitants. You have no expectations of others, and you generously provide a light, exultant touch to all. It is your nature; you don't even have to give it a thought to emanate sweetness. We also call you Flower because of the beauty of your presence everywhere you go. Unlike a flower, your essence does not fade away; it stays alive. You are a flower which does not wilt and brings serenity when needed. We will send increased energy to your heart center when an individual or situation is in need of this serenity. You will feel a deep tranquility sinking into and then springing from your heart ... that placidity will in turn soothe others' hearts. Thank you, our gracious flower.

JUNE

You are stronger than you think. Please stop degrading yourself. We are sad that you hold back so much and find it difficult to show your feelings. We see your exterior strength masking your secret inner feelings of weakness. We will help you embrace the authentic strength that you are. Just ask, and we will assist you to become what others already believe you to be. It will not be as difficult as you think. We are holding you up, always. You are destined to exude confident humility, which is seen in visionaries. Yes, you are destined for such.

JUSTIN

Search and Rescue. Search for the love inside your heart and rescue yourself. Search for the knowledge lying deep within your soul, and know yourself. Redeem the gifts you have been given to love and to be loved. You have suppressed love, the inner knowledge, and the miracles of your spiritual gifts in past life times. You are destined to rise above the worldly chains to realize your full spiritual influence upon your own soul. Consequently, you will spread this love into the vast universe. Your immediate purpose, however, is to spread the love during this lifetime, on this Earth plane, to the souls here who are impoverished from love. We will shower them with the energy of Rose Quartz and open their heart centers as you reveal the pure love you were sent to teach. You, as well, are nourished and supported by us with this pure, loving energy.

KALEB

The rails are what keep the trains on track. Each railroad car is dependent on well-maintained tracks. We say to you: Maintain each track in your life so as to minimize the possibility of being derailed. Do not depend on your powerful engine to get you through to your destinations. Pay attention to the details (rails) of your life to ensure that there are no major mishaps along the way. The rails are your core group of family and friends, and also include your career path. Your train may jump the track occasionally. This life on Earth cannot be free from being derailed now and then. We want you to know, however, that we are here with you to help mend the track and maintain safety to the degree possible from our realm. Your lesson is to learn that, despite any malfunctioning rails, you are able to reach your intended stations, yet rails that have been unattended will slow you down. Neglect increases the odds for "accidents" and delays. Your purpose is to alert those closest to you to pay attention to their rails, too, as this will result in a smoother ride for all.

KAMRON

Pragmatism is practical. However, pragmatism used too diligently and consistently may take some of the fun out of life that you deserve. You did not come to this Earth to be serious and exercise conservatism in your life on a daily basis. However, we say to you that you may have the tendency to do so. Your lesson is to observe the mundane situations objectively, take the actions you know are proper, and move on to lighter life experiences. You will learn to remove yourself from the rut of the concrete, black-and-white decision making and practical mode. You will learn to remove your blinders and see the panoramic view of the world and its charm. Further, you will learn when to remove the blinders … when to approach life with prudence and when to simply enjoy yourself. In doing so, you will serve as an example of responsibly living this life to the fullest.

KARA

Your lesson is to avoid throwing your pearls to the swine. Not that there is anything bad about swine—all creatures are valuable. We refer to the symbolism to which the word "swine" is known. There are those who will muddy up your pure and clear intentions … as well as your talents. Be cautious with whom you share. "Sign up" with only those who have your best interests at heart. We will assist with decisions along your path. When in doubt, ask and we will provide you with guidance. Resist any person or situation that does not represent what is in your best interest as well as their own. Remember, we will help and send the guidance for your direction. You will realize that your pearls are gifts from the angels, and you will treasure them, not allowing them to go to waste.

KAREN

Your strength is both a blessing and a curse. You came here with the ability to be firm, to speak up, and to run the show, both behind the scenes and on stage. Your exceptional strength and assertiveness (sometimes interpreted as abrasiveness) will off put others at times. Do not worry on this matter. These are the times when those who are offended are also learning needed lessons for their own path. They see your caring and generous ways and know that providing kindness does not equate with weakness. You are here to break down the false paradox that kindness and direct strength are always separate.

KARL

Stringing things, or people, along is not your style. You have the gift of Directness with a Smile, even if the news is not desirable. You deliver with grace and have an uncanny ability to make an undesirable situation tolerable with your charming nature. We say charming as with an innocent manner, not a deceiving manner. This authentic, caring charm is so helpful to lift others up at times when no one else could do the same. We caution you to take this responsibility seriously, as some with this gift fall into a temptation to use it for their benefit, even when they are not being deceitful. Hang on to the trustworthy charm you came here to share. It will bring smiles and uplift spirits.

Intensity is a trait you also possess. Know when it is necessary and when you must temper it, else you stand the risk of your purpose backfiring on you. Hence, you would need to work on learning this lesson in your next life. You have learned much on your journeys; we do not want to see you take any steps backward. We place a garland of lilies around your heart to keep it pure and to allow you to feel our unconditional love.

KARMEN

Start it up! You have a knack for igniting and setting things in motion. We call you our Initiator and Accelerator, as you are among the ones who are sent here to put things in motion and then move them forward. We caution you, too, that there are times to put on the brakes, and this is the lesson you are here to learn. We may add that you have been doing well with both this life's purpose and this life's lesson. You have arrived here with the knowledge instilled within your soul that, once something is ablaze, you are aware of exactly when to stoke the fire. Conversely, you know when to let the coals dim and fade out, because some blazes are not for the common good. Karmen, we have provided you with our gift of cedarwood and spruce energy for your need to stay both heightened and grounded; you have such a high calling. Visit Cedarwood and Spruce when you feel the need to elevate your consciousness and when you feel the need to get back to Earth. Share this message with others who you will know require it. Thank you for your response to the call to step out, step up, and ignite! We cherish you.

KASEY

Descending on you daily are angels of consequence. They bring you blessings for all the good things and the care that you bring to people on a regular basis. You cannot help but have good consequences, as you came here for the express purpose of bringing happiness and contentment to those around you, and you are able to do this in many ways, at many levels. You are versatile, and this versatility and adaptability will benefit you as well, all through the times of this life. Your chameleon-like demeanor is rare and priceless, as you have the foresight and ability to adapt when needed. This is a gift we have given you to help with your work here.

KATE

Your strength is both a blessing and a curse. You came here with the ability to be firm, to speak up, and to run the show, both behind the scenes and on stage. Your exceptional strength and assertiveness (sometimes interpreted as abrasiveness) will off put others at times. Do not worry on this matter. These are the times when those who are offended are also learning needed lessons for their own path. They see your caring and generous ways and know that providing kindness does not equate with weakness. You are here to break down the false paradox that kindness and direct strength are always separate.

KATELYN

Surrey, surrey. You feel you would love the traveling style of yesteryear. The hustle and bustle of highways pale in comparison to the byways of old. You would prefer to ride in a beautiful surrey or walk down a sidewalk with a parasol, through a quaint town lined with trees and lampposts. Such charm, and not racing to and fro, as it seems is the norm at this time. We say to you: Your purpose is to teach others to slow down and look around ... to soak in the natural beauty of truly being alive and acknowledging surroundings. There is always something eloquent to find in the environment if only the current pace is reduced. You know how to embellish the daily humdrum of busy-ness with beholding the quiet beauty among society's noise. Yes, ride your symbolic surrey and carry your symbolic parasol. This elegant energy will help you cope with the world's fast pace and set a good example for those who heed your advice.

KATHERINE / KATHRYN

Never fear the wrath from those you may perceive to be your enemies. Your genuine kindness and the pure light that emanates from your being will almost always divert anyone who has ill intentions. Your light is so bright that it deflects threatening energies and attracts all things positive. Your purpose is manifested through your nurturing mannerisms that convert hard-shelled souls into baby-like souls wishing to be held in pure light. Should you be confronted by wrong doers despite your demeanor, please know that you are protected when you call on us, your angels.

KATHY

Never fear the wrath from those you may perceive to be your enemies. Your genuine kindness and the pure light that emanates from your being will almost always divert anyone who has ill intentions. Your light is so bright that it deflects threatening energies and attracts all things positive. Your purpose is manifested through your nurturing mannerisms that convert hard-shelled souls into baby-like souls wishing to be held in pure light. Should you be confronted by wrong doers despite your demeanor, please know that you are protected when you call on us, your angels.

KATIE

Ask and you shall receive ... you must learn to make your needs known, dear Katie. Your quiet, still nature is endearing and brings soulfulness when needed. Do not change this ...

you came here to provide this stillness for others. Please always remember to ask when in need. Never worry about how to ask, as your humility will shine through no matter what you say or how you say it. Your lesson is to be open to receive. Your personal contributions will continue, and more so when you are willing to have your own needs met.

KAYLA

Sky-lit, you are able to see a vast panorama of possibilities, unlike most on this Earth walk. You carry with you the secrets and the magic of a million stars, the power of the sun, and the stillness of the moon ... not all at once ... rather when whichever of these promotes well-being and brings answers that are being sought. Allow others to look to you for inspiration in finding their answers and to realize that some mysteries must remain mysteries. In so doing, they too will embrace the universe's panorama.

KAYLEE

Sky-lit, you are able to see a vast panorama of possibilities, unlike most on this Earth walk. You carry with you the secrets and the magic of a million stars, the power of the sun, and the stillness of the moon – not all at once - rather when whichever of these promotes well-being and brings answers that are being sought. Allow others to look to you for inspiration in finding their answers and to realize that some mysteries must remain mysteries. In so doing, they too will embrace the universe's panorama.

KEITH

All hands on deck! We call you The Captain because of your ability to assemble a diverse group to work toward a common goal. You are respected, yet not feared. You provide momentum severally and wholly. We ask you to step out and step into areas where group cooperation is desired. You are gifted in directing projects, whether it be Spring cleaning, a street fair, or a corporate undertaking. Organizers and motivators, like you who bring progress without conflict, are much needed. This is your purpose. You are appreciated, and we are grateful that you chose this role. We support you with a spiral of chakra colors to keep you grounded, creative, confident, open to unconditional and mutual acceptance, clearly spoken, intuitive, and connected to the divine.

KELLY

Juice it up! You are the resourceful and appreciative one. Rather than simply garnishing with beauty, such as a lime or lemon slice attached to a glass, you squeeze the juice into the glass. Yes! Is not the content improved with the flavor of the juice? Of course, and you realize this fact. Show and savor all of the fruits of life, not just the appearances. Such an example you are, and in this regard you are serving your purpose.

Experience the whole. "Oooo" and "ahhh" at the aesthetics, and at the same time, appreciate the nuts and bolts that make the piece of furniture useful and beautiful. Enjoy the orange, and drink the juice which remains. Behold the art, and be attentive to the nuances of the work. Celebrate the music; use it to sing and dance. Notice its rhythm and each of the instruments. What you illustrate is the opposite of greed. You reflect a zest for total experience versus a pleasant glance, taste, or dance step. You, with your deep gratitude for all aspects of the gifts the universe brings, will influence others to reach a new level of appreciation, thus embracing life to a fuller extent.

KELSEY

Sky-lit, you are able to see a vast panorama of possibilities, unlike most on this Earth walk. You carry with you the secrets and the magic of a million stars, the power of the sun, and the stillness of the moon ... not all at once ... rather when whichever of these promotes well-being and brings answers that are being sought. Allow others to look to you for inspiration in finding their answers and to realize that some mysteries must remain mysteries. In so doing, they too will embrace the universe's panorama.

KEN / KENNETH

Our sophisticated one, we revel in your auric presence, as do the fortunate souls who recognize your blue light of compassion and truth. Yes, Ken, Archangel Michael and his band of protective angels are a major influence in your life ... your everyday life as well as your purpose in this lifetime. Your purpose is to radiate comfort and warmth with a strength that cannot be ignored or questioned. This powerful warmth results in those who need to feel protected ... those who need to know unconditional love ... those who need to feel blessed by angelic presence. Those who are touched by your strength will transform from their insecurities. Fear will melt away from their Earthly suppositions.

We want you to know that not everyone who you would hope to benefit from the light you have been provided will see you, or sense this angelic love in which you are surrounded. We beseech you to allow Archangel Michael's influence to take its spiritually directed course. You are in good hands. We send gratefulness to you for choosing this role, and the angels reciprocate with warmth, compassion, truth, and unfaltering love. You have chosen to be here and have allowed us to enable you for this work. While you are in touch with this amazing appointment, we wish to say that you are spirit, personified. Yes, it is true that all human form is spirit at a most often unrecognized level; however, it is rare to take on this role in human form.

KENDALL

Fly your kites. Fly all colors and shapes of kites. Let the world know you are capable of rising above the mundane, and that the variety of life is truly what brings people to new and exciting heights. When you choose to fly your kites, you will serve your purpose of demonstrating that a passion for living life in full color is so much more fulfilling than settling for whatever people feel is handed to them for mere existence. You exist, evolve, and excite. You soar, and revel in all the possibilities for happiness at heights many never realize. Fly your kite and invite others to not only observe, but to also participate with their own kites.

KENDRA

Flowing from the stream to the pond to the lake and to the ocean ... allowing yourself to be carried through the tributaries of life without question is quite difficult. However, your lesson is to learn to float to your destinations and to your destiny during this life without resistance or question. Indeed, this is seemingly impossible to the human experience. However, you will learn and you will feel the freedom and exhilaration of "going with the flow," as the saying goes. You will reach both small and great goals along the way, and you will swim easily in all types of currents with ease once you simply allow your river of life to unfold. We send you invisible, weightless life jackets of courage and rafts of comfort to help you along the way.

KENNEDY

In the quagmire of Earth's society, you are one who knows how to use the sometimes perplexing map therein to find treasures. You have the gift of staying on course in the midst of the maze of human life experiences. Some become lost inside a labyrinth and some find that it offers time to reflect, to gain insight, to meditate, to discover deeper truth, and to receive epiphanies. In essence, the labyrinth will either cause confusion and anxiety or it will bring tremendous blessings. You are equipped to not only traverse easily through the maze; you could even build one if you so desired. However, it is not your desire to bring strife. You arrived here with the gift of knowing the "in's and out's" required to discern which direction to take at any given moment and with every surprising twist or turn. Therefore, your purpose is to be a leader of those who have lost direction. On the light side, you can even be a tour guide of life, pointing out highlights along the way. We provide you with an eternal sense of right direction, because we know you will use it to the best advantage and the correct advantage for all. If you ever feel you may slip (after all, you are in human form), call on us and you will receive immediate navigation assistance.

KENNY

We hope you never tire or feel offended by being what some refer to as the Class Clown. That is merely a convenient label. Refreshing moments and reminders to stray away from too much seriousness are greatly needed on the Earth plane. What a gift you have chosen to bring to this lifetime: To elicit the healing properties of laughter. When you are referred to as the comic relief or comedian or jokester, it is in essence a gratitude phrase from those who derive uplifting moments from your positive presence. Notice the energy shift when you contribute your gift. You are frequently present when most needed. Your lesson is to follow your instincts about when your purpose to elevate is queued by us. This is how you will bring much healing. Yes, laughter is truly good medicine, and you are endowed with thousands of prescriptions. We say to you: Those who have chosen this purpose may often feel pressure to sustain their healing amusement. We want you to know that we realize this difficulty and will pave a restful road from the possible feeling of being responsible for glee on a constant basis. These will be respites from what you may feel to be a demanding role, and they will be plentiful. We guarantee this, and we assure you that we will assist in bringing you balance.

KENT

In the quagmire of Earth's society, you are one who knows how to use the sometimes perplexing map therein to find treasures. You have the gift of staying on course in the midst of the maze of human life experiences. Some become lost inside a labyrinth and some find that it offers time to reflect, to gain insight, to meditate, to discover deeper truth, and to receive epiphanies. In essence, the labyrinth will either cause confusion and anxiety or it will bring tremendous blessings. You are equipped to not only traverse easily through the maze; you could even build one if you so desired. However, it is not your desire to bring strife. You arrived here with the gift of knowing the "in's and out's" required to discern which direction to take at any given moment and with every surprising twist or turn. Therefore, your purpose is to be a leader of those who have lost direction. On the light side, you can even be a tour guide of life, pointing out highlights along the way. We provide you with an eternal sense of right direction, because we know you will use it to the best advantage and the correct advantage for all. If you ever feel you may slip (after all, you are in human form), call on us and you will receive immediate navigation assistance.

KERRY

Diamonds in the sand. Yes, your lesson during this lifetime is to not only realize that there are diamonds among the trillions of grains of sand ... you will learn to recognize those sparkling individuals who are precious, yet possess an indestructible spirit. Your purpose is to bring to attention their worth and help them to shine, as only they can. There are an endless number of diamonds in the sand, and most are unaware of their value. They are easily found. In fact, all grains are gleaming gems. However, some are just not ready to glisten with impenetrable endurance. They are here to learn different lessons. You are one such diamond who is aware of your value, and you will recognize those who are unaware or feel cracked. They are not marred, and you will know exactly how to transform their inferior mentality to that of gleaming intention for the benefit of the planet. We will help transport you to the many beaches where these dear jewels are waiting to be discovered.

KEVIN

Brass knuckles are never needed, and you arrived here with that internal knowledge. No boxing gloves, no abrasive actions or words ... simply speaking your truth with no fear or hesitancy. This trait is often considered an art. We say to you: You arrived with the gift of speaking your truth, and we praise our Kevin's for not faltering with this gift. Leaving no questions regarding your approach, your philosophy, or any solutions required, your calm truth transforms confusion and catapults it to resolution. Grieve not when your truth doesn't result in a progression toward solving conflict of any type; these are times when the lessons offered to others are seeded for future growth.

Your influence will sometimes take hours, months, or years. Nevertheless, this gift of yours is to be shared as a purpose for your life on this Earth. We protect your throat energy center and your center of intuition at all times. Do not fret when your throat feels irritated. It may feel overused to you at times. We will clear this for you and soothe you. We love you too much to allow you to become or remain hoarse for any extended period of time. Ask for Archangel Michael to surround you with his blue protective light when you feel compromised or vulnerable.

KIM

Layers upon layers. Don't forget about the layers, else you may become impatient and possibly careless about building in a cumulative manner. This is your lesson ... to learn how to build without leaving out any steps. Your patience will prevail as long as you are in touch with the spiritual energy we provide you with every step of the way. You will build in many areas of life, with strong footings and successful outcomes. Please do not forget about the layers, our builder and creator of dreams.

KIMBERLY / KIMBERLEE

Layers upon layers. Don't forget about the layers, else you may become impatient and possibly careless about building in a cumulative manner. This is your lesson ... to learn how to build without leaving out any steps. Your patience will prevail as long as you are in touch with the spiritual energy we provide you with every step of the way. You will build in many areas of life, with strong footings and successful outcomes. Please do not forget about the layers, our builder and creator of dreams.

KIRK

Burn unit. Scars. You heal the burns and scars that others sustain from abuse of one kind or another. You are the miracle salve to soothe and nurture. Not only do you offer healing energy—you perform corrective surgery for the soul.

The invisible stitches you provide also pull together torn hearts and merge the pieces into a whole. Being a nurse for injured souls does not come without its difficulties. Some will not welcome your care. Some will expect more than you can give. But, ah, many will both want and need your "treatments." Do not concern yourself with those who do not welcome or appreciate your care. Simply live your life as the surgeon you chose to be before you arrived here. The patients will come. There will never be too many so as to overwhelm you. This purpose will be served easily by you. We honor you for this service to humankind.

KIT / KITTY

Totality of being is your lesson. Fragmented souls have fragmented energy. You arrived here with residual disintegration from past lives. This served as a lesson which you brought to this current lifetime. You are now equipped with the knowledge you need to solidify your essence and become grounded in consciousness. This lifetime will complete the lesson in totality of being so that your purpose of being a mentor to the spiritually and emotionally oppressed and confused will be realized. This will continue until you are an old age in Earth years, and you may wish to return with the same divine purpose multiple times. The choice will be yours. We support you regardless of what you choose to contribute.

KOBI / KOBY

Our darling aristocrat, you emanate both charm and class. Sometimes you present yourself as the magnetic, flirtatious one, and at other times you appear to be noble and of higher echelon, as the Earth's population may see it. It is not true that there are differences in levels of "class" when speaking of spiritual matters. However, we address it in this form because you are in a human vehicle. The wonderful thing about you is that you, unlike most, can be charming and elegant at one and the same time. Because of this, you are charismatic. We say to you: Be mindful of this rare combination and do not use it to gain unfair advantage. Your lesson is to discover that positive combinations of traits can be used for the betterment of all. This is a difficult lesson while being in this Earth world today. We will help you exercise humility with your charm and dignity. This combination will provide you with fun, inner joy, and self-fulfillment while also serving a higher good.

KRYSTAL

Krystal, you are as the evergreen, always exhibiting beauty throughout the seasons of your life. Your lesson is to learn how to be consistent. This will help you be able to count on yourself to always "BE" when you feel you may be less than your true value. Your purpose is to demonstrate this consistency. Too many plant themselves in a comfortable spot. They do grow; however, they do not always reach their full potential of enjoying the constant beauty of life. They go through the seasons and often allow the winter seasons to freeze their glamour and their goals. So, our splendid evergreen, stand tall, display your eternal beauty, and provide nurturing to others who can also be evergreen, with your nudge.

KYLE

Our persistent one, as the old saying goes, *"some things are just not meant to be."* We are not at all saying there is anything wrong with being persistent—it is one of your greatest traits. Trying and trying again is what creates our great achievers, and we relish you as a great achiever. What we are saying is: You may feel that fate at times creates certain circumstances, events, or developments no matter what. This is true if they are meant to be. You are well aware of this. Your lesson is to distinguish when something just isn't meant to be and to have the ability and foresight to move on, allowing the things that are meant to happen. We say to you, your Pollyanna-like soul, when you need assistance in determining if something is not meant to be, please ask us. We love it when you communicate with us.

Ask, and we will send signs that will be unmistakable. Once you learn this lesson, you will be able to fulfill your purpose of having a contagious, positive attitude. Keep smiling! We send you the energy of Citrine as a token of our loving guidance and protection.

KYLIE

Our persistent one, as the old saying goes, "*some things are just not meant to be.*" We are not at all saying there is anything wrong with being persistent—it is one of your greatest traits. Trying and trying again is what creates our great achievers, and we relish you as a great achiever. What we are saying is: You may feel that fate at times creates certain circumstances, events, or developments no matter what. This is true if they are meant to be. You are well aware of this. Your lesson is to distinguish when something just isn't meant to be and to have the ability and foresight to move on, allowing the things that are meant to happen. We say to you, your Pollyanna-like soul, when you need assistance in determining if something is not meant to be, please ask us. We love it when you communicate with us. Ask, and we will send signs that will be unmistakable. Once you learn this lesson, you will be able to fulfill your purpose of having a contagious, positive attitude. Keep smiling! We send you the energy of Citrine as a token of our loving guidance and protection.

KYRA

You have a heart of gold, stone, crystals, and flowers. Your heart responds in kind to however it needs in all the books, chapters, paragraphs, and sentences of your life. The most miraculous part of your heart is that however you respond, it is always filled with love. Even when your heart must turn temporarily to stone, the stone is covered with and grows in love. The stone response simply assists with boundaries and with the lessons required for both you and the individuals who receive this response. Later, your heart can respond from another perspective when it is time. This multi-dimensional heart of yours is enchanting. The gold aspect is pure; the stone aspect is strong; the crystal aspect is amplifying, and the flower aspect reflects beauty and gratitude. We ask you to always honor your heart and its responses, as your heart will be your greatest teacher. In turn, it will create you as a gracious mentor.

LACEY / LACY

Do not wait for the mountain to come to you; go to the mountain. What seems to be immovable can transform with your diligence. Your lesson is to learn how to move mountains through sheer determination. Yes, you can do it. You can be a fiery force that can transmute dirt to gold because of your strong constitution and inner strength. We say to you: Remember that, even though you develop great confidence as a result of your fortitude, no one is immune to this world's destructive ways, especially from humankind. Your lesson is to use your strength wisely, where it will result in only good, and to avoid being drawn into ventures that would take advantage of others or of the land. Stay strong, our Atlas, and we will guide you toward the most auspicious and positive adventures.

LADONNA

Dear one, do not let the soulful sound of your name fool you. Others are at times surprised, as they have expectations of softness from you. This is not true. You are assertive in every way, and will deflect destructive energy in all forms, especially every-day hurtful actions and words. You are actually a hero, which is your chosen path. Steadfast, you are one who others look to for sound answers and frank responses. You are guided and surrounded by many angels for the strength to be a citadel in your home, work, and play. What a gallant role you have chosen. We give you the energy of Garnet for grounding and loyalty to your calling. We respect you so much.

LAHNA / LONNA

You carry with you the energy of the dove ... the white dove of peace. You have the natural capacity to bring peaceful feelings, calmness, and even at times the peace needed to resolve conflict or confrontation. We also give you the energy of moonlight—the soft light upon any harsh environment in which you may enter.

We plead with you to not allow the ways of the unawakened to draw you into a non-peaceful existence. We know this is difficult, and it happens temporarily from time to time ... for moments, days, weeks, months, or longer. It would be a tragedy in our eyes should you fall into a lifetime of being drawn into this type of unfruitful energy. Please be mindful of this and avoid being thwarted from your soul's purpose, which is to be a bringer of peaceful energy. Hold the moonlight dove close to your heart, and we will help you do your work with a peaceful, healing luminosity.

LAINE / LAYNE / LAINEY

Tender is the heart of those with your name, and when you love, the love is pure. Your lesson is to discern on whom you grace your tenderness and love. Look and watch for those who cherish and care for the flowers of life that have been granted to them. The flower within your heart can wilt quickly from neglect; protect this sacred space by allowing only kindred hearts as permanent parts of this life. Those who have not reached this level of loving tenderness are welcome to be in your life on a different level. They will take away a lesson in genuine caring, yet they will not weaken your blossoms. Therefore, all of your relationships in human form will be for the betterment because of your pristine intentions.

LANA / LANNA

You carry with you the energy of the dove...the white dove of peace. You have the natural capacity to bring peaceful feelings, calmness, and even at times the peace needed to resolve conflict or confrontation. We also give you the energy of moonlight—the soft light upon any harsh environment in which you may enter.

We plead with you to not allow the ways of the unawakened to draw you into a non-peaceful existence. We know this is difficult, and it happens temporarily from time to time ... for moments, days, weeks, months, or longer. It would be a tragedy in our eyes should you fall into a lifetime of being drawn into this type of unfruitful energy. Please be mindful of this and avoid being thwarted from your soul's purpose, which is to be a bringer of peaceful energy. Hold the moonlight dove close to your heart, and we will help you do your work with a peaceful, healing luminosity.

LANCE

Your open arms are what attract the essence of the souls who enter your life to stay. These souls respond to your acceptance and your helpful nature. You are also able to build ladders of hope that are easy to climb, and can take seekers to new heights. You can set an example of hope if you so choose. You do have a choice to extend the ladders, or to simply provide a footstool. We say again: It is your choice. Your primary lesson is to learn to recognize your own compassion and then act on it, expand it. You will either continue to grow as an empathetic soul or stay comfortable where you are; it is up to you. Thank you for where you are now, with your welcoming gestures. We will assist you to build on this, if you request our guidance.

LANI

Strait jackets or other restraints are meant for no one, our dear one. We ask that you release and free yourself from the confines of any chains you may have created for yourself. Break out? Yes, please do! Some of you with these names are reserved and shy. Others with these same names are bold, sometimes brazen, yet don't always jump over the right hurdles. They land confidently...on the wrong track. We want to tell you that your lesson here on Earth is to find the most auspicious direction and move forward with clarity and focus, neither in a withdrawn manner, nor with too bold of a manner. Set your own bar and then jump. We will guide your sprint, or your standing jump, and will clear the track for you. It is not a track for racing or running. It is a long distance track with hurdles to jump. Once you are on it, you will have accomplished this lesson and will move purposefully in the direction of your calling: To awaken others to their own dreams and free themselves from restraints.

LARRY

Tether ball is not your thing. Rather, you are the type to go for the gusto and to take things to the limit. All things good and all things kind are what you seek, and you amplify these values in your daily life with strangers, friends, and loved ones. We caution you to be discreet, as your powerful ways can be misinterpreted. We will assist, if you ask, in guiding you to people and situations that are open to your grand personality. We do not mean your way is imposing, boastful or larger than life. Strength and enthusiasm can also be subtle. Continue to be the part in this movie of life as the doer and motivator. In so doing, you will realize your purpose.

LAUREN

Juice it up! You are the resourceful and appreciative one. Rather than simply garnishing with beauty, such as a lime or lemon slice attached to a glass, you squeeze the juice into the glass. Yes! Is not the content improved with the flavor of the juice? Of course, and you realize this fact. Show and savor all of the fruits of life, not just the appearances. Such an example you are, and in this regard you are serving your purpose. Experience the whole. "Oooo" and "ahhh" at the aesthetics, and at the same time, appreciate the nuts and bolts that make the piece of furniture useful and beautiful. Enjoy the orange, and drink the juice which remains. Behold the art, and be attentive to the nuances of the work. Celebrate the music; use it to sing and dance. Notice its rhythm and each of the instruments.

What you illustrate is the opposite of greed. You reflect a zest for total experience versus a pleasant glance, taste, or dance step. You, with your deep gratitude for all aspects of the gifts the universe brings, will influence others to reach a new level of appreciation, thus embracing life to a fuller extent.

LAURIE

Juice it up! You are the resourceful and appreciative one. Rather than simply garnishing with beauty, such as a lime or lemon slice attached to a glass, you squeeze the juice into the glass. Yes! Is not the content improved with the flavor of the juice? Of course, and you realize this fact. Show and savor all of the fruits of life, not just the appearances. Such an example you are, and in this regard you are serving your purpose. Experience the whole. Oooo and "ahhh" at the aesthetics, and at the same time, appreciate the nuts and bolts that make the piece of furniture useful and beautiful. Enjoy the orange, and drink the juice which remains. Behold the art, and be attentive to the nuances of the work. Celebrate the music; use it to sing and dance. Notice its rhythm and each of the instruments.

What you illustrate is the opposite of greed. You reflect a zest for total experience versus a pleasant glance, taste, or dance step. You, with your deep gratitude for all aspects of the gifts the universe brings, will influence others to reach a new level of appreciation, thus embracing life to a fuller extent.

LAVERNE

Refrain from keeping all of your options open, LaVerne. The world is full of potentially rewarding life paths, entertainment, and friendships. Your lesson is to explore before you make decisions, especially major ones. You are such a diversified soul that it will be difficult to zone in to the correct choices that will best enhance your life here. The good news for you is that, should you make a decision you do not end up liking, your flexibility will see you through until you can step away and move toward another, more desirable, one. Of course, you want to avoid as many of these glitches as possible. Therefore, we will send you additional resilience to withstand the errors in judgment, and especially additional wisdom to complement your varied curiosities. This will help keep you grounded and focused on what truly excites your being.

LAWRENCE

Tether ball is not your thing. You rather are the type to go for the gusto and to take things to the limit. All things good and all things kind are what you seek, and you amplify these values in your daily life with strangers, friends, and loved ones. We caution you to be discreet, as your powerful ways can be misinterpreted. We will assist, if you ask, in guiding you to people and situations that are open to your grand personality. We do not mean your way is imposing, boastful or larger than life. Strength and enthusiasm can also be subtle. Continue to be the part in this movie of life as the doer and motivator. In so doing, you will realize your purpose.

LAYLA

Your destiny calls, as it always has. Most do feel the urge to reach a destiny ... a destiny most often unknown. This is a mysterious factor of life on the Earth plane. For many, it is a knowing that there must be some kind of destiny, yet a question of what it may be or how to reach it. For others, destinies are revealed at some point, and they are gratified at a deep level with the discovery. Then there are those who arrived here with a passionate drive, with a knowledge of why they are here. You, Layla, are one such passion-filled soul. You have a clear awareness of your purpose to bring mostly unknown information to the forefront. This information is at a level that some have not experienced. The information is about introducing others to levels of consciousness that they may otherwise never recognize. The best part of this revelation is that, once introduced to these levels, they will discover their own individual destinies. Thank you for this unique, yet important work. We send light to your third eye to direct you on your course.

LEAH

We admire you, as do others, for your ability to so easily float through life and its sometimes rough circumstances. You were given this ability before arriving here because you chose to experience more placid travel after having lived in other tumultuous lifetimes. We say to you: Not all who are given this gift actually remember or implement it. Some drift into the worldly challenges and lose their awareness of the gentle waves in which they can undulate and flow with the issues, and may actually sink into heavy, murky mud. You will come across some of these souls, and you will lift them up out of their quicksand, reminding them with your ease of effort that they, too, share this gift. This is your purpose: To recognize those who have forgotten, and bring them to their remembrance of the gift of ease.

LEE / LEIGH

Your acceptance of others is your greatest gift. It brings healing at a level unseen, but felt at the core. Even when you disagree or are disappointed with another, you unfailingly continue to provide support, but not without at least sharing your thoughts. The world needs so many such as you ... to help bring about the peace sought after by most. You do bring inner peace through your non-judgmental approach and self-discovery through your candidness. Your strength walks beside your acceptance, and your shield of personal power is ever present, allowing no one to cross your own peaceful boundaries or self-knowledge. This is difficult to attain, yet you possess these qualities. We congratulate you for this accomplishment.

LEEANNE

Your acceptance of others is your greatest gift. It brings healing at a level unseen, but felt at the core. Even when you disagree or are disappointed with another, you unfailingly continue to provide support, but not without at least sharing your thoughts. The world needs so many such as you ... to help bring about the peace sought after by most. You do bring inner peace through your non-judgmental approach and self-discovery through your candidness. Your strength walks beside your acceptance, and your shield of personal power is ever present, allowing no one to cross your own peaceful boundaries or self-knowledge. This is difficult to attain, yet you possess these qualities. We congratulate you for this accomplishment.

LENORE

Sink your feet deep into the sand. Feel the energy of a million particles that will stabilize you, and at the same time remind you of how many actions it takes to become one with the All That Is. You long for a purpose, and we want to direct you to meditation. If you are unable to stand motionless in the sand, stand on the Earth. Feel its nurturing energy. Feel the millions of vibrations that resonate as one world. You are the same. Your many steps, your countless thoughts and actions—all are manifesting as one. YOU—One with the All That Is.

LEO / LEONARDO

Step it up! You may find yourself thinking this or actually saying this to those you feel are not giving it their best, or are procrastinating about any number of things. Your lesson is to learn that patience can indeed be a virtue, especially if you are assuming that all have equal skills and abilities to perform. You will learn not to be quick to judge, rather to see each person's capabilities. Regarding those who aren't as adept as you or others, you will circumvent the others from criticizing and demanding that performance be improved. You will learn to allow others to live this life at their pace, and you will only encourage them to improve only when you know they have the capability to do so. There will be those who are simply not motivated, or who want to take the path of least resistance. These will be the times when you can say, "step it up," and provide the motivation and positive reinforcement for them to improve not only their performance, but their self-worth. This is your purpose: To be a coach and to encourage those who are capable of doing more.

LEON

Step it up! You may find yourself thinking this or actually saying this to those you feel are not giving it their best, or are procrastinating about any number of things. Your lesson is to learn that patience can indeed be a virtue, especially if you are assuming that all have equal skills and abilities to perform. You will learn not to be quick to judge, rather to see each person's capabilities. Regarding those who aren't as adept as you or others, you will circumvent the others from criticizing and demanding that performance be improved. You will learn to allow others to live this life at their pace, and you will only encourage them to improve only when you know they have the capability to do so. There will be those who are simply not motivated, or who want to take the path of least resistance. These will be the times when you can say, "step it up," and provide the motivation and positive reinforcement for them to improve not only their performance, but their self-worth. This is your purpose: To be a coach and to encourage those who are capable of doing more.

LES

Tell me something good. This is your mantra. You do like good news, as does everyone. This, however, is about your love for others' life stories. You thrive on listening, learning, and acquiring knowledge. You apply others' life lessons to yourself and share them (anonymously) so that others can also glean wisdom, delight, and practical applications. Some stories, of course, will revolve around unpleasant experiences, yet there are always lessons or reversals of circumstances from which to grow. This is your purpose: To accumulate personal accounts that will benefit the majority. We call you The Journalist, as you ... with permission ... share diaries in a responsible and informative manner. We give you the energy of a flock of geese so that you will always travel in the right direction to fulfill your purpose.

LESLIE

Tell me something good. This is your mantra. You do like good news, as does everyone. This, however, is about your love for others' life stories. You thrive on listening, learning, and acquiring knowledge. You apply others' life lessons to yourself and share them (anonymously) so that others can also glean wisdom, delight, and practical applications. Some stories, of course, will revolve around unpleasant experiences, yet there are always lessons or reversals of circumstances from which to grow. This is your purpose: To accumulate personal accounts that will benefit the majority. We call you The Journalist, as you ... with permission ... share diaries in a responsible and informative manner. We give you the energy of a flock of geese so that you will always travel in the right direction to fulfill your purpose.

LESTER

Tell me something good. This is your mantra. You do like good news, as does everyone. This, however, is about your love for others' life stories. You thrive on listening, learning, and acquiring knowledge. You apply others' life lessons to yourself and share them (anonymously) so that others can also glean wisdom, delight, and practical applications. Some stories, of course, will revolve around unpleasant experiences, yet there are always lessons or reversals of circumstances from which to grow. This is your purpose: To accumulate personal accounts that will benefit the majority. We call you The Journalist, as you ... with permission ... share diaries in a responsible and informative manner. We give you the energy of a flock of geese so that you will always travel in the right direction to fulfill your purpose.

LILY/ LILLY

Tender is the heart of those with your name, and when you love, the love is pure. Your lesson is to discern on whom you grace your tenderness and love. Look and watch for those who cherish and care for the flowers of life that have been granted to them. The flower within your heart can wilt quickly from neglect; protect this sacred space by allowing only kindred hearts as permanent parts of this life. Those who have not reached this level of loving tenderness are welcome to be in your life on a different level. They will take away a lesson in genuine caring, but they will not weaken your blossoms. Therefore, all of your relationships in human form will be for the betterment because of your pristine intentions.

LINDA

No, it isn't anything in the water. The productivity you create, and the increase therefrom, is contagious. In every situation, with most in your immediate circle, productivity abounds. You chose to arrive here as an enthusiast for enthusiasm, and what a splendid job you are doing in serving this purpose. You and those you affect find self-reward and satisfaction in positive accomplishments. Look around you at any given moment and see the results of the energy you have brought and continue to bring. We call you the Rabbit of Progress. You create and continue to create. To assist with this purpose, we surround you with the energy of Citrine to help you sustain confidence in fulfilling your role and for physical strength at the human level. Your spiritual strength is well intact.

LINDSEY

Your life, just like everyone's, is built upon layers. Each chapter creates a layer, and the layers combine to make you who you are today. You are keenly attuned with your stories and how they have created the individual that you are today. More so, you will be mindful of the tiers you are creating that will add to your uniqueness. Although everyone is a walking novel, you pay more attention to what the chapters contain so that your story will be interesting, plus serve as a model that reveals significant lessons. You are willing to make errors and to rise above them in order to illustrate these lessons. Although you are attentive to each stage as your life story is developed, you have chosen to teach through your life's course of layers, both directly and indirectly. You are like the sun as well as its shadow. One cannot exist without the other. The knowledge that one must experience the shadows of life, if the light is to also always exist, is difficult to internalize. To take rest in the cool shadows is a valuable tool which you are here to demonstrate.

LISA

Tell me something good. This is your mantra. You do like good news, as does everyone. This, however, is about your love for others' life stories. You thrive on listening, learning, and acquiring knowledge. You apply others' life lessons to yourself and share them (anonymously) so that others can also glean wisdom, delight, and practical applications. Some stories, of course, will revolve around unpleasant experiences, yet there are always lessons or reversals of circumstances from which to grow. This is your purpose: To accumulate personal accounts that will benefit the majority. We call you The Journalist, as you ... with permission ... share diaries in a responsible and informative manner. We give you the energy of a flock of geese so that you will always travel in the right direction to fulfill your purpose.

LIZ

The albatross you feel you carry is for a noble reason, yet you need not feel this weight. Align yourself with angelic lightness, and this burden you have taken on will feel feathery. Release the serious nature you may have attached to your purpose of lifting the lost from their self-created despair. Acknowledge the valuable direction and tenderness you willingly give. Treat your purpose as a welcomed spiritual gift and enjoy the manifestations of healing the darkened hearts that need your light. Once you do this, we will be much more able to help you soar with no feelings of heavy, Earth angel wings. Being willing is the secret that you need to make this happen.

LLOYD

Stone cold. At times, this is how you are seen. However, it is only because you are intrinsically shy. You often appear distant and unfeeling. We know it may take some effort for you to emerge from your shell when needed, and at times when you would rather not be outgoing at all. We say to you: Reassess what this world sees as outgoing or gregarious. Instead, think of your public personality as simply interactive at a helpful level, with a smile. That is all that is needed. It matters not if you are perceived as aloof, or even stone cold.

What will matter is the warmth you naturally emanate when comfortably stepping into your role as an Ambassador of Truth. Your manner of fulfilling your role will be pleasant to others and natural for you. We also wish to point out that with intimate relationships such as close friends, family, and romantic companions, there is no perception of stone cold. You are as a warm blanket on a winter's day to the people who are close to you.

LOIS

Stone cold. At times, this is how you are seen. However, it is only because you are intrinsically shy. You often appear distant and unfeeling. We know it may take some effort for you to emerge from your shell when needed, and at times when you would rather not be outgoing at all. We say to you: Reassess what this world sees as outgoing or gregarious. Instead, think of your public personality as simply interactive at a helpful level, with a smile. That is all that is needed. It matters not if you are perceived as aloof, or even stone cold. What will matter is the warmth you naturally emanate when comfortably stepping into your role as an Ambassador of Truth. Your manner of fulfilling your role will be pleasant to others and natural for you. We also wish to point out that with intimate relationships such as close friends, family, and romantic companions, there is no perception of stone cold. You are as a warm blanket on a winter's day to the people who are close to you.

LOLA

Clear all the decks, Lola. It gets too crowded. Too many interests dilute your richness. Clear the decks and give your attention to a few. You will know which one or which ones to devote your loyalty. They are the interests which are not merely interests; they are the ones that fire such a passion that you cannot clear them from any decks. Let the ones go that are intriguing, yet do not ignite that fire. This goes for people in your life as well. Your striking presence makes people gravitate toward you. Crowds do not serve you well. Limit the seating at your personal stadium. Allow all to visit, and allow only a limited number of back stage passes. Those with passes are those who will share with you mutually enriching experiences. Your life lesson is to achieve clarity. We say to you: Learn what is extraneous and what is pertinent to your life's purpose. Your purpose is to pass along this ability.

LONNIE

Strait jackets or other restraints are meant for no one, our dear one. We ask that you release and free yourself from the confines of any chains you may have created for yourself. Break out? Yes, please do! Some of you with these names are reserved and shy. Others with these same names are bold, sometimes brazen, yet don't always jump over the right hurdles. They land confidently...on the wrong track. We want to tell you that your lesson here on Earth is to find the most auspicious direction and move forward with clarity and focus, neither in a withdrawn manner, nor with too bold of a manner. Set your own bar and then jump. We will guide your sprint, or your standing jump, and will clear the track for you. It is not a track for racing or running. It is a long distance track with hurdles to jump. Once you are on it, you will have accomplished this lesson and will move purposefully in the direction of your calling: To awaken others to their own dreams and free themselves from restraints.

LOREN

Tell it like it is. Do not hesitate. You have been bestowed a gift of knowledge, insight, and foresight. As grains of sand accumulate to create a vast beach, your words of knowledge lay a soft covering of small lessons which build on each other to create a library. This collection of lessons can be called upon whenever needed. These are times to never withhold; these are times to always share the words so that you can tell it like it is. Souls who hear will prosper from your lessons. Keep telling and building.

LORENZO

Juice it up! You are the resourceful and appreciative one. Rather than simply garnishing with beauty, such as a lime or lemon slice attached to a glass, you squeeze the juice into the glass. Yes! Is not the content improved with the flavor of the juice? Of course, and you realize this fact. Show and savor all of the fruits of life, not just the appearances. Such an example you are, and in this regard you are serving your purpose. Experience the whole. "Oooo" and "ahhh" at the aesthetics, and at the same time, appreciate the nuts and bolts that make the piece of furniture useful and beautiful. Enjoy the orange, and drink the juice which remains. Behold the art, and be attentive to the nuances of the work. Celebrate the music; use it to sing and dance. Notice its rhythm and each of the instruments.

What you illustrate is the opposite of greed. You reflect a zest for total experience versus a pleasant glance, taste, or dance step. You, with your deep gratitude for all aspects of the gifts the universe brings, will influence others to reach a new level of appreciation, thus embracing life to a fuller extent.

LORETTA

A taste of hospitality is what you bring to your world. You embody the essence of refreshing, sweet tea on a sweltering hot day that makes the heat more tolerable. You reflect the elegance of a parasol, twirling whimsically while protecting and welcoming the elements to join the naturally occurring fun. You bring the coziness of cinnamon rolls to welcome the morning. You are the open door, inviting all to partake of wholesome gatherings. Your purpose is to enrich and vitalize family and friends through your warmth, friendliness, and openness. There is a great need in this world for graciousness and pureness of heart. You help to fulfill that need, and your reward is the knowledge that you take the edge off of the oftentimes harsh human existence.

LORI

Tell it like it is. Do not hesitate. You have been bestowed a gift of knowledge, insight, and foresight. As grains of sand accumulate to create a vast beach, your words of knowledge lay a soft covering of small lessons which build on each other to create a library. This collection of lessons can be called upon whenever needed. These are times to never withhold; these are times to always share the words so that you can tell it like it is. Souls who hear will prosper from your lessons. Keep telling and building.

LOUISE

Reap and harvest! You are the essence of work and play to the utmost. Because you seem tireless in all you do, we give you the energy of aquamarine to soothe you, calm you, and bring forth relaxed energy at any time you feel the need. Your zest for many facets of life is unparalleled at times, and this brings elation, laughter, and inspiration wherever you go. Your harvest—what you reap—is reciprocal bliss. You are lifted up in no better way than from this type of happiness given back to you on different levels. We say to you: Take rest on a regular basis and take pauses when tasks or events—no matter how large or small—begin to lessen your excitement or feel like too much of a job. We delight in your delight, and our desire is to maintain your excitement in living to the fullest extent during this lifetime on the Earth plane. You have brought with you energy which ignites many when they otherwise would have fizzled out like a dampened matchbook. Thank you for your fire and for lighting the way through your enormous flame.

LUCAS

Yes, you are able-bodied and able-minded as your name in this society often implies. You are aware, though, that there is so much more than what your name implies as to level of mind and body strength. You know that you *are* your purpose, you *are* your soul's path, and you *are* your spirit incarnate. Even better ... you know that this is everyone's truth. We assist you always in dispelling society's myth associated with the type of strength attached to your name. If your purpose is to be a virulent protector, so be it and you will fulfill it. If your purpose is to be a meek servant, so be it and you will fulfill it. In other words, despite what the world in general expects you to be and pressures you to be, we help you to continue BEING unabashedly YOU. Your purpose is to be a reflection of the necessity of being the truth of who you are – for everyone.

LUCILLE

Reap and harvest! You are the essence of work and play to the utmost. Because you seem tireless in all you do, we give you the energy of aquamarine to soothe you, calm you, and bring forth relaxed energy at any time you feel the need. Your zest for many facets of life is unparalleled at times, and this brings elation, laughter, and inspiration wherever you go. Your harvest—what you reap—is reciprocal bliss. You are lifted up in no better way than from this type of happiness given back to you on different levels. We say to you: Take rest on a regular basis and take pauses when tasks or events—no matter how large or small—begin to lessen your excitement or feel like too much of a job. We delight in your delight, and our desire is to maintain your excitement in living to the fullest extent during this lifetime on the Earth plane. You have brought with you energy which ignites many when they otherwise would have fizzled out like a dampened matchbook. Thank you for your fire and for lighting the way through your enormous flame.

LUCY

You carry with you the energy of the dove ... the white dove of peace. You have the natural capacity to bring peaceful feelings, calmness, and even at times the peace needed to resolve conflict or confrontation. We also give you the energy of moonlight—the soft light upon any harsh environment in which you may enter.

We plead with you to not allow the ways of the unawakened to draw you into a non-peaceful existence. We know this is difficult, and it happens temporarily from time to time - for moments, days, weeks, months, or longer. It would be a tragedy in our eyes should you fall into a lifetime of being drawn into this type of unfruitful energy. Please be mindful of this and avoid being thwarted from your soul's purpose, which is to be a bringer of peaceful energy. Hold the moonlight dove close to your heart, and we will help you do your work with a peaceful, healing luminosity.

LUKE

Yes, you are able-bodied and able-minded as your name in this society often implies. You are aware, though, that there is so much more than what your name implies as to level of mind and body strength. You know that you are your purpose, you are your soul's path, and you are your spirit incarnate. Even better ... you know that this is everyone's truth. We assist you always in dispelling society's myth associated with the type of strength attached to your name. If your purpose is to be a virulent protector, so be it and you will fulfill it. If your purpose is to be a meek servant, so be it and you will fulfill it. In other words, despite what the world in general expects you to be and pressures you to be, we help you to continue BEING unabashedly YOU. Your purpose is to be a reflection of the necessity of being the truth of who you are – for everyone.

LYNN

Curiosity has never killed anyone, has never thwarted or resulted in the imagination's demise, and has never stopped inventive endeavors in its tracks. Your curiosity, our creative one, has served as a catalyst for your purpose of introducing new spins and twists on old paradigms. Your curiosity has also resulted in new projects and learning experiences ... projects and experiences which would have occurred, anyway ... however, in a less interesting and exciting manner. Your lesson, and the lesson you teach through others' observation of your life, is: As long as curiosity is nourished, there is no need to be studious. There are some areas of life that simply shine brighter in the absence of academics, and you have a knack at finding those subjects. Our dear, never lose your illusion, for it is where, in the magical impressions, you find your light and shine forth.

LYNETTE

Curiosity has never killed anyone, has never thwarted or resulted in the imagination's demise, and has never stopped inventive endeavors in its tracks. Your curiosity, our creative one, has served as a catalyst for your purpose of introducing new spins and twists on old paradigms. Your curiosity has also resulted in new projects and learning experiences ... projects and experiences which would have occurred, anyway ... however, in a less interesting and exciting manner. Your lesson, and the lesson you teach through others' observation of your life, is: As long as curiosity is nourished, there is no need to be studious. There are some areas of life that simply shine brighter in the absence of academics, and you have a knack at finding those subjects. Our dear, never lose your illusion, for it is where, in the magical impressions, you find your light and shine forth.

MADISON

Sorghum molasses. You may feel that your journey has been sticky, slow, and frustrating. You may feel you have the residual stickiness and messiness of past difficult or preposterous experiences on your life path, making it difficult to step forward freely, without obstruction. We have news for you: Without the mess there would be no sweetness. We say to you that no matter how messy, the sweetness is what holds together your path. The sugar experiences do make things sticky and serve as a reminder that, although the path at times seems like scalding concrete or filled with icy shards, it is seasoned with the sweetness which makes you go, "Yum." You must remember the yums. They overpower the sour taste that life sometimes hands you. You must remember that the sweetness of life pours slowly throughout your time here ... so slowly that you may not even notice it. Do remember that messiness is merely a reminder of the sweetness that accompanies it and embellishes your life. We will send you delectable reminders of real molasses and honey along your way. Even better, we always surround you with the innocent energy of the sweetest cherubs of the universe, fluttering and smiling upon you.

MADONNA

Dear one, do not let the soulful sound of your name fool you. Others are at times surprised, as they have expectations of softness from you. This is not true. You are assertive in every way, and will deflect unpleasant energy in all forms, especially every-day hurtful actions and words. You are actually a hero, which is your chosen path. Steadfast, you are one whom others look to for sound answers and frank responses. You are guided and surrounded by many angels for the strength to be a citadel in your home, work, and play. What a gallant role you have chosen. We give you the energy of Garnet for grounding and loyalty to your calling. We respect you so much.

MAGGIE

Rain falling beautifully like a fountain overflowing, or a quiet waterfall hugging a rock embankment. Calming. Soul cleansing. Refreshing. This is what you bring to those who are willing to appreciate you and your gifts. There are those who will resist. Pay no mind; they are on their individual, chosen path. Allow your healing energy to flow naturally. You do not have to think on this or try to implement your gifts. We direct your steps and provide you the same comfort that your presence gives to others. We call you our Natural Balm.

MALLORY

Stars are meant to shine. Your lesson is to always remember that you do shine, and that no person or circumstance will darken your brightness. It may seem at times that your light is about to forever fade. Know that this is only temporary. Liken these times as turning off or dimming lights in order to sleep, to be restored, and to be refreshed through rest. After rest, the lights go back on. So, our dear star, you will come to the understanding that you indeed shine and have the magnitude you need at any given moment. Know that during any time when you feel dimness, we are surrounding you with our light to protect and encourage you. We repeat: Never forget that you shine.

MANDY

To be or not to be? Mandy, you find yourself often having difficulty with decision making. You try and try to change this about yourself. We say to you: It is your nature to weigh everything ... to assess the pros and cons, to achieve a perfect answer. It often times appears to you as indecisiveness;

however, always remember your purpose of bringing about balance in your life and your work, and therefore serving as a role model. You are appreciated by many for this gift because you show them the benefits of looking at both sides of whatever coin they are thinking of tossing, or at the cards they may be choosing along their path.

MARCELLA

Lay it on the line, our candid one. Your gifts are the ability to speak your truth without harshness, and to analyze situations, events, and individuals with concise precision. Because you are known for your consistent frankness and accurate perceptions, you are honored by most as a voice of reason. We say to you: Take care to avoid getting lost in a world that is so full of opportunities to step in and summarize. Pay attention also to your own life path on a daily basis to ensure you are living your own truth. This is your lesson: To share your gifts and shower yourself with the love of truth.

MARCIA / MARSHA

Strange things are happening! Not really! It just may seem strange to you at times when what seems to be ESP or extreme serendipity ... or when things way beyond coincidence, happen. Marcia/Marsha, you simply have an extra keen intuition. Do not discount it or fear it. Do not think it makes you too unusual. Instead, accept the gifts it offers you, including the refreshing smiles it brings. You will find that this will not only be enlightening—it will help serve others should you choose to share this gift for the higher good. The choice is yours. Regardless of your choice, you are an Ambassador of Insight and Intuition. Butterflies we send you when in doubt. Carry our butterfly reminders wherever you go.

MARCY

Lay it on the line, our candid one. Your gifts are the ability to speak your truth without harshness, and to analyze situations, events, and individuals with concise precision. Because you are known for your consistent frankness and accurate perceptions, you are honored by most as a voice of reason. We say to you: Take care to avoid getting lost in a world that is so full of opportunities to step in and summarize. Pay attention also to your own life path on a daily basis to ensure you are living your own truth. This is your lesson: To share your gifts and shower yourself with the love of truth.

MARGARET

Rain falling beautifully like a fountain overflowing, or a quiet waterfall hugging a rock embankment. Calming. Soul cleansing. Refreshing. This is what you bring to those who are willing to appreciate you and your gifts. There are those who will resist. Pay no mind; they are on their individual, chosen path. Allow your healing energy to flow naturally. You do not have to think on this or try to implement your gifts. We direct your steps and provide you the same comfort that your presence gives to others. We call you our Natural Balm.

MARGE / MARGIE

Crystalline caves surround you when you feel your energy waning. You receive their strength, wisdom, and ancient truths. However, we say to you: Be aware when we send you these timeless healers, and be quiet with them. Honor this honor. Allow the cleansing, balancing, knowledge and healing to be immersed within, and experience transformation after transformation. Yes, the particular journey you have chosen is indeed a superb one, as you will learn more than ever to prepare for your next big adventure (a most important one).

MARIA

The albatross you feel you carry is for a noble reason, yet you need not feel this weight. Align yourself with angelic lightness, and this burden you have taken on will feel feathery. Release the serious nature you may have attached to your purpose of lifting the lost from their self-created despair. Acknowledge the valuable direction and tenderness you willingly give. Treat your purpose as a welcomed spiritual gift and enjoy the manifestations of healing the darkened hearts that need your light. Once you do this, we will be much more able to help you soar with no feelings of heavy, Earth angel wings. Being willing is the secret that you need to make this happen.

MARIAN / MARION

Lavender fields are what you represent ... the soft, subtle, graceful beauty that brings about relaxation and appreciation of the All That Is ... the lullaby for the heart when the heart needs soothing ... the contrast needed against the sometimes harsh existence on this plane. Your natural balm to troubled souls is not always present. We provide this for you to grace those in need at the appointed times, just as we provide this harmonious state of being to you when needed. We want you to know that you are here for the sole purpose of being the embrace that elicits a sigh of relief from angst. Your calming elixir is priceless, yet a complimentary gift from the angels through you. Thank you for coming into existence to assist us in providing this valuable level of healing.

MARIE

You wear it well. Whether it be a formal gown or casual jeans, you exude elegance. Whether it be a smile or a sad face, you radiate love. There is nothing paradoxical about you. It may be said about you that what you see is what you get. What the world gets from you is authenticity regardless of where you are, who you are with, or what you are doing. You are true to your ideals, your goals, your beliefs, and your relationships. Your lesson for this lifetime is to simply accept those who have not reached the spiritual truths with which you arrived. Your purpose, no matter how unintentional on your part, is to be a shining example of living your own truth. We honor you, especially for your genuine smiles.

MARILYN

Give me your weak, give me your poor, give me your hungry. This is the kind of saint-like soul you are. You do great and wonderful works, yet you have no quest for recognition. We chose "Marilyn" to represent unselfishness. Be cautious, however, not to be selfless in your work, as this can easily happen. You need to maintain your well-being. Acknowledge yourself for the benevolent spirit you are, and accept acknowledgment when offered. This will in no way impede your unselfish work. We bring you the strength of ten thousand elephants – creatures who support, remember, and maintain friendships. This energy assists you to carry on and to help you bring forth the best of your compassion.

MARIS

You are the colorful hot air balloon that helps people realize they can rise to new heights, and have an adventure in doing so. You provide the moral support and the feeling of safety as they lift off, trusting the process while they learn the ropes, so to speak. Who says it's a self-defeating mindset to have one's head in the clouds? Not according to you. Liftoff is not only possible, but exhilarating and productive. You are the epitome of rising above and breaking through the paradigm of limited goals. Fortunate are those who have the presence of mind and the fortitude to follow your lead.

MARISSA

An umbrella of protection from sadness is what you bring to share. When there are sad feelings, where there may be a depression setting in, your positive umbrella of smiles and praise will not only protect from low frequencies—it will bring a shower of bright frequencies. You most often open your umbrella without conscious awareness, but you will become aware of your role of alleviating mental anguish with your bright bursts of encouragement. You know exactly how and where to position yourself to shield with your special umbrella.

MARJORIE / MARJE

All hands on deck! We call you The Captain because of your ability to assemble a diverse group to work toward a common goal. You are respected, yet not feared. You provide momentum severally and wholly. We ask you to step out and step into areas where group cooperation is desired. You are gifted in directing projects, whether it be Spring cleaning, a street fair, or a corporate undertaking. Organizers and motivators like you, who bring progress without conflict, are much needed. This is your purpose. You are appreciated, and we are grateful that you chose this role. We support you with a spiral of chakra colors to keep you grounded, creative, confident, open to unconditional and mutual acceptance, clearly spoken, intuitive, and connected to the divine.

MARLENA

Old school is not your thing, although some may mistake you for such. Your purpose is to raise the frequency of old school thoughts, protocol, philosophy, and procedures when it appears obvious to you that there will be benefit to all. We are not saying you will perpetually be reinventing the wheel. Actually, you won't be reinventing many, if any, wheels at all. What you will be doing is opening minds to question old school ways, and accelerating progress. When you are mistaken for old school, the perception will soon fall away once your advanced method of doing things are naturally revealed. We give you bright light energy as though fueled by Quartz Crystal to enhance and amplify your work here.

MARLENE

Old school is not your thing, although some may mistake you for such. Your purpose is to raise the frequency of old school thoughts, protocol, philosophy, and procedures when it appears obvious to you that there will be benefit to all. We are not saying you will perpetually be reinventing the wheel. Actually, you won't be reinventing many, if any, wheels at all. What you will be doing is opening minds to question old school ways, and accelerating progress. When you are mistaken for old school, the perception will soon fall away once your advanced method of doing things are naturally revealed. We give you bright light energy as though fueled by Quartz Crystal to enhance and amplify your work here.

MARK

A treasure you are. We say this because there is no better friend than you. Although you bring a variety of talents to this world, the gift most valuable is that of abiding friendship for some, and temporary, yet memorable friendship to others. Those who have the honor of having you in their lives—whether for a short while or a lifetime—will not forget the manner in which you demonstrate and personify the word *friend*. We genuinely care for you in the same way you care for your fellow souls, and beyond. We pour star streaks of the pure energy of Rose Quartz upon you.

MARTHA

Come to us Martha, when you weep. Come to us when your soul is hungry for love. We will remind you of your innocence and your vast ability to love. We will infuse you with twice the love that you give. We will give you smiles that will grace your being. We will give you the faith you seek, for this is the lesson you came here to learn. Your faith, then, will propel your purpose of being a mentor for knowing and believing. Doubt not; we are with you at all times, and your bliss will ring out for eternity.

MARTIN

You are so personable and kind that some may want to name their pets or children after you. Oh, did we also mention that you are a loyal friend? Your treasure lies in the self-fulfillment of your role, which is to bring smiles and comfort as often as possible. Merry you are, and just as attentive. You can be as a court jester one moment and a caring giver the next. This role can be tiring, as you may feel the expectations of others to always be performing in order to uphold and uplift. We ask that you retreat for respite often. This will be necessary for you. Your lesson for this life is directly related to your role: To know when to provide the self-care of respite.

We send you our songs of merriment and our melodies of peacefulness with divine timing. Lean on us to always know how to balance your energy.

MARTY

You are so personable and kind that some may want to name their pets or children after you. Oh, did we also mention that you are a loyal friend? Your treasure lies in the self-fulfillment of your role, which is to bring smiles and comfort as often as possible. Merry you are, and just as attentive. You can be as a court jester one moment and a caring giver the next. This role can be tiring, as you may feel the expectations of others to always be performing in order to uphold and uplift. We ask that you retreat for respite often. This will be necessary for you. Your lesson for this life is directly related to your role: To know when to provide the self-care of respite. We send you our songs of merriment and our melodies of peacefulness with divine timing. Lean on us to always know how to balance your energy.

MARY

A soulful name you have, Mary, and soulfulness you bring when you choose. Do not feel pressure to exhibit soulfulness always, as this would surely snuff out your pure effect. Instead, relax with this life. Know you are guided in your purpose to be the presence of calmness, caring, and nurturing in each divine moment of timing that embraces another with healing energy. You do carry soulfulness with you always. We provide it. You will feel our warmth of love, guidance, and protection when most needed.

MARYANNE

Lavender fields are what you represent ... the soft, subtle, graceful beauty that brings about relaxation and appreciation of the All That Is...the lullaby for the heart when the heart needs soothing ... the contrast needed against the sometimes harsh existence on this plane. Your natural balm to troubled souls is not always present. We provide this for you to grace those in need at the appointed times, just as we provide this harmonious state of being to you when needed. We want you to know that you are here for the sole purpose of being the embrace which elicits a sigh of relief from angst. Your calming elixir is priceless, yet a complimentary gift from the angels through you. Thank you for coming into existence to assist us in providing this valuable level of healing.

MATT

You have a knack at looking back ... looking back to see what worked, what didn't, and what may have worked. In other words, Matt, you have analytical skills that will greatly assist in all you do. Used properly, you will serve your purpose of teaching about the delicate balance between analysis and rumination. You deduce at the ultimate level of competency toward arriving at the best conclusions. Urge others to not look back too often or too much about too many things. Your own lesson is to look back but not cling to the past. You have, in other lifetimes, lived in the past. This time you will be able to move forward after assessing the past.

MATTHEW

You have a knack at looking back ... looking back to see what worked, what didn't, and what may have worked. In other words, Matthew, you have analytical skills that will greatly assist in all you do. Used properly, you will serve your purpose of teaching about the delicate balance between analysis and rumination. You deduce at the ultimate level of competency toward arriving at the best conclusions. Urge others to not look back too often or too much about too many things. Your own lesson is to look back but not cling to the past. You have, in other lifetimes, lived in the past. This time you will be able to move forward after assessing the past.

MAUREEN

Old school is not your thing, although some may mistake you for such. Your purpose is to raise the frequency of old school thoughts, protocol, philosophy, and procedures when it appears obvious to you that there will be benefit to all. We are not saying you will perpetually be reinventing the wheel. Actually, you won't be reinventing many, if any, wheels at all. What you will be doing is opening minds to question old school ways, and accelerating progress. When you are mistaken for old school, the perception will soon fall away once your advanced method of doing things are naturally revealed. We give you bright light energy as though fueled by Quartz Crystal to enhance and amplify your work here.

MEGAN / MEGHAN

Stoke the fires of your passions often. We advise you of this because we know you are prone to becoming discouraged or jaded after having tended to your flames of interests for an extended period of time. Rest, yes, rest ... but we say to you: Sit back, stoke the fire, watch the fire rise again, and become the flames. You have amazing potential to excel in whatever you choose. Your lesson is to choose what will best serve your personal and spiritual growth and then focus on those things. Your purpose is to reflect the truth that success with more than one interest is possible, and through those successes, the true calling will be revealed. Once the true calling is revealed, there will be no need to stoke the fires of passion to bring them higher or stronger, as they will never wane.

MELANIE

Shhh. Listen. You have so much to say, and others do listen to you. You counsel well, with valuable insight and information to many in need, who may otherwise have gone without assistance. Although your destiny is being fulfilled in this manner, we need to remind you to listen. You can be your own counsel often ... if you take your wisdom within. We, of course, are always here to guide you if you ask.

Truths can fall silently. Within that silence is the depth of your lessons. Go within, with the shadows of the silence that follow you. It is there where your inner wisdom will mingle with the silence—and the answers you seek will be clear as they make their way to the light between the shadows. This light represents you and your helpfulness to others who turn to you. We thank you for being this welcomed light, and you will remain so as long as you take the time to listen.

MELISSA

Lavender fields are what you represent ... the soft, subtle, graceful beauty that brings about relaxation and appreciation of the All This Is ... the lullaby for the heart when the heart needs soothing. The contrast needed against the sometimes harsh existence on this plane. Your natural balm to troubled souls is not always present. We provide this for you to grace those in need at the appointed times, just as we provide this harmonious state of being to you when needed. We want you to know that you are here for the sole purpose of being the embrace which elicits a sigh of relief from angst. Your calming elixir is priceless; it is a complimentary gift from the angels through you. Thank you for coming into existence to assist us in providing this valuable level of healing.

MELINDA

Lavender fields are what you represent ... the soft, subtle, graceful beauty that brings about relaxation and appreciation of the All This Is ... the lullaby for the heart when the heart needs soothing. The contrast needed against the sometimes harsh existence on this plane. Your natural balm to troubled souls is not always present. We provide this for you to grace those in need at the appointed times, just as we provide this harmonious state of being to you when needed. We want you to know that you are here for the sole purpose of being the embrace which elicits a sigh of relief from angst. Your calming elixir is priceless; it is a complimentary gift from the angels through you. Thank you for coming into existence to assist us in providing this valuable level of healing.

MELODY

For you, the top of the mountain isn't that exhilarating. We smile when we see you become mesmerized by all the beauty along the way to the top. The wildflowers, the wildlife in nature, the views of the sky above … all are rewards for you along the way. These rewards would not be realized, and would go unappreciated without your observation, and if you were not tuned in to the all-encompassing beauty of the mountain. For this reason, you will derive more gratitude and awe for this mortal lifetime than most. Your purpose is to always remind others that the view on the way to the goal is a valuable part of the reward. Without it, the goal is not entirely whole. Thank you for being this reminder for others.

MEREDITH

How saucy you can be! Life on this Earth needs spice, and you have the ability to bring it. When you feel the need to temper your blend of spicy, caring nature, call on us and you will be given the means to remain true to your soul self while conducting your Earthly business. It is your sauciness, however, that enhances your world and those in it—even if it is while standing in a checkout lane. The angels thank you for bringing zest to the mundane when most needed.

MICHAEL / MIKE

Although we are unable to give a message for all those with the name of Michael, we want to include this name. There are so many! We do want to say that it is one of the most spiritual names on your Earth realm. It carries a high frequency, and those with this name are highly capable of fulfilling their purposes. This is only true, however, for those who choose, upon arriving here on this plane, to use their spiritual gifts to the best of their ability. We want to note that there is a smaller group of Michaels who chose a higher purpose before arriving here. This particular group has been given the highest frequencies possible to function in their role.

There are some—especially including those who are called Mike—who choose to repress this high spiritual vibration. This is okay—it is their choice to learn the results of repression, and the lessons needed will be internalized.

Many, if not all Michaels, can appear to have lofty goals. They may be said to have their heads in the clouds. Not to worry, Michael—it is true because you function at such a high frequency that you cannot help but be in touch with the elevated frequencies of spiritual stewardship. Neither the Michaels nor the Mikes ever need to be dismayed. Instead, hold to this knowledge that you are here either to experience elevated spirit and all the ways in which it can be manifested for the betterment of yourself and ALL ... or to learn the lesson that to repress your gifts will deter your evolvement. If you are the latter, it is a valuable lesson you need, and chose, in order to become what you wish in the future.

MICHELLE

Slow burn. Don't let this misconception alter your path. You are not a victim of a slow burn. You are not a victim at all. Your graciousness may, at times, result in unappreciative opportunists gravitating toward you. However, this is in no way a detriment to your pure and light-filled soul. Continue always on your path of service. You have the ability to discern how to veer away from the misled, and therefore you will not *be* misled. Teaching others the importance of discernment, and how to listen to their heart, is your purpose. We exalt you for your pure heart and your authentic desire to share your time and your gifts to benefit where they may.

MICK

Your life and your work is like a game of jacks, our deft one. Your dexterity is superior; you can have a ball in the air, yet maintain your focus on the ground. In other words, you can pitch your dreams to the stars while attending to one or more multi-faceted parts of your dreams until you are able to realize all the parts at once. When and if you wish, you can move on to the next "game of jacks" to achieve yet another dream. We give you the skill to pitch up and pick up simultaneously. We say to you: Keep your humility, else you will overestimate yourself and could become greedy, which will tarnish your lesson. Your lesson is to know when to stop.

Your purpose is to assist others with the dexterity needed for their lives' jack games.

MICKEY

Your life and your work is like a game of jacks, our deft one. Your dexterity is superior; you can have a ball in the air, yet maintain your focus on the ground. In other words, you can pitch your dreams to the stars while attending to one or more multi-faceted parts of your dreams until you are able to realize all the parts at once. When and if you wish, you can move on to the next "game of jacks" to achieve yet another dream. We give you the skill to pitch up and pick up simultaneously. We say to you: Keep your humility, else you will overestimate yourself and could become greedy, which will tarnish your lesson. Your lesson is to know when to stop. Your purpose is to assist others with the dexterity needed for their lifes' jack games.

MILDRED

Spin no more, our lady. You often feel that you are spinning in circles, getting nowhere fast. Spin no more. Instead, recognize that each step you take is indeed taking you somewhere. It is taking you to self-realization. Stay off your self-built merry-go-round, as you have much to contribute and create. Yes, many pauses for rest will be needed, but your lesson here is to learn the value of goals and moving toward them. We will keep you refreshed. The golden ring is in each cycle of success. Your purpose is to demonstrate how to stop spinning, and to recognize the cycles of success.

MILLIE

Spin no more, our lady. You often feel that you are spinning in circles, getting nowhere fast. Spin no more. Instead, recognize that each step you take is indeed taking you somewhere. It is taking you to self-realization. Stay off your self-built merry-go-round, as you have much to contribute and create. Yes, many pauses for rest will be needed, but your lesson here is to learn the value of goals and moving toward them. We will keep you refreshed. The golden ring is in each cycle of success. Your purpose is to demonstrate how to stop spinning, and to recognize the cycles of success.

MINDY

Shadows falling softly from the sweet light create floating patterns. This is what we want you to remember: Even when the shadows of life seem to be a hindrance, there can be elegant beauty in this subsided light. Without the light there cannot possibly be shadows, and shadows are interesting, containing beauty and design. Remember always that there are some circumstances and some individuals or groups of individuals that need the reflection from the light to create the beauty in the shadow. Be that light. Create the beauty and gracefulness from what may appear to be darkness, yet in essence, is simply a result of experiencing the light from a different aspect. Be the sweet light, casting the consciousness of finding serenity where some perceive as dusk leading to a dark night. There is elegance in dusk. There is peaceful rest within the shadows of dusk—a calm pause for regeneration to greet the dawn. Bring that elegance with your sweet light so that those around you may relax into a consciousness of appreciation for both dusk and dawn ... for rest, contemplation, and renewed energy to continue moving forward. Be the balancing, sweet light.

MIRANDA

Stoke the fires of your passions often. We advise you of this because we know you are prone to becoming discouraged or jaded after having tended to your flames of interests for an extended period of time. Rest, yes, rest ... but we say to you: Sit back, stoke the fire, watch the fire rise again, and become the flames. You have amazing potential to excel in whatever you choose. Your lesson is to choose what will best serve your personal and spiritual growth and then focus on those things. Your purpose is to reflect the truth that success with more than one interest is possible, and through those successes, the true calling will be revealed. Once the true calling is revealed, there will be no need to stoke the fires of passion to bring them higher or stronger, as they will never wane.

MIRIAM

A soulful name you have, Miriam, and soulfulness you bring when you choose. Do not feel pressure to exhibit soulfulness always, as this would surely snuff out your pure effect. Instead, relax with this life. Know you are guided in your purpose to be the presence of calmness, caring, and nurturing in each divine moment of timing that embraces another with healing energy. You do carry soulfulness with you always. We provide it. You will feel our warmth of love, guidance, and protection when most needed.

MISTY

Shadows falling softly from the sweet light create floating patterns. This is what we want you to remember: Even when the shadows of life seem to be a hindrance, there can be elegant beauty in this subsided light. Without the light there cannot possibly be shadows, and shadows are interesting, containing beauty and design. Remember always that there are some circumstances and some individuals or groups of individuals that need the reflection from the light to create the beauty in the shadow. Be that light. Create the beauty and gracefulness from what may appear to be darkness, yet in essence, is simply a result of experiencing the light from a different aspect. Be the sweet light, casting the consciousness of finding serenity where some perceive as dusk leading to a dark night. There is elegance in dusk. There is peaceful rest within the shadows of dusk—a calm pause for regeneration to greet the dawn. Bring that elegance with your sweet light so that those around you may relax into a consciousness of appreciation for both dusk and dawn ... for rest, contemplation, and renewed energy to continue moving forward. Be the balancing, sweet light.

MITCH

Spartan you are, lad. We say this because you possess the masculine qualities of a warrior and the childlike wonder of a boy. Seek not solace in the arena of the highest position of work. Seek not the power in the hierarchy of society. Stay attuned to your youthful strength and use the maturity of your mind to rise above the ordinary without the need for recognition. You are able to withstand the darts of Earthly society and stand strong as you protect your integrity and your truth ... unwavering, yet with a smile. Your purpose is to advocate for those who have not learned how to escape the arrows pointed their way by this society's unlearned warriors.

MITCHELL

Spartan you are, lad. We say this because you possess the masculine qualities of a warrior and the childlike wonder of a boy. Seek not solace in the arena of the highest position of work. Seek not the power in the hierarchy of society. Stay attuned to your youthful strength and use the maturity of your mind to rise above the ordinary without the need for recognition. You are able to withstand the darts of Earthly society and stand strong as you protect your integrity and your truth ... unwavering, yet with a smile. Your purpose is to advocate for those who have not learned how to escape the arrows pointed their way by this society's unlearned warriors.

MITZI

Shadows falling softly from the sweet light create floating patterns. This is what we want you to remember: Even when the shadows of life seem to be a hindrance, there can be elegant beauty in this subsided light. Without the light there cannot possibly be shadows, and shadows are interesting, containing beauty and design. Remember always that there are some circumstances and some individuals or groups of individuals that need the reflection from the light to create the beauty in the shadow. Be that light. Create the beauty and gracefulness from what may appear to be darkness, yet in essence, is simply a result of experiencing the light from a different aspect. Be the sweet light, casting the consciousness of finding serenity where some perceive as dusk leading to a dark night. There is elegance in dusk. There is peaceful rest within the shadows of dusk—a calm pause for regeneration to greet the dawn. Bring that elegance with your sweet light so that those around you may relax into a consciousness of appreciation for both dusk and dawn ... for rest, contemplation, and renewed energy to continue moving forward. Be the balancing, sweet light.

MOLLY / MOLLIE

Stand tall, yet not with arrogance. Walk strong, yet with humility. You inherently know the difference between pride and humility, and you have an uncanny ability to hover right in between. Because of this harmony of emotion and how you yourself emote, you are able to connect with every Earthly personality. This is not only a wonderful asset for your journey—it helps relax people and situations to the point where the best outcome is reached more easily. You are the scales that balance interactions at every level. Congratulations. This is seen in but a few.

MONICA

Sorghum molasses. You may feel that your journey has been sticky, slow, and frustrating. You may feel you have the residual stickiness and messiness of past difficult or preposterous experiences on your life path, making it difficult to step forward freely, without obstruction. We have news for you: Without the mess there would be no sweetness. We say to you that no matter how messy, the sweetness is what holds together your path. The sugar experiences do make things sticky and serve as a reminder that, although the path at times seems like scalding concrete or filled with icy shards, it is seasoned with the sweetness which makes you go, "Yum." You must remember the yums. They overpower the sour taste that life sometimes hands you. You must remember that the sweetness of life pours slowly throughout your time here ... so slowly that you may not even notice it. Do remember that messiness is merely a reminder of the sweetness that accompanies it and embellishes your life. We will send you delectable reminders of real molasses and honey along your way. Even better, we always surround you with the innocent energy of the sweetest cherubs of the universe, fluttering and smiling upon you.

MORGAN

Come hither, our cooperative diplomat. We will be frequently asking you this so that you will continue to glean from our subtle direction the means and ways for your interactions. You are noted by us as the Liberator of Dissension, and this is because of your gift of diplomacy. This gift, and your genuine desire to be a peacemaker, makes you among the cherished ones. Continue with your gentle arbitrating, and your world ... this world ... will be positively influenced. We are deeply grateful for you and your work here.

MORRIS

Strike up the band. Orchestrate. Entertain and lead. You are the conductor of life symphonies. You will always have this role of leading the band, so to speak, because you understand how many different parts create the whole. Someone must keep the instruments in harmony so as to manifest symphonies when there could have been chaos. You do all this without being appointed as a superior or without being charged with the "authority over others," as the world puts it. The Humble Conductor is what we call you. Your purpose is to create and maintain congruence between everyone within all your life's groups.

𝒩

NADEEN / NADINE

Tell it like it is. Do not hesitate. You have been bestowed a gift of knowledge, insight, and foresight. As grains of sand accumulate to create a vast beach, your words of knowledge lay a soft covering of small lessons, which build on each other to create a library. This collection of lessons can be called upon whenever needed. These are times to never withhold; these are times to always share the words so that you can "tell it like it is." Souls who hear will prosper from your lessons. Keep telling and building.

NADIA

Tell it like it is. Do not hesitate. You have been bestowed a gift of knowledge, insight, and foresight. As grains of sand accumulate to create a vast beach, your words of knowledge lay a soft covering of small lessons, which build on each other to create a library. This collection of lessons can be called upon whenever needed. These are times to never withhold; these are times to always share the words so that you can "tell it like it is." Souls who hear will prosper from your lessons. Keep telling and building.

NAN / NANETTE

How saucy you can be! Life on this Earth needs spice, and you have the ability to bring it. When you feel the need to temper your blend of spicy, caring nature, call on us and you will be given the means to remain true to your soul self while conducting your Earthly business. It is your sauciness, however, that enhances your world and those in it—even if it is while standing in a checkout lane. The angels thank you for bringing zest to the mundane when most needed.

NANCY

Oh, to be Nancy and require nudges from your guides and angels to get in step with your plan. Your energy flows in more than one direction at any given moment. This is your lesson: It is good to study in many areas; however, you must learn to focus on what best serves you and those around you during certain phases of this lifetime. Do not concern yourself with the frustration of how you may perceive a lack of focus on any one thing may affect others. This is actually endearing and interesting. You will learn how to bring your interests into one center, and all will be well. Your purpose is to open closed minds.

NAOMI

You may be told that you have your head in the clouds, and that you have goals that are too lofty. We say to you: There is nothing wrong with reaching for the stars. Our moonstruck one, we behold you for keeping your aspirations alive, even in what may seem to be the darkest of days. Your lesson here is to learn that your thoughts about yourself are more powerful than your perceptions of what others think about you. Also, dedicated focus on a dream creates progress and desirable results. We give you the grounding energy you will need to stay balanced with your high ... and commendable ... vision. Your purpose is to encourage others to hold on to their dreams.

NATALIE

Tender is the heart of those with your name, and when you love, the love is pure. Your lesson is to learn to whom you grace your tenderness and love. Look and watch for those who cherish and care for the flowers of life that have been granted to them. The flower within your heart can wilt quickly from neglect; protect this sacred space by allowing only kindred hearts as *permanent* parts of this life. Those who have not reached this level of loving tenderness are welcome to be in your life on a different level. They will take away a lesson in genuine caring, yet they will not weaken your blossoms. Therefore, all of your relationships in human form will be for the betterment because of your pristine intentions.

NATASHA

Wind chimes and windmills, bringing forth music from seemingly nowhere, and energy from the same source. You are seen to be mysterious in the ways which you bring both melody and power. You do so in everyday, personal interactions as well as your profession. It is because you arrived here with this gift to share. At times we know you will feel lacking in the source of your melodic yet powerful mannerisms. We recognize this and allow you time to rest from your ultimate purpose of bringing your gift to the Earth plane. Never dwell on your ability to continue with your "personality," as it is called here.

You have an endless supply of the mysterious, unknown force behind the gentle, wind chime-like song and the strong, windmill-like energy. We honor you for choosing this dichotomous ability. You are viewed by many as paradoxical. We will always soothe you when needed. Lullabies from us are always only a prayer away for you.

NATE

"Come to your senses!" You may hear that a lot along the way. Your ideas are generally viewed as a little absurd by others, however, we say to you: Your thoughts are often directed by troops of angels who give you ideas about others and their ability to understand. Be strong in spirit and follow through, knowing you are directed to do grand things ... things that become grand when the thoughts are brought to fruition. Never fight your ideas. Use them for your benefit and the benefit of others. It may take time. However, know you are always directed. Both your gift and your lesson are Endurance. Thank you for enduring. You are always on the right path.

NATHAN

"Come to your senses!" You may hear that a lot along the way. Your ideas are generally viewed as a little absurd by others, however, we say to you: Your thoughts are often directed by troops of angels who give you ideas about others and their ability to understand. Be strong in spirit and follow through, knowing you are directed to do grand things ... things that become grand when the thoughts are brought to fruition. Never fight your ideas. Use them for your benefit and the benefit of others. It may take time. However, know you are always directed. Both your gift and your lesson are Endurance. Thank you for enduring. You are always on the right path.

NATHANIEL

"Come to your senses!" You may hear that a lot along the way. Your ideas are generally viewed as a little absurd by others, however, we say to you: Your thoughts are often directed by troops of angels who give you ideas about others and their ability to understand. Be strong in spirit and follow through, knowing you are directed to do grand things ... things that become grand when the thoughts are brought to fruition. Never fight your ideas. Use them for your benefit and the benefit of others. It may take time. However, know you are always directed. Both your gift and your lesson are Endurance. Thank you for enduring. You are always on the right path.

NEAL / NEIL

Falling like thunder is how we see you ... the kind of soft thunder which is so welcomed by those who desire the tranquility experienced by nature sounds. Your calming yet distant presence is just what is needed by your friends and loved ones. Your quiet thunder and your comforting, safe presence helps stress surrender to serenity. This soft thunder also is a reminder that a cleansing rain may be nigh. How refreshing and nurturing you are to those who will savor your gentleness and the hope for a cleansing of stress.

NEENAH / NINA

"How dare you?!" Yes, you may hear this often throughout your time here. Why? You may be well aware by now that you rock the boat with your risk taking, with your direct approach, and with your free-spirited mannerisms. Your approach is filled with zest and fervor, something which is not always welcomed in conditions of social, professional, political, and yes—even day-to-day restraints. You do not always understand these restraints, and we say to you: Cherish your boldness. It may not be endearing to some, but do not let these different energies thwart you. Your boldness is necessary for you to carry out your purpose of discovering the freedom you so desire – to be your authentic self.

NEL / NELLIE

You have been instructed by this world that throwing caution to the wind is not prudent and can have disastrous results. The instruction has not resulted in what the world has been hoping you would learn. Instead, you are a free spirit, led by divine inspiration. Yes, there are many times when you have not chosen the right course of actions or made the right decisions. However, your lesson is to continue with what is incorrectly said to be your impulsiveness, because you learn from trial and error. Most do not have enough courage to live this life with a great amount of trial and error. Those who do are able to abandon their fear of moving forward and embracing uncertainties while never being so brave or impetuous as to make moves which could cause dangerous or harmful results. Impulsiveness with rationale is a rare combination, and you are gifted with such an ability. Despite your impulse on any unsafe direction, we are your constant compass, light and guidepost.

NELSON

You have been instructed by this world that throwing caution to the wind is not prudent and can have disastrous results. The instruction has not resulted in what the world has been hoping you would learn. Instead, you are a free spirit, led by divine inspiration. Yes, there are many times when you have not chosen the right course of actions or made the right decisions. However, your lesson is to continue with what is incorrectly said to be your impulsiveness, because you learn from trial and error. Most do not have enough courage to live this life with a great amount of trial and error. Those who do are able to abandon their fear of moving forward and embracing uncertainties while never being so brave or impetuous as to make moves which could cause dangerous or harmful results. Impulsiveness with rationale is a rare combination, and you are gifted with such an ability. Despite your impulse on any unsafe direction, we are your constant compass, light and guidepost.

NICK

Slowly, we say to you ... slowly. You have a tendency to move a little too quickly through things that need more time in order to best perform the task at hand, and to more thoroughly derive joy from your work. Your lesson here is to learn to savor every action you take as though it is of importance to your soul's development of peace within yourself. This particular life lesson is learned through appreciation of your moments.

We also want you to know that "rattling the cage" gets you nowhere, plus it can agitate the very people who would love you most. Your other lesson is to find the ability to tame your restlessness, which leads to your purpose. Once achieved, you will be of great help to those who also need to be in touch with a milder approach. Call on us when you need respite from your head-on tendencies. We will bring you tolerance and comfort.

NILES

Behold the newness in all things...in the present, the past, and later. Like a work of art, knowledge is perceived from the learners' perceptions, which is either assimilated or ignored. You will know what applies to you and what to ignore. You are divinely guided to the precise knowledge you need that will add to your already deeply-rooted wisdom. Yes, you have learned in many lifetimes and we bid you success, as now you have acquired enough to propel others into the endless sea of wise currents and waves. It is your time to enjoy ... to observe the newness arise in those who derive benefits from your natural way of directing them to the knowledge they most need.

NICOLE

Your lesson is to learn how to sift situations, acting as a sieve to eliminate as many imperfections as possible in this Earthly world. You also will learn to act as a spatula, recovering and implementing as much as possible of the positive yield. Your ability to do so will not only prevent sour, rocky experiences; it will ensure the best quality of life for you. Know that we are with you, coaching you in ways you may not realize. Know that you will realize the gifts of this lesson and will be able to sort through any circumstance to find the even flow. Of course, as with all lessons, you can share and help others realize a better quality of life.

NIKKI

Your lesson is to learn how to sift situations, acting as a sieve to eliminate as many imperfections as possible in this Earthly world. You also will learn to act as a spatula, recovering and implementing as much as possible of the positive yield. Your ability to do so will not only prevent sour, rocky experiences; it will ensure the best quality of life for you. Know that we are with you, coaching you in ways you may not realize. Know that you will realize the gifts of this lesson and will be able to sort through any circumstance to find the even flow. Of course, as with all lessons, you can share and help others realize a better quality of life.

NINA / NEENAH

"*How dare you?!*" Yes, you may hear this often throughout your time here. Why? You may be well aware by now that you rock the boat with your risk taking, with your direct approach, and with your free-spirited mannerisms. Your approach is filled with zest and fervor, something which is not always welcomed in conditions of social, professional, political, and yes—even day-to-day restraints. You do not always understand these restraints, and we say to you: Cherish your boldness. It may not be endearing to some, but do not let these different energies thwart you. Your boldness is necessary for you to carry out your purpose of discovering the freedom you so desire – to be your authentic self.

NISSA / NYSSA

Clover attracts the bees, which bring us honey. You, our flower, have great ability to turn what may appear to be menacing circumstances into sweet results. Although you do not attract negativity, certain people and situations may falsely appear to be threatening. Always realize that, if meant to be, the situation will transform to the best result. It may, as with the pollination from bees, take the involvement of more than what appears on the surface. It will, in time, be transmuted as long as it is in divine order. You may ask why you are a conduit for such change for the better. It is because you are not only the clover that attracts bees; you are also a four-leaf clover for many, and you seek out good fortune. Be comforted in knowing you are an optimist at heart and a changer of conditions. We will send you four-leaf clovers to remind you that you are a good luck charm, and that we will provide you with the sometimes unexpected means you need to carry forth your purpose of transforming circumstances.

NITA

Clover attracts the bees, which bring us honey. You, our flower, have great ability to turn what may appear to be menacing circumstances into sweet results. Although you do not attract negativity, certain people and situations may falsely appear to be threatening. Always realize that, if meant to be, the situation will transform to the best result. It may, as with the pollination from bees, take the involvement of more than what appears on the surface. It will, in time, be transmuted as long as it is in divine order. You may ask why you are a conduit for such change for the better. It is because you are not only the clover that attracts bees; you are also a four-leaf clover for many, and you seek out good fortune. Be comforted in knowing you are an optimist at heart and a changer of conditions. We will send you four-leaf clovers to remind you that you are a good luck charm, and that we will provide you with the sometimes unexpected means you need to carry forth your purpose of transforming circumstances.

NOAH

The moon holds mysteries, and so do you. You gaze at the moon and wonder. We say to you: Gaze within to discover the wondrous mystery of You. You are looked upon by the world around you as curious and mysterious. In others' eyes, you gracefully waltz through your days and glide across your personal dance floor. For this, you are sometimes admired and are sometimes found to be perplexing. Your philosophical nature compels and repels, depending on the individuals who notice your enigmatic presence. Your lesson is to understand that, despite what you may see as a larger mystery of the moon, or the universe in general, it is the realization that you hold the universe within. Revel in your truth. Celebrate the ancient truths that you hold. Let the moonlight of your very soul softly shine within, and then outward. For this you will be doubly blessed, and you will be a catalyst for others to look within.

NOEL / NOELLE

The moon holds mysteries, and so do you. You gaze at the moon and wonder. We say to you: Gaze within to discover the wondrous mystery of You. You are looked upon by the world around you as curious and mysterious. In others' eyes, you gracefully waltz through your days and glide across your personal dance floor. For this, you are sometimes admired and are sometimes perplexing. Your philosophical nature compels and repels, depending on the individuals who notice your enigmatic presence. Your lesson is to understand that, despite what you may see as a larger mystery of the moon, or the universe in general, it is the realization that you hold the universe within. Revel in your truth. Celebrate the ancient truths that you hold. Let the moonlight of your very soul softly shine within, and outward. For this you will be doubly blessed, and you will be a catalyst for others to look within.

NORA

The moon holds mysteries, and so do you. You gaze at the moon and wonder. We say to you: Gaze within to discover the wondrous mystery of You. You are looked upon by the world around you as curious and mysterious. In others' eyes, you gracefully waltz through your days and glide across your personal dance floor. For this, you are sometimes admired and are sometimes perplexing. Your philosophical nature compels and repels, depending on the individuals who notice your enigmatic presence. Your lesson is to understand that, despite what you may see as a larger mystery of the moon, or the universe in general, it is the realization that you hold the universe within. Revel in your truth. Celebrate the ancient truths that you hold. Let the moonlight of your very soul softly shine within, and outward. For this you will be doubly blessed, and you will be a catalyst for others to look within.

NORM / NORMAN

You are among the rather rare, paradoxical ones. Pragmatic and practical, yet with a sense of humor that can bring comic relief at the drop of a hat. Further, your humor is of an intelligent type, which keeps others thinking while chuckling. Those of you with this name make stellar educators. If you are not a teacher or professor, you likely are (and should be) teaching through seminars, presentations, or workshops. Of course, friends and family (especially the children in your family) are included in your teaching mannerisms. You make learning fun. This world is in much need of necessary, yet light-hearted information that can be assimilated, and thus internalized for present and future reference. To help you with your purpose, we surround you with the wisdom of ancient philosophers and the comedic genius of a laugh-a-teer.

NORMA

You are among the rather rare, paradoxical ones. Pragmatic and practical, yet with a sense of humor that can bring comic relief at the drop of a hat. Further, your humor is of an intelligent type, which keeps others thinking while chuckling. Those of you with this name make stellar educators. If you are not a teacher or professor, you likely are (and should be) teaching through seminars, presentations, or workshops. Of course, friends and family (especially the children in your family) are included in your teaching mannerisms. You make learning fun. This world is in much need of necessary, yet light-hearted information that can be assimilated, and thus internalized for present and future reference. To help you with your purpose, we surround you with the wisdom of ancient philosophers and the comedic genius of a laugh-a-teer.

NORRIS

Strike up the band. Orchestrate. Entertain and lead. You are the conductor of life symphonies. You will always have this role of leading the band, so to speak, because you understand how many different parts create the whole. Someone must keep the instruments in harmony so as to manifest symphonies when there could have been chaos. You do all this without being appointed as a superior or without being charged with the authority over others, as the world puts it. The Humble Conductor is what we call you. Your purpose is to create and maintain congruence between everyone within all your life's groups.

OLGA

Some perceive the characteristic of your name to reflect sternness. This is not true of you at all. Although you have the ability to be easily assertive, you speak your truth with gentleness. It's the kind of gentleness that is soft yet strong, with no room for anyone to guess what it is you really mean. You know how to ask for what you want, and you know how to correct harsh action from others while avoiding arguments. Your purpose is to help your closest family members and friends learn that there is strength in inoffensive assertiveness, and that this brings positive results. When these loved ones learn to respect themselves enough to speak up, their lives will improve. We give you the energy of baby blue skies to embellish your communication skills and to stay calm when storms come your way.

OLIVER

Stories upon stories. This is your purpose: To be a storyteller who brings joy and wisdom to your audiences, whether they be immediate family, friends, or any other group. Your stories act much like Aesop's Fables, with lessons in each tale. Some of your accounts of happenings will be true; some will be fiction with profound meaning. Regardless of factual or creative tales, you will deliver the best and will always, instinctively know the tone needed. We say to you: If you are so inclined, write your work so that the wisdom contained therein can be permanently referenced for the good of all who do not have the privilege of hearing your personal presentations.

OLIVIA

Stories upon stories. This is your purpose: To be a storyteller who brings joy and wisdom to your audiences, whether they be immediate family, friends, or any other group. Your stories act much like Aesop's Fables, with lessons in each tale. Some of your accounts of happenings will be true; some will be fiction with profound meaning. Regardless of factual or creative tales, you will deliver the best and will always, instinctively know the tone needed. We say to you: If you are so inclined, write your work so that the wisdom contained therein can be permanently referenced for the good of all who do not have the privilege of hearing your personal presentations.

OLLIE / OLLY

Stories upon stories. This is your purpose: To be a storyteller who brings joy and wisdom to your audiences, whether they be immediate family, friends, or any other group. Your stories act much like Aesop's Fables, with lessons in each tale. Some of your accounts of happenings will be true; some will be fiction with profound meaning. Regardless of factual or creative tales, you will deliver the best and will always, instinctively know the tone needed. We say to you: If you are so inclined, write your work so that the wisdom contained therein can be permanently referenced for the good of all who do not have the privilege of hearing your personal presentations.

OMAR

Striated hearts are drawn to you, as your heart is kindred to theirs. The striations have been formed throughout lifetimes of broken or interrupted relationships with loved ones. We do not speak solely of heartache from unhappy transitions. We do not speak of only romantic relationships, or betrayals, or perceived failures. We speak of scars upon the heart that have been carried forward to your kindred hearts from past lifetimes, as well as the new scars during this present time on the Earth plane. We say to you: It is your purpose, and it is vital, that you respond to those who have striated hearts. You have the healing energy to brush away the scars with your patience, unconditional love, and kindness. You can also set the example of Phoenix-like strength. These kindred hearts can only respond to one such as yours. You are their hearts' salvation as to healing from losses while understanding their loved ones can still be honored and kept sacred within. Here is the other critical part: In responding and assisting others, your own striated heart will be healed.

OPAL / OPEL

Ne'er do wells seem to be attracted to you. We want to, on one hand, commend you for your altruistic nature. On the other hand, we ask you to heed our caution signal to evaluate each relationship and interaction carefully. Take time for decisions—more time than you may think is necessary. This will help direct your steps. Lean on us...your angels and guides...to assist when you are in doubt. Your purpose is to be an example of prudent decision making. You will help divert your loved ones from making many wrong or harmful decisions through your own experiences.

ORVILLE

Stalwart as you may be, there is a cuddly side of you that few see, yet sense that it is there. You are excellent at choosing who will see this soft side, and you are just as keen at maintaining your strong stance on any subject you feel needs an unrelenting position. Quiet as you may at times be, when you speak, others want to know what you have to say, as they become aware that you do not over-use words nor do you speak idly. Your task here is to teach the art of discrimination when speaking.

OTIS

We are serious about this when we say to you that you are sometimes too serious. You may often hear others ask you why you are so serious. While you frequently mask your deep thoughts and depth of feeling with surface humor, it is difficult for you to stay light (internally) for long. Therefore, we reveal your lesson: To have the ability to remain serious about your desires and longing for the world to rise above difficulties, yet allow yourself time to enjoy its wonders. Permit yourself to enjoy your time here more often. This will raise your vibration and consequently assist the environment around you. Actually, it will send higher frequency waves farther than you may realize. Our dear, concerned one, we in turn lift you and bring "happenchances" that will make you smile, elicit laughter from your caring soul, and imprint those smiles. These imprinted smiles are there for you to revisit when you feel you are sinking into an extended period of worried reflection. We encourage you to continue your work for the better good of all, and to be mindful of the ALL THAT IS. This awareness will transform your soul to approach your chosen work to that of more joy.

OTTO

We are serious about this when we say to you that you are sometimes too serious. You may often hear others ask you why you are so serious. While you frequently mask your deep thoughts and depth of feeling with surface humor, it is difficult for you to stay light (internally) for long. Therefore, we reveal your lesson: To have the ability to remain serious about your desires and longing for the world to rise above difficulties, yet allow yourself time to enjoy its wonders. Permit yourself to enjoy your time here more often. This will raise your vibration and consequently assist the environment around you. Actually, it will send higher frequency waves farther than you may realize. Our dear, concerned one, we in turn lift you and bring "happenchances" that will make you smile, elicit laughter from your caring soul, and imprint those smiles. These imprinted smiles are there for you to revisit when you feel you are sinking into an extended period of worried reflection. We encourage you to continue your work for the better good of all, and to be mindful of the ALL THAT IS. This awareness will transform your soul to approach your chosen work to that of more joy.

OWEN

Stars are meant to shine. Your lesson is to always remember that you do shine, and that no person or circumstance will darken your brightness. It may seem at times that your light is about to forever fade. Know that this is only temporary. Liken these times as turning off or dimming lights in order to sleep, to be restored, and to be refreshed through rest. After rest, the lights go back on. So, our dear star, you will come to the understanding that you indeed shine and have the magnitude you need at any given moment. Know that during any time when you feel dimness, we are surrounding you with our light to protect and encourage you. We repeat, never forget that you shine.

OWENA

Stars are meant to shine. Your lesson is to always remember that you do shine, and that no person or circumstance will darken your brightness. It may seem at times that your light is about to forever fade. Know that this is only temporary. Liken these times as turning off or dimming lights in order to sleep, to be restored, and to be refreshed through rest. After rest, the lights go back on. So, our dear star, you will come to the understanding that you indeed shine and have the magnitude you need at any given moment. Know that during any time when you feel dimness, we are surrounding you with our light to protect and encourage you. We repeat, never forget that you shine.

PAGE / PAIGE

You have a heart of gold, stone, crystals, and flowers. Your heart responds in kind to however it needs in all the books, chapters, paragraphs, and sentences of your life. The most miraculous part of your heart is that however you respond, it is always filled with love. Even when your heart must turn temporarily to stone, the stone is covered with and grows in love. The stone response simply assists with boundaries and the lessons required for both you and the individuals who receive this response. Later, your heart can respond from another perspective when it is time. This multi-dimensional heart of yours is enchanting. The gold aspect is pure; the stone aspect is strong; the crystal aspect is amplifying, and the flower aspect reflects beauty and gratitude. We ask you to always honor your heart and its responses, as your heart will be your greatest teacher. In turn, it will create you as a gracious mentor.

PAM /PAMELA

Your life, just like everyone's, is built upon layers. Each chapter creates a layer, and the layers combine to make you who you are today. You are keenly attuned with your stories and how they have created the individual that you are today. More so, you will be mindful of the tiers you are creating that will add to your uniqueness. Although everyone is a walking novel, you pay more attention to what the chapters contain so that your story will be interesting, plus serve as a model that reveals significant lessons. You are willing to make errors and to rise above them in order to illustrate these lessons. Although you are attentive to each stage as your life story is developed, you have chosen to teach through your life's course of layers, both directly and indirectly. You are like the sun as well as its shadow. One cannot exist without the other. The knowledge that one must experience the shadows of life if the light is to also always exist is difficult to internalize. To take rest in the cool shadows is a valuable tool which you are here to demonstrate.

PAT

You are not one for false bravado. You wear your shield of confidence like a banner, announcing that you have overcome fear-based beliefs. Your courage is not as a bandy rooster, puffed up. It is as a solid mountain, unmoved by turmoil. We give you the strength of mountains, treed with oaks, to sustain your valor. You are aware at a level beyond your consciousness of this space of strength within. Your internal dialog is not moved or disturbed by the external events of this worldly existence. Your purpose is to provide courage and confidence to those who are in most need. Some of them will receive your help on a temporary basis; others will present themselves as family members and close friends. Do not worry about who, when, where, or how. We will take care of that part, and your inner knowledge will guide you.

PATRICIA

A wandering gypsy you are not. You prefer a grounded home base from which to extend all of your activities. Yes, you are an active sort, both physically (unless incapable of certain things), and mentally. You delve into whatever has sparked your interest, and you stick with it until you are ready to move on to the next area of focus ... always with the knowing that you have a secure home ground to which you can return. You are driven to finish what you start, and at times you can be intense with your focus, yet you keep from becoming overly serious. This would be uncomfortable for you.

On another level, you delight in socialization and spark excitement at any gathering, whether it be with one other person or at a large gathering. Therefore, you possess a healthy type of duality, so to speak, that brings admiration and emulation from those you came here to influence and teach from your actions alone. Thank you for your dedication to whatever you do and to whatever milieu in which you are present at any given time.

PATRICK

You are not one for false bravado. You wear your shield of confidence like a banner, announcing that you have overcome fear-based beliefs. Your courage is not as a bandy rooster, puffed up. It is as a solid mountain, unmoved by turmoil. We give you the strength of mountains, treed with oaks, to sustain your valor. You are aware at a level beyond your consciousness of this space of strength within. Your internal dialog is not moved or disturbed by the external events of this worldly existence. Your purpose is to provide courage and confidence to those who are in most need. Some of them will receive your help on a temporary basis; others will present themselves as family members and close friends. Do not worry about who, when, where, or how. We will take care of that part, and your inner knowledge will guide you.

PATSY

When the heat is on, you are the one to cool things off. You are a mediator at heart, and objective mediation is your purpose. Others turn to you for your ability to assess all angles, all sides, and to do so objectively. You favor no one person over another. Those who are fortunate enough to know you are blessed with loving peacekeeping from you. You are truly an equalizer who brings stability, and we assist you in maintaining your own sense of equality.

PATTI / PATTY

A wandering gypsy you are not. You prefer a grounded home base from which to extend all of your activities. Yes, you are an active sort, both physically (unless incapable of certain things), and mentally. You delve into whatever has sparked your interest, and you stick with it until you are ready to move on to the next area of focus ... always with the knowing that you have a secure home ground to which you can return. You are driven to finish what you start, and you at times can be intense with your focus, yet you keep from becoming overly serious. This would be uncomfortable for you.

On another level, you delight in socialization and spark excitement at any gathering, whether it be with one other person or at a large gathering. Therefore, you possess a healthy type of duality, so to speak, that brings admiration and emulation from those you came here to influence and teach from your actions alone. Thank you for your dedication to whatever you do and to whatever milieu in which you are present at any given time.

PAUL

Carry on. One step after another. For you, it will take many steps to reach the pinnacle of your self-realization, because you have so many interests, and the talents to pursue each one. Your fulfillment will come once you have explored enough to realize your calling. Do not become dismayed about your many quests—each one is significant. You will gain useful information, and you will gain ground toward your ultimate role. Your lesson and purpose are one and the same: The art of exploration and creating maps to find destinations. Carry on, and we will carry you to great heights.

PAULA

Strike up the band. Orchestrate. Entertain and lead. You are the conductor of life symphonies. You will always have this role of leading the band, so to speak, because you understand how many different parts create the whole. Someone must keep the instruments in order to manifest symphonies when there could have been chaos. You do all this without being appointed a superior or without being charged with the authority over others, as the world puts it. The Humble Conductor is what we call you. Your purpose is to create and maintain harmony between everyone within all your life's groups.

PEARL

Sticking to the basics is something you have never liked to do, and never will. You have a knack of transforming the ordinary to unusual and boredom to excitement. Because of this, children flock to you to stimulate their minds. Adults who are jaded from the conventional gravitate toward you to experience a bigger picture. You may be viewed as eccentric; however, you are simply using the full gamut of availability ... availability of color, sound, texture, and data ... the vastness of possibilities. You realize that this life can be a work of art at every turn. You are among the creative geniuses who see life as a series of canvases and musical instruments. You relish all genres, and you make each work distinctive. Your purpose is to bring zest to the oftentimes blandness of life.

PEG

Like a loaf of freshly-baked bread, you draw family, friends, and other visitors to your welcoming, cozy home and remind them of the nurturing they crave through connection with the home base. Star light, star bright, all's well and good tonight ... this is the peaceful countenance you exude. You will always be surrounded with people who gravitate toward and embrace the energy of a home with the welcome mat always available. This Earth on which you live is in grave need of wholesome connections. Thank you for serving this purpose.

PEGGY

Like a loaf of freshly-baked bread, you draw family, friends, and other visitors to your welcoming, cozy home and remind them of the nurturing they crave through connection with the home base. Star light, star bright, all's well and good tonight ... this is the peaceful countenance you exude. You will always be surrounded with people who gravitate toward, and embrace the energy of, a home with the welcome mat always available. This Earth on which you live is in grave need of wholesome connections. Thank you for serving this purpose.

PENELOPE

Outgoing people are needed; they are sought after; they are appreciated. You are one who brings these desired energies. You are depended upon to be the catalyst of optimism and the creator of positive atmosphere. More so, you enjoy this role and share your personality freely. We do know that you cannot possibly be on key continuously. Therefore, we provide you with solace when you need to escape from this demanding role, even though you feel driven to be the joy bringer. At times you will feel the need for a weekend in the middle of the week. We understand the vast amount of energy used to create happy environments. We surround you with the color blue to remain calm and the color gold to restore your vitality. We also give you the energy of Celestite and Citrine to reinforce you. Thank you for choosing such a role to uplift those around you.

PENNY

Outgoing people are needed; they are sought after; they are appreciated. You are one who brings these desired energies. You are depended upon to be the catalyst of optimism and the creator of positive atmosphere. More so, you enjoy this role and share your personality freely. We do know that you cannot possibly be on key continuously. Therefore, we provide you with solace when you need to escape from this demanding role, even though you feel driven to be the joy bringer. At times you will feel the need for a weekend in the middle of the week. We understand the vast amount of energy used to create happy environments. We surround you with the color blue to remain calm and the color gold to restore your vitality. We also give you the energy of Celestite and Citrine to reinforce you. Thank you for choosing such a role to uplift those around you.

PETE / PETER

We are serious about this when we say to you that you are sometimes too serious. You may often hear others ask you why you are so serious. While you frequently mask your deep thoughts and depth of feeling with surface humor, it is difficult for you to stay light (internally) for long. Therefore, we reveal your lesson: To have the ability to remain serious about your desires and longing for the world to rise above difficulties, yet allow yourself time to enjoy its wonders. Permit yourself to enjoy your time here more often. This will raise your vibration and consequently assist the environment around you. Actually, it will send higher frequency waves farther than you may realize. Our dear, concerned one, we in turn lift you and bring "happenchances" that will make you smile, elicit laughter from your caring soul, and imprint those smiles. These imprinted smiles are there for you to revisit when you feel you are sinking into an extended period of worried reflection. We encourage you to continue your work for the better good of all, and to be mindful of the ALL THAT IS. This awareness will transform your soul to approach your chosen work to that of more joy.

PHIL / PHILLIP

Stories upon stories. This is your purpose: To be a storyteller who brings joy and wisdom to your audiences, whether they be immediate family, friends, or any other group. Your stories act much like Aesop's Fables, with lessons in each tale. Some of your accounts of happenings will be true; some will be fiction with profound meaning. Regardless of factual or creative tales, you will deliver the best and will always, instinctively know the tone needed. We say to you: If you are so inclined, write your work so that the wisdom contained therein can be permanently referenced for the good of all who do not have the privilege of hearing your personal presentations.

PHYLLIS

Phyllis, you are rare among the names, as you have decided to follow a path of service—and oh how many are the ways in which you can serve. Take your pick, but you will likely choose to serve in more than one capacity. Those with the name of Phyllis are able to function at multiple levels simultaneously and stay focused on the moment. We have braced you with the gifts of determination and energy to carry out your chosen purposes of service AND to carry out the pursuit of sharing your own spirit-given gifts with humanity. You actually chose these gifts. It is an honorable combination, and you have the fortitude to see it through. To enhance your abilities, we give you the deep, loving pink and the secure, grounding energies of Rhodonite. We add Chrysocolla for expression. You will always feel our grounding love and our assistance with expressing your gifts in whatever areas you have chosen; there are so many! The gifts you have chosen to express during this lifetime are perfect now, and the gifts that are not being fully expressed will carry through to the future lifetimes. None will be lost. Thank you for taking on this incarnation's multiple purpose. Know that you will never lack in the strength you need as long as you wish to walk this path.

POLLY

Search and Rescue. Search for the love inside your heart and rescue yourself. Search for the knowledge lying deep within your soul, and know yourself. Redeem the gifts you have been given to love and to be loved. You have suppressed love, the inner knowledge, and the miracles of your spiritual gifts in past lifetimes. You are destined to rise above the worldly chains to realize your full spiritual influence upon your own soul. Consequently, you will spread this love into the vast universe. Your immediate purpose, however, is to spread the love during this lifetime, on this Earth plane, to the souls here who are impoverished from love. We will shower them with the energy of Rose Quartz and open their heart centers as you reveal the pure love you were sent to teach. You, as well, are nourished and supported by us with this pure, loving energy.

PRISCILLA

Do not wait for the mountain to come to you; go to the mountain. What seems to be immovable can transform with your diligence. Your lesson is to learn how to move mountains through sheer determination. Yes, you can do it. You can be a fiery force that can transmute dirt to gold because of your strong constitution and inner strength. We say to you: Remember that, even though you develop great confidence as a result of your fortitude, no one is immune to this world's destructive ways, especially from humankind. Your lesson is to use your strength wisely, where it will result in only good, and to avoid being drawn into ventures that would take advantage of others or of the land. Stay strong, our Atlas, and we will guide you toward the most auspicious and positive adventures.

QUIN / QUINTON

Fly your kites. Fly all colors and shapes of kites. Let the world know you are capable of rising above the mundane, and that the variety of life is truly what brings people to new and exciting heights. When you choose to fly your kites, you will serve your purpose of demonstrating that a passion for living life in full color is so much more fulfilling than settling for whatever people feel is handed to them for mere existence. You exist, evolve, and excite. You soar, and revel in all the possibilities for happiness at heights many never realize. Fly your kites and invite others to not only observe, but to participate with their own kites.

QUINCY

Expectations, expectations, expectations. Your lesson is to release from your mind any and all expectations from the world, from those in your life, and from yourself. You, of course, will have dreams you wish to fulfill ... *your* dreams, not anyone else's dreams for you. You can work toward your dream without letting others down who perceive your dream differently. We say to you: Your dream is your purpose, and your purpose will be fulfilled whether you or others expect it to manifest or not. This is why we advise you to be easy on yourself while you follow the joy of your vision. What you may think you need to do, or what you must do, may deter your advancement. The old expression, "follow your heart, not your head," is perfectly fitting for you, as overthinking can create self-expectations. We wish also for you to be cautious of outside expectations in everyday living. If you are told you should wear the green shirt and you want to wear the orange shirt, wear the orange shirt. If you are "expected" to meet a goal (such as peer pressure to own a flashy car) but it is not your goal, then meet *your own* goal. Once you free yourself from expectations, your journey will be relaxed. We send you gold dust to build and preserve your resolve.

RACHEL

Ne'er do wells seem to be attracted to you. We want to, on one hand, commend you for your altruistic nature. On the other hand, we ask you to heed our caution signal to evaluate each relationship and interaction carefully. Take time for decisions—more time than you may think is necessary. This will help direct your steps. Lean on us...your angels and guides...to assist when you are in doubt. Your purpose is to be an example of prudent decision making. You will help divert your loved ones from making many wrong or harmful decisions through your own experiences.

RAE /RAY

Story time is something you cherish and enjoy to the hilt. As a child on this Earth, you were held in fascination at the stories which were read to you and told to you by relatives and friends. When you learned to read, you were captivated by the marvels found in the written word and at the vastness of subject matters ... especially the words that told a good story. You grew to love hearing others tell interesting stories, and your gift is that of sharing a good story, whether it be amusing, informational, or that it contains a lesson of sort. This is not to say that you crave the attention of a storyteller ... you simply convey your stories in a natural, low-key manner. However, no matter what the surroundings or the style of delivery, and no matter how small or large the audience, the interest and benefit is always enjoyed. Thank you for sharing and contributing to the enjoyment of everyday life ... it is an important gift for many to receive.

RALPH

"Come 'round, everyone; hear what he has to tell." We see you as a great messenger of wisdom through parables, which is your purpose. You are humble enough as a student of life on Earth to also be a pillar among teachers. You are sought out when sound advice is deemed necessary; you are also a source of laughter, and insightful thinking to any age group. You are guided by Archangel Gabriel for this journey when you are commissioned to impart truth through allegories and analogies. We say to you: Do not doubt the wisdom and direction provided to you. Your lesson is to realize you arrived here with this calling, and to relax into it. Once you do, you will lose all doubt and easily, without effort, accomplish your mission.

RANDY

Always a jokester, you do have a serious side. Ride it out when you feel too serious, and your smile will return. You may come to think others rely on your upbeat, fun nature. We say to you: Do not allow this perception to make you feel pressure. Always, we say always ride it out, whatever the situation may be. Never force yourself to be either upbeat or serious. This will thwart your spirit. Your lesson is to be comfortable with yourself in your jolly moments as well as your somber ones. In loving kindness we uphold you.

RAYMOND

Story time is something you cherish and enjoy to the hilt. As a child on this Earth, you were held in fascination at the stories which were read to you and told to you by relatives and friends. When you learned to read, you were captivated by the marvels found in the written word and at the vastness of subject matters ... especially the words that told a good story. You grew to love hearing others tell interesting stories, and your gift is that of sharing a good story, whether it be amusing, informational, or that it contains a lesson of sort. This is not to say that you crave the attention of a storyteller ... you simply convey your stories in a natural, low-key manner. However, no matter what the surroundings or the style of delivery, and no matter how small or large the audience, the interest and benefit is always enjoyed. Thank you for sharing and contributing to the enjoyment of everyday life ... it is an important gift for many to receive.

REBECCA / REBEKAH

Child of grace, Rebecca, you have the ability to give direction to others. If there is a storm, others can find their way with your help—with your beam as of a lighthouse. You may have a challenge about your choice to use this gift. There will be times when you just do not feel strong enough, and you wonder if others will even want to pay heed to your guiding light, which comes so naturally to you. We say to you: Do not give much thought to this. Your gift will shine to those who can see. And Rebecca, we shine our love to you always.

RENEE

Streaming light, streaming information, streaming introspection ... you arrived here to be a powerful bringer of knowledge, truth, and awakening. We call you the Comet of Reflection and Enlightenment. You will appear on thousands of scenes, brightly and briefly, leaving behind a plethora of effects to be either considered or embraced. The effects of the temporary brilliance you bring may often be ignored, but not forgotten. The memory of such a bright phenomenon for those who have witnessed it may come forth to consciousness at a later time and result in an instant enlightenment of sorts. This illumination will occur as swiftly as a comet, yet the effect and awe will remain permanently, just as the comet's. We surround you with the energy of a thousand other comets to maintain your own awareness of your purpose: To increase awakening.

RHONDA /RONDA

Astute, yet fun. Biting, yet soft-hearted. You are an enigma. If you observe a need, worthy of a cause or not, you may feel compelled to assist. If you sense a wrong doing, guilty or not, you will confront it with full force. You are full of surprises because of your reserved mannerisms that can change in an instant to one of spontaneous humor and fun or assertive advocacy. Although you may or may not consider that variety is the spice of life, you bring variety to your inner circle, and at times show a glimpse of this rare variety to the public and more distant acquaintances. This is your purpose: To teach through your various actions that there is no one correct way to approach life. Each moment may be most handled and blessed with the approach most appropriate. Know that you are guided.

RICH

To be Rich is to want for nothing. You will reach this fulfillment ... this gratitude for whatever is surrounding you ... during your lifetime here. Your lesson (which you chose) is to be aware of the richness of life regardless of possessions, and yes, even comfort levels. You may experience feast and you may experience famine this time around—your choice. You may be surrounded with fine embellishments and accessories or with only bare necessities. We extend to you our congratulations for choosing the lesson of gratitude. This is a big step in the process of loving, giving, receiving, and most of all—acceptance.

RICHARD

To be Rich is to want for nothing. You will reach this fulfillment ... this gratitude for whatever is surrounding you ... during your lifetime here. Your lesson (which you chose) is to be aware of the richness of life regardless of possessions, and yes, even comfort levels. You may experience feast and you may experience famine this time around—your choice. You may be surrounded with fine embellishments and accessories or with only bare necessities. We extend to you our congratulations for choosing the lesson of gratitude. This is a big step in the process of loving, giving, receiving, and most of all—acceptance.

RICK / RICKY

Twirl a wand, a baton, a pizza dough, or your own body in a circle—it's all about movement—movement with rhythm complementary to whatever the moment is holding. Your lesson is to stay "in time" and recognize the beat of the day, the encounters, the meetings, the weather, the errands—all of it. There are so many beats in time ... so much singing without music. Listen to the musical beat of each bird's song, to the ocean's tides, to the traffic, and to the silence. Yes, there is a sacred rhythm to silence. Find the tempo to each moment and flow with it. Your understanding and appreciation for all of life will be elevated to heights you never felt possible.

RITA

You have a heart of gold, stone, crystals, and flowers. Your heart responds in kind to however it needs in all the books, chapters, paragraphs, and sentences of your life. The most miraculous part of your heart is that however you respond, it is always filled with love. Even when your heart must turn temporarily to stone, the stone is covered with and grows in love. The stone response simply assists with boundaries and the lessons required for both you and the individuals who receive this response. Later, your heart can respond from another perspective when it is time. This multi-dimensional heart of yours is enchanting. The gold aspect is pure; the stone aspect is strong; the crystal aspect is amplifying, and the flower aspect reflects beauty and gratitude. We ask you to always honor your heart and its responses, as your heart will be your greatest teacher. In turn, it will create you as a gracious mentor.

ROB / ROBBIE

You become the breath of fresh air, which is a normal thing for you to bring to a normal day. The unusual thing is that you are unaware of this natural ability to lift up a moment at any given time. You may be equally unaware that this gift of yours will be, and is, taken for granted—after all, that's just who you are! We say to you: Appreciation at the highest level is always upon you and elevates you to a realm not "normally" experienced by those on this Earth plane. We raise your consciousness, yet we keep you grounded with our support and love. You have the strength, intertwined with the compassion, of elephant energy from which all walking this Earth can learn. We will bring those to you who will learn this meaningful way of the elephant and who will value the lessons, modeling themselves after this type of community. You arrived here with these admirable qualities—these naturally pure qualities. We are so happy that you have not ignored this gift and have brought it forth to share. With thanks, we give you the energy of Frankincense to sustain your higher consciousness.

ROBERT

Subtleties are your specialty, Robert. By that we mean that you have no need to say or do anything with brashness. You are by nature not one of many words, which is why when you do speak, others want to hear what you have to say. You do not feel the need to do things with a great deal of liveliness. Therefore, others watch you. They take your quiet lead, and they want to mirror you. You do not demand respect; however, your very nature gains respect. Your purpose is to lead by example, and you quietly perform this role quite well. We shower you with the energy of Amethyst to assist you in connecting with your source, which you so desire.

ROBERTA

Unlike your counterpart (Robert), you do speak up and speak out, comfortably. You are animated in actions and words, and you are audacious with your endeavors. You have another, different side, however. Your maternal instinct flows over into your everyday life, with everyday people. You are unique in that you are an outgoing nurturer. You have the ability to give both cheer and comfort simultaneously. For this we thank you, as you chose this purpose before arriving here. Most would find it difficult to carry out a dichotomous role such as this one. You, Roberta, thrive on it. You have learned in past life times that it is possible to be deeply kind *and* jovial. You are carrying out this lesson now. We surround you with the energies of Rose Quartz to keep your heart soft, and Citrine to sustain your fortitude.

ROBIN

Slow, rolling waves over motionless rocks create a contrast of strength ... strength of flow and power of stance. The waves learn that they can continue to move despite the resolute stones. The stones learn that when a position is required to maintain balance, the movement around and over them will not adversely affect them in the present moment, yet over time will create polished beauty.

Your lesson is to learn how to be the wave and how to be the stone. Bring refreshing, cleansing beauty to the undaunted. Allow yourself to view threats to your convictions as an addition of peace to what must be unwavering in the now moment. You do have an understanding that, over time, the resolute may be altered or transformed by the beauty of a natural course of change. Embrace this understanding while you are being a mainstay of peaceful existence during this lifetime. We support you with the grace of Earth angels who we send to you throughout your time here.

ROCHELLE

Ne'er do wells seem to be attracted to you. We want to, on one hand, commend you for your altruistic nature. On the other hand, we ask you to heed our caution signal to evaluate each relationship and interaction carefully. Take time for decisions—more time than you may think is necessary. This will help direct your steps. Lean on us...your angels and guides...to assist when you are in doubt. Your purpose is to be an example of prudent decision making. You will help divert your loved ones from making many wrong or harmful decisions through your own experiences.

ROGER

You are a faraway star that only certain people can see— the ones whose light, although possibly shining at a different brightness, is nonetheless appreciative of the frequency you emit. They are the fortunate ones who are guided by your streaming glow, as it will lead to right and blessed actions, reaping rewards for the soul, just as a rainbow's light helps to access the golden reward at its perceived end. Your bright guidance may also be perceived to have an ending point; however, it is eternal. You have accepted this purpose more than once from us to arrive on the Earth plane as a guiding light in human form. There is no need to study on how to direct this sacred light—it is done for you, always. You merely need to continue to accept this position for those who see you, to guide them on to their destined paths.

ROD / RODMAN

You may be viewed as a little different. Friendly, yet discriminating, selective. Artistic, yet commonplace. Not wanting, but wanting. Proud, yet humble. What these contradictions mean is that you are flexible, resilient. We revel in those with this name, as they offer a variety of life's aspects to those in their circle. A carefree attitude is predominant, but watch for your limited ability to process angry feelings. We encourage you to respond to these feelings after your reaction has subsided. In that way you can maintain your relationships and the variety of your personality aspects they love. Your purpose is to teach variety as an example of an exciting, fulfilling life. We endearingly call you the Chameleon.

RODNEY

You may be viewed as a little different. Friendly, yet discriminating, selective. Artistic, yet commonplace. Not wanting, but wanting. Proud, yet humble. What these contradictions mean is that you are flexible, resilient. We revel in those with this name, as they offer a variety of life's aspects to those in their circle. A carefree attitude is predominant, but watch for your limited ability to process angry feelings. We encourage you to respond to these feelings after your reaction has subsided. In that way you can maintain your relationships and the variety of your personality aspects they love. Your purpose is to teach variety as an example of an exciting, fulfilling life. We endearingly call you the Chameleon.

RON / RONALD

Stalwart as you may be, there is a cuddly side of you that few see, yet sense that it is there. You are excellent at choosing who will see this soft side, and you are just as keen at maintaining your strong stance on any subject you feel needs an unrelenting position. Quiet as you may at times be, when you speak, others want to know what you have to say, as they become aware that you do not over-use words, nor do you speak idly. Your task here is to teach the art of discrimination when speaking.

RONETTE

Stalwart as you may be, there is a cuddly side of you that few see, yet sense that it is there. You are excellent at choosing who will see this soft side, and you are just as keen at maintaining your strong stance on any subject you feel needs an unrelenting position. Quiet as you may at times be, when you speak, others want to know what you have to say, as they become aware that you do not over-use words, nor do you speak idly. Your task here is to teach the art of discrimination when speaking.

RONNIE

Stalwart as you may be, there is a cuddly side of you that few see, yet sense that it is there. You are excellent at choosing who will see this soft side, and you are just as keen at maintaining your strong stance on any subject you feel needs an unrelenting position. Quiet as you may at times be, when you speak, others want to know what you have to say, as they become aware that you do not over-use words, nor do you speak idly. Your task here is to teach the art of discrimination when speaking.

RORY

Slow, rolling waves over motionless rocks create a contrast of strength ... strength of flow and power of stance. The waves learn that they can continue to move despite the resolute stones. The stones learn that when a position is required to maintain balance, the movement around and over them will not adversely affect them in the present moment, yet over time will create polished beauty. Your lesson is to learn how to be the wave and how to be the stone. Bring refreshing, cleansing beauty to the undaunted. Allow yourself to view threats to your convictions as an addition of peace to what must be unwavering in the now moment. You do have an understanding that, over time, the resolute may be altered or transformed by the beauty of a natural course of change. Embrace this understanding while you are being a mainstay of peaceful existence during this lifetime. We support you with the grace of Earth angels who we send to you throughout your time here.

ROSE / ROSIE

Throw away your jewels—by that we mean superfluous things. You are doing so well gaining the lessons you came here to learn and then to share. In fact, you learned it quickly, at a young age. Tend to the necessities. The adornments of your life will come in ways you could not imagine as you go about the priorities. The small, immediate picture becomes a grand masterpiece, framed eloquently. Know this truth and convey it. We honor you.

ROWENA

Stars are meant to shine. Your lesson is to always remember that you do shine, and that no person or circumstance will darken your brightness. It may seem at times that your light is about to forever fade. Know that this is only temporary. Liken these times as turning off or dimming lights in order to sleep, to be restored, and to be refreshed through rest. After rest, the lights go back on. So, our dear star, you will come to the understanding that you indeed shine and have the magnitude you need at any given moment. Know that during any time when you feel dimness, we are surrounding you with our light to protect and encourage you. We repeat, never forget that you shine.

ROXANNE

Roxanne, you're the fabric of progress within the microcosmic world to which you came ... which you chose. You help the ones immediately around you to progress. Your friends and family look to you for assistance with any type of progress needed, at any particular time, for any particular reason. You're a great facilitator. The lessons that you come here to teach are perseverance and commitment.

The light you bring is directional. You are as the lighthouse ... strong, steady, standing firm yet showing the way via the light. You show the way also by providing the example of being the person to effect progress. You might ask, "*Progress of which type of things?*" Anything. Progress with any type of work, project ... even life path progress. Progress on passion, progress on child rearing, progress on building anything that people want to build or to accomplish. Although you, at times, feel the need for someone else to be the strength, you do not need this for long. We send you individuals, souls, and spirits to give you that boost, that comfort, and that nurturing you so need at times. And then you carry on. No one sees when you need the nurturing, but we do, and we arrange for your reinforcement. Although it is temporary, it's all you need.

ROY

Sometimes it seems as though things will never work out. However, your purpose is to demonstrate to many that, despite the appearance, there is always a suitable outcome. You are here to allow others to see that when the outcome they desire eludes them, it may not have been what they truly needed. You are here to teach others the appreciation of prayers unanswered for their ultimate good, and about the prayers, though never spoken, that reveal the best results and unexpected gifts. Continue to be willing to let the process of best interests and appreciation of what IS unfold for yourself, and you will see and experience the ALL THAT IS.

RUBY

"This could be the start of something big." This lyric is similar to how you feel about small matters that may need to remain small. Your lesson here is to learn the art of evaluating situations and conclude if they are as they should remain, or if there is a larger outcome needed. The sparrow is perfect as a sparrow; it does not need to become an eagle. The egg, on the other hand, needs to be warmed to the point of hatching to the sparrow or the eagle, whichever it is destined to be. You will easily learn how to discern what things to nurture and to build, and which things to leave as they are. You will see that an anthill needs to be an anthill, not a mountain. Once this lesson is integrated, you will feel the peace within which you will have been seeking and will be more equipped to move forward with your life purpose of sharing excellent judgment.

RUTH

Frilly, frilly, frilly. "Why do some people like frills all the time, every day?" You may ask yourself that question often, as you prefer few or no flashy accessories with almost anything. Our realist, your lesson is to discover and appreciate the confetti, the streamers, and the sequins of life. You chose this lesson so that you can be complete with your experience of life on this plane. Your self-assignment of pragmatism for the sake of progress, as well as assisting your soul family with this type of approach to progress, has been met. You can relax a little now. It has been difficult at times to like the ribbons and the bows of life, yet you are now aware you need to be delighted in these things that elevate the experience of living. Use the lace, plant the flowers, accent with glitter. There are those who will teach you about the frills and the smiles brought forth through a more light-hearted approach. You will learn to incorporate the ribbons with a plain tradition, and you will smile as you continue assisting your circle. This is a completion of sorts for you, and you will have more variety from which to choose when the time comes to incarnate again.

SABRINA

Like a chunk of butter in the warm sun, you melt hearts with your rays of light. You shine forth tenderness with sunbeams that promote growth and awareness of the benefits from allowing the light in. You then provide rain showers for additional growth. It is your purpose to reveal the substance necessary for self-love and self-actualization. Unlike hot and cold, this substance is gentle, yet paradoxical, with the warmth of sun and coolness of raindrops. You are a healer of the heart and teach that growth is possible without harshness. This is indeed something that, if not natural, could not be accomplished by most. This gift for you *is* natural, and fortunate are those who are blessed to receive your presence.

SADIE

You came to Earth to spread your sweetness, because you knew that this special type of kindness is so needed by its inhabitants. You have no expectations of others, and you generously provide a light, exultant touch to all. It is your nature; you don't even have to give it a thought to emanate sweetness. We also call you "Flower" because of the beauty of your presence everywhere you go. However, unlike a flower, your essence does not fade away; it stays alive. You are a flower which does not wilt and brings serenity when needed. We will send increased energy to your heart center when an individual or situation is in need of this serenity. You will feel a deep tranquility sinking into and then springing from your heart ... that placidity will in turn soothe others' hearts. Thank you, our gracious flower.

SALLY

"Get a grip." This is a slogan *for* you, not *about* you, as you already are solid. You help others to realize they must get a grip, and you do so in such a way that it is firm yet not offensive...nurturing, yet not too tender. Incarnates of this world need souls like yours to help them realize that they need not swim in their muddy water, but create their own life jacket, grip their buoy, and swim rather than sink. Be careful not to become their buoy. They need their own.

SAM / SAMUEL

"Let's Dance!" Sam/Samuel, our rhythmic one, you are in touch with all of life's rhythms ... the atmosphere, the oceans, all sights, all sounds. And so it is with relationships. You strike up the right rhythm with your inner circle as well as those with whom you work. Consequently, you teach others the importance and joy of flow. We treasure the rhythm of the universe ... and we also treasure you for exuding the ebb and flow, the light and shadows, the undulating rhythm of life on the realm where you currently live, which is in such need of harmonic rhythm. We are dancing with you as you sing and play your life's song.

SAMANTHA

This we say to you: Carry on with your whys and wherefores. You depend on these answers that come from within yourself ... and from us. Others also depend on your whys and wherefores to help bring balance and discipline to their own lives ... based on your confident manner of providing information. Stay steadfast and take it to the limit with all you do. We guide you with all the whys and wherefores of your journey so that there will be no limits.

SAMMIE / SAMMY

"Let's Dance!" Sammie/Sammy our rhythmic one, you are in touch with all of life's rhythms . . . the atmosphere, the oceans, all sights, all sounds. And so it is with relationships. You strike up the right rhythm with your inner circle as well as those with whom you work. Consequently, you teach others the importance and joy of flow. We treasure the rhythm of the universe ... and we also treasure you for exuding the ebb and flow, the light and shadows, the undulating rhythm of life on the realm where you currently live, which is in such need of harmonic rhythm. We are dancing with you as you sing and play your life's song.

SANDRA

Sandra, we send you frequent sources of strength, because you feel compelled to step up to the plate much more often than your kindred spirits, who are also advocates. Be careful, however, about the expectations that may come about regarding your quickness to jump in and help. When you feel overwhelmed ... and you will...ask us for guidance in choosing when and whom to help at any given moment. We will give you the inner knowing, and will continue providing you with the mental and physical sustenance to carry out your work. Your lesson is to derive self-respect for all you do and avoid any feeling of guilt about any situations when you were unable to step up to the plate. All is in divine order, and we remind you of unconditional love for yourself.

SANDY

Sandy, we send you frequent sources of strength, because you feel compelled to step up to the plate much more often than your kindred spirits, who are also advocates. Be careful, however, about the expectations that may come about regarding your quickness to jump in and help. When you feel overwhelmed ... and you will...ask us for guidance in choosing when and whom to help at any given moment. We will give you the inner knowing, and will continue providing you with the mental and physical sustenance to carry out your work. Your lesson is to derive self-respect for all you do and avoid any feeling of guilt about any situations when you were unable to step up to the plate. All is in divine order, and we remind you of unconditional love for yourself.

SARA / SARAH

Sturdy is your resolve, as it should be ... you were sent here to stand strong in the face of adversity when it presents itself to you and to anyone you love or serve. Your purpose is to work for others in a position of advocacy and healing. We call you our Social Worker for Wounded Souls. You can be compared to social workers because of their commitment to the higher good of those they are called to assist, for their empathy, and for their fierce, lion-like, protective nature. These divinely appointed individuals may be mistaken for having constant, bleeding hearts. However, they cannot be shaken from their stand to advocate for others' rights to fairness. Yes, they are among the gentle giants in this world. Yes, you too are among the gentle and strong giants. We say to you: There is no need to literally become a "professional" social worker. One can see these accomplished individuals in all walks of this life ... the ones who are firm in their pure intent to help empower those in need. Your lesson here is to accept this role with unwavering passion, pure intent, and total reassurance that we guide you and are committed to YOUR highest good.

SAVANNAH

Like a chunk of butter in the warm sun, you melt hearts with your rays of light. You shine forth tenderness with sunbeams that promote growth and awareness of the benefits from allowing the light in. You then provide rain showers for additional growth. It is your purpose to reveal the substance necessary for self-love and self-actualization. Unlike hot and cold, this substance is gentle, yet paradoxical, with the warmth of sun and coolness of raindrops. You are a healer of the heart and teach that growth is possible without harshness. This is indeed something that, if not natural, could not be accomplished by most. This gift for you *is* natural, and fortunate are those who are blessed to receive your presence.

SCOTT

Our subtle one, you are not comfortable with billowing through life's situations, as you witness others doing so often. Instead, you prefer a softer approach to any interpersonal or group challenge. This is your purpose: To bring harmony to discord within your circles. You accomplish this through asking us to provide you with the words and actions to bring forth peace. Once you release your *self* from your response, your healing language will flow as easily as the stream flows over the rocks therein. And yes, your words and actions will be as healing as the sounds of the stream. Stay focused on the fact that, without the rocks, the beauty of the brook would remain; however, the rocks are what create the wonderment of the peacefulness felt by sitting beside it ... a tributary to larger bodies of flow. We repeat, stay focused on the stream, on the quietness, the subtle strength ... the tranquility. The rivers and oceans depend on this.

SEAN / SHAWN

Urgency. You have learned how to put back a sense of urgency in favor of level-headed approaches to all matters, from household chores to finding enlightenment. You know that enlightenment arises from the lack of urgency to find it, and to simply allow the unfolding of your connection to the All That Is ... to the Divine. We have graced you with patience and, in turn, you have prevented others, with your calm demeanor, from experiencing the angst of impatience. In order to help you quickly revert back from episodes of urgency, we bring you the essence of Amber to ground you and to prevent you from falsely giving up your personal will. You are here to reflect the tranquility that comes from removing urgency about life's matters and to be an example of the peacefulness of flow.

SELENA

Like a chunk of butter in the warm sun, you melt hearts with your rays of light. You shine forth tenderness with sunbeams that promote growth and awareness of the benefits from allowing the light in. You then provide rain showers for additional growth. It is your purpose to reveal the substance necessary for self-love and self-actualization. Unlike hot and cold, this substance is gentle, yet paradoxical, with the warmth of sun and coolness of raindrops. You are a healer of the heart and teach that growth is possible without harshness. This is indeed something that, if not natural, could not be accomplished by most. This gift for you *is* natural, and fortunate are those who are blessed to receive your presence.

SERENA

Like a chunk of butter in the warm sun, you melt hearts with your rays of light. You shine forth tenderness with sunbeams that promote growth and awareness of the benefits from allowing the light in. You then provide rain showers for additional growth. It is your purpose to reveal the substance necessary for self-love and self-actualization. Unlike hot and cold, this substance is gentle, yet paradoxical, with the warmth of sun and coolness of raindrops. You are a healer of the heart and teach that growth is possible without harshness. This is indeed something that, if not natural, could not be accomplished by most. This gift for you *is* natural, and fortunate are those who are blessed to receive your presence.

SETH

The albatross you feel you carry is for a noble reason; however, you need not feel this weight. Align yourself with angelic lightness, and this burden you have taken on will feel feathery. Release the serious nature you may have attached to your purpose of lifting the lost from their self-created despair. Acknowledge the valuable direction and tenderness you willingly give. Treat your purpose as a welcomed spiritual gift and enjoy the manifestations of healing the darkened hearts that need your light. Once you do this, we will be much more able to help you soar with no feelings of heavy Earth angel wings. Being willing is the secret that you need to make this happen.

SHANE

Urgency. You have learned how to put back a sense of urgency in favor of level-headed approaches to all matters, from household chores to finding enlightenment. You know that enlightenment arises from the lack of urgency to find it, and to simply allow the unfolding of your connection to the All That Is ... to the Divine. We have graced you with patience and, in turn, you have prevented others, with your calm demeanor, from experiencing the angst of impatience. In order to help you quickly revert back from episodes of urgency, we bring you the essence of Amber to ground you and to prevent you from falsely giving up your personal will. You are here to reflect the tranquility that comes from removing urgency about life's matters and to be an example of the peacefulness of flow.

SHANNON

You are the colorful hot air balloon that helps people realize they can rise to new heights, and have an adventure in doing so. You provide the moral support and the feeling of safety as they lift off, trusting the process while they learn the ropes, so to speak. Who says it's a self-defeating mindset to have one's head in the clouds? Not according to you. Liftoff is not only possible, but exhilarating and productive. You are the epitome of rising above and breaking through the paradigm of limited goals. Fortunate are those who have the presence of mind and the fortitude to follow your lead.

SHARON

Your Life as Sharon is about strength. Strength of character, body, spirit, and mind. Some may perceive you as having a strong will ... which *is* true ... and that you are concerned with power and control ... which is *not* true. Know this, and do not pay heed to those who will say such things. Instead, let their words and thoughts blow away with the wind ... the same wind that ushers in yet more strength to you. It is a gentle strength which, at times, needs to appear as iron. This is so, because in this manner, when necessary, it assists you in achieving your work here ... to be a role model for strength. And yes, we are forever assisting you. Know that your mission will be accomplished and that there is no need to alter your strength. It is exactly as it needs to be. You are *in* love, dear Sharon, and this is all that matters now, then, and beyond. We Bless You.

SHAWN / SEAN

Urgency. You have learned how to put back a sense of urgency in favor of level-headed approaches to all matters, from household chores to finding enlightenment. You know that enlightenment arises from the lack of urgency to find it, and to simply allow the unfolding of your connection to the All That Is ... to the Divine. We have graced you with patience and, in turn, you have prevented others, with your calm demeanor, from experiencing the angst of impatience. In order to help you quickly revert back from episodes of urgency, we bring you the essence of Amber to ground you and to prevent you from falsely giving up your personal will. You are here to reflect the tranquility that comes from removing urgency about life's matters and to be an example of the peacefulness of flow.

SHAUNA / SHAWNA

Urgency. You have learned how to put back a sense of urgency in favor of level-headed approaches to all matters, from household chores to finding enlightenment. You know that enlightenment arises from the lack of urgency to find it, and to simply allow the unfolding of your connection to the All That Is ... to the Divine. We have graced you with patience and, in turn, you have prevented others, with your calm demeanor, from experiencing the angst of impatience. In order to help you quickly revert back from episodes of urgency, we bring you the essence of Amber to ground you and to prevent you from falsely giving up your personal will. You are here to reflect the tranquility that comes from removing urgency about life's matters and to be an example of the peacefulness of flow.

SHEILA / SHELIA

Lo and behold, our Sun-ray, you are basking in our light and in the success of your individuality. The reflection you shed on others of independence, inner strength, and striving for personal best is welcomed, as like the warmth of the midday sun. Your purpose is to show others their best reflection. Your lesson is to be grounded and stable with your uniqueness. You have had many moments of self-doubt. We want to remind you that you need not spend much time in that mindset. We will always lead you away from that and into the magnificent.

SHELBY

Sober as you may appear at times, you do have a sense of humor that lifts people and situations out of their doldrums. More than this, when you instinctively know that your lighthearted approach is needed, you bring resolution to conflicts more easily than had you not been present. Your natural ability to use humor without being offensive ... and to apply your words to be relevant to the situation ... is indeed a gift. Your purpose is to use this gift when you have a knowing that through your happy, diplomatic approach, peaceful outcomes will be realized. In turn, you will have great joy in knowing that you have made a difference that many could not have accomplished alone.

SHELLEY / SHELLY

For each and every detrimental experience, we give you at least three positive experiences. And this is as it should be. Some would say that for proper balance, there would be one for one. We say *not* ... as with so many, including you, it takes much to overcome the unpleasant occurrences. The troubling events, people, and circumstances take a toll on your consciousness for you in human form. We elevate your spiritual connection by augmenting all of your uplifting moments ... some moments which last for an extended period of time throughout your life here on this planet. We simply ask that you allow us to expand the positive—the light—and bathe in the moments of wonder, of calm, of nurturing, of exhilaration. We also ask that you share these uplifting areas of consciousness by focusing on that feeling you have when all things wonderful are embraced. This will in turn deflect any darkness, yet will assist in maintaining the balance we all need in order to understand the ebb and flow of worldly existence. Never fear—we have your back, literally. We stand behind you in all difficult moments and beside you, always. You will know we are there when you take pause to feel the warmth of the golden light with which we surround you. We send you the energy of a thousand gentle sunrises for you to maintain your warmth and to always be aware of the positive flow. Yes, balance is achieved by accentuating the positive!

SHERRY

A Blast from the Past. All the things taught by those who are wise about not holding on to the past—they are correct. You possess the ability ... which so many do not ... to glean happy thoughts and memories, and to hold the lessons—both good and not-so-good—in your soul. You can visit the past briefly and move on without interrupting your present moment. You are also gifted at creating good memories for yourself and your loved ones ... memories which bring joy to the moment being experienced. Congratulations on being so adept with this purpose.

SHERYL

A Blast from the Past. All the things taught by those who are wise about not holding on to the past—they are correct. You possess the ability...which so many do not...to glean happy thoughts and memories, and to hold the lessons—both good and not-so-good—in your soul. You can visit the past briefly and move on without interrupting your present moment. You are also gifted at creating good memories for yourself and your loved ones ... memories which bring joy to the moment being experienced. Congratulations on being so adept with this purpose.

SHIRLEY

Like a loaf of freshly-baked bread, you draw family, friends, and other visitors to your welcoming, cozy home and remind them of the nurturing they crave through connection with the home base. Star light, star bright, all's well and good tonight ... this is the peaceful countenance you exude. You will always be surrounded with people who gravitate toward and embrace the energy of a home with the welcome mat always available. This Earth on which you live is in grave need of wholesome connections. Thank you for serving this purpose.

SONIA / SONYA

Tell us, how do you maintain your calm demeanor? This is something you may hear often on this life path of yours. We help you with your chosen ability to be the one who prevents chaos, or decreases it. Your purpose is valuable in a world so engulfed by stress, anger, and greed. Any time others can feel less of the worldly woes and angst is one step toward their peace. Thank you for this indirect and subtle influence which reduces the volume of disagreements, tension, and rage. You may not see the value in your part, but you are a giant diamond in the rough. Keep glistening.

SOPHIA

Stately you are at times. At other times, you are a roll-up-your-sleeves-and-get-your-hands-dirty kind of girl. Your lesson is to understand that there is no delineation between those born with the proverbial silver spoon and those born to humble, plebeianistic circumstances. You are learning this equality-consciousness role well, which is critical for the Earth. It may still take a long while before you realize this lesson, and you are among those who *have* been, are *now*, and *will be* establishing the mentality of fairness for all. Keep up the dichotomy of your appearance; for in the world's recognition of contrast will come acceptance that all are significant and essential.

SOPHIE

You are like colorful thread, delicately weaving strong connections between people. We call you The Networker. You easily see which strengths and challenges can be balanced by linking them together. Also, merging strengths with strengths multiply successful outcomes, and you match these up as well. Some may say you should be in marketing or human resources. We say to you: Follow whatever interests you have that will fuel the fire in your heart. You will recognize those who will offer mutual enhancement, and you will always be a weaver of coordination between those who need reinforcement.

STACEY / STACY

"Who goes there? Is it you?" Or is it a masquerade? We see that you do not like the necessity of donning masks to fit the occasion. This is a discomfort that you must experience in order to step into your purpose here as effectively as possible. You have known the discomfort of conforming at all costs, and because of this, you will now be able to achieve authenticity with the same level of comfort as the discomfort you have felt. This is your lesson: To be comfortable with who you are, with no apologies and no regrets. We are well aware of how difficult it is to maintain a genuine persona in the midst of all this worldly activity. Be assured that we will reinforce you with the courage needed to follow your true nature. You will learn this lesson in order to fulfill your purpose, which is to be a mirror of authenticity to others. Thus, they will want to emanate a true reflection of themselves. We remind you: We give you the needed strength to accomplish this, and we celebrate with you the glorious freedom of its result.

STAN / STANLEY

"Hey there!" That's what we feel when we think of you and when we see you, because it is the same reaction of others when they see you. You are so approachable; others are always happy to see you and are uplifted by your mere presence. Never doubt your positive effect on others. We know you often do have this doubt, but be assured you have invisible amber light around you that makes people happy. They are unaware of your light, yet it certainly has an uplifting effect. Also, do not concern yourself with meeting this purpose ... don't worry that it may deplete your energy. It will not. It never has, lifetime after lifetime. Yes, you have an eternal purpose of lifting others' spirits. We give you the energy of Carnelian and of Gold Calcite. Carry these stones if you wish, but we are surrounding you with these energies, with their radiance, and with our happiness. Thank you, dear Stanley; we are smiling.

STELLA

Our Stella, you are like a velvet chain—you have the ability to raise a family and correct your children with soft sternness. This ability is difficult for other parents to achieve, but you arrived here with the sole purpose of turning negative behavior into acceptable behavior without severity. This also applies to other individuals with whom you communicate throughout this lifetime ... especially those in your family and others with whom you have frequent contact. You are the Gentle Teacher of your inner circle.

STEPHANIE

Coal mines are fiery and treacherous. We ask you to avoid placing yourself in positions where discomfort and jeopardy exist. Your lesson here is to realize the simplicities of life. You may have a tendency to make mountains from molehills, as is the common expression. There are safe and secure paths to realize goals without entering or walking through dangerous mines. We are not saying there exist no challenges or degrees of difficulty; those are a part of evolving and becoming. We are stressing that we wish you to approach life step-by-step rather than jumping into the fire. We are here to protect you and nudge you with the wisdom of minimalism.

STEPHEN / STEVEN

Top it off, Stephen / Steven. You have a knack at topping things off for yourself, for your family events, for work ... for just about any of your endeavors. You even have a reputation of topping things off for friends and colleagues. That extra touch, that extra whipped cream with a cherry on top—it is what you do in life. You put the added touch that makes a positive and uplifting difference. Because of you, those around you can learn how positive the results can be by topping things off with the extra touch. Yes, going the extra mile, as is the saying, is your forte. Cherish it—you are among the few. We honor you.

STEVE

Top it off, Steve. You have a knack at topping things off for yourself, for your family events, for work … for just about any of your endeavors. You even have a reputation of topping things off for friends and colleagues. That extra touch, that extra whipped cream with a cherry on top—it is what you do in life. You put the added touch that makes a positive and uplifting difference. Because of you, those around you can learn how positive the results can be by topping things off with the extra touch. Yes, going the extra mile, as is the saying, is your forte. Cherish it—you are among the few. We honor you.

STEWART / STUART

Wind chimes and windmills, bringing forth music from seemingly nowhere, and energy from the same source. You are seen to be mysterious in the ways which you bring both melody and power. You do so in everyday, personal interactions as well as your profession. It is because you arrived here with this gift to share. At times we know you will feel lacking in the source of your melodic yet powerful mannerisms. We recognize this and allow you time to rest from your ultimate purpose of bringing your gift to the Earth plane. Never dwell on your ability to continue with your "personality," as it is called here.

You have an endless supply of the mysterious, unknown force behind the gentle, windchime-like song and the strong, windmill-like energy. We honor you for choosing this ability. We will always soothe you when needed. Lullabies from us are always only a prayer away for you.

STU

Wind chimes and windmills, bringing forth music from seemingly nowhere, and energy from the same source. You are seen to be mysterious in the ways which you bring both melody and power. You do so in everyday, personal interactions as well as your profession. It is because you arrived here with this gift to share. At times we know you will feel lacking in the source of your melodic yet powerful mannerisms. We recognize this and allow you time to rest from your ultimate purpose of bringing your gift to the Earth plane. Never dwell on your ability to continue with your "personality," as it is called here.

You have an endless supply of the mysterious, unknown force behind the gentle, windchime-like song and the strong, windmill-like energy. We honor you for choosing this ability. We will always soothe you when needed. Lullabies from us are always only a prayer away for you.

SUE

Juice it up! You are the resourceful and appreciative one. Rather than simply garnishing with beauty, such as a lime or lemon slice attached to a glass, you squeeze the juice into the glass. Yes! Is not the content improved by adding the flavor of the juice? Of course it is; and you realize this fact. Show and savor all of the fruits of life, not just the appearances. Such an example you are, and in this regard you are serving your purpose.

Experience the whole. "Oooo" and "ahhh" at the aesthetics, and also appreciate the nuts and bolts that make the piece of furniture useful and beautiful. Enjoy the orange, and drink the juice which remains. Behold the art, and be attentive to the nuances of the work. Celebrate the music; use it to sing and dance. Notice its rhythm and each instrument. What you illustrate is the opposite of greed. You reflect a zest for total experience versus a pleasant glance, taste, or dance step. You, with your deep gratitude for all aspects of the gifts the universe brings, will influence others to reach a new level of appreciation, thus embracing life to a fuller extent.

SUMMER

You are so personable and kind that some may want to name their pets or children after you. Oh, did we also mention that you are a loyal friend? Your treasure lies in the self-fulfillment of your role, which is to bring smiles and comfort as often as possible. Merry you are, and just as attentive. You can be as a court jester one moment and a caring giver the next. This role can be tiring, as you may feel the expectations from others to always be performing in order to uphold and uplift. We ask that you retreat for respite often. This will be necessary for you. Your lesson for this life is directly related to your role: To know when to experience your own joy and when to provide self-care and serene respite. We send you our songs of merriment and our melodies of peacefulness with divine timing. Lean on us to always know how to balance your energy.

SUSAN

Soft curtains of flowing rainbow beams showering around you make life colorful, brilliant, and overwhelmingly beautiful for you. Like a waterfall reflecting prisms from the sun's kisses, we help you see, experience, and deeply appreciate the power of love and the exciting carousel of life. Your delight with the simplest to the most complex things is contagious and helps those around you to notice and appreciate the glory of the All That Is, if they choose to see. You are fulfilling your purpose of beholding all.

The splendor and the abundant elation is ever present through us, even if on uncommon occasion you close your eyes and become blind to it. We will pour over you the delicate, warm, and reflective rainbow of unbridled love for it all when you ask.

SUSANNE

Soft curtains of flowing rainbow beams showering around you make life colorful, brilliant, and overwhelmingly beautiful for you. Like a waterfall reflecting prisms from the sun's kisses, we help you see, experience, and deeply appreciate the power of love and the exciting carousel of life. Your delight with the simplest to the most complex things is contagious and helps those around you to notice and appreciate the glory of the All That Is, if they choose to see. You are fulfilling your purpose of beholding all.

The splendor and the abundant elation is ever present through us, even if on uncommon occasion you close your eyes and become blind to it. We will pour over you the delicate, warm, and reflective rainbow of unbridled love for it all when you ask.

SUSIE

Find the golden morsels in everyday life. Avoid the tendency to look above or below the daily golden nuggets. They're all around you, each and every day. Avoid the tendency to get stuck in worry and fear. You do have the tendency to mull over things that don't really matter in the big picture. Do what you must; do not fret over it, and please do look for those morsels of wonder. They're all around you. Every day you will see them, and you may need to be more alert. Increase your awareness; that's why you came here ... to increase your awareness of the wonder and the glory and the miracles that are all around you, constantly. You will learn this lesson during your current lifetime. When you do, you will be able to share with others who are unable to see. You will be able to help them open their eyes and awaken to those morsels that are all around them, all the time, every day. They will thank you for the examples you set ... for the little things you say to them that help them awaken and see the glory, and to see that they do not have to fret needlessly. They do not have to dwell on what appear to be problems that are in the long run unimportant. They will see the importance of their day-to-day life being equally important as the grand picture of their life. You will teach them to take each moment and make it glorious in some way.

We thank you for taking on this seemingly heavy duty, and remind you that you have chosen this, and you will rise above your mulling. You will rise above it, and you will be so filled ... so filled with laughter and smiles. We give you clear

Quartz crystal to enhance every positive thought and observation. You are programmed to not increase negative thoughts and observations. They will not be enhanced ... only the positive will be augmented. We also give you Gold Quartz to enhance your happiness and your self-confidence. Go now, do your job; you chose it. You have all the capabilities to see, to feel, and to hear the glorious.

SUZANNE

Trip the light fantastic! *Easy does it* is your motto. You go about this life on Earth in a confident manner with the innate knowledge that worry is counterproductive, and you know how to incorporate fun into your job. You delight in all you do, as you find purpose and excitement in all your endeavors. Starlight and fireflies are magic to your eyes, and you in turn reflect light amid darkness for others to see. You can lead the way because your 'light' attitude negates worry about outcomes. Stay amazed with this life. It is your destiny to be shining with happiness.

SUZY / SUZIE

Find the golden morsels in everyday life. Avoid the tendency to look above or below the daily golden nuggets. They're all around you, each and every day. Avoid the tendency to get stuck in worry and fear. You do have the tendency to mull over things that don't really matter in the big picture. Do what you must; do not fret over it, and please do look for those morsels of wonder. They're all around you. Every day you will see them, and you may need to be more alert. Increase your awareness; that's why you came here ... to increase your awareness of the wonder and the glory and the miracles that are all around you, constantly. You will learn this lesson during your current lifetime. When you do, you will be able to share with others who are unable to see. You will be able to help them open their eyes and awaken to those morsels that are all around them, all the time, every day. They will thank you for the examples you set ... for the little things you say to them that help them awaken and see the glory, and to see that they do not have to fret needlessly. They do not have to dwell on what appear to be problems that are in the long run unimportant. They will see the importance of their day-to-day life being equally important as the grand picture of their life. You will teach them to take each moment and make it glorious in some way.

We thank you for taking on this seemingly heavy duty, and remind you that you have chosen this, and you will rise above your mulling. You will rise above it, and you will be so filled ... so filled with laughter and smiles. We give you Clear Quartz crystal to enhance every positive thought and observation. You are programmed to not increase negative thoughts and observations. They will not be enhanced ... only the positive will be augmented. We also give you Gold Quartz to enhance your happiness and your self-confidence. Go now, do your job; you chose it. You have all the capabilities to see, to feel, and to hear the glorious.

SYBIL

"All's well that ends well." This is, or could be, your motto. You are focused on the end result. No matter what happens between point A and point Z, your ultimate goal is to bring the objective to fruition. The world needs you, as you are the one who gets things done, who achieves the task at hand and the projects which may take a while. You are the glue that holds together what may, at times, seem to be intricacies. You are a leader who takes on your role with pleasure. Your example is seen by others and acted upon, although you may not realize this.

We are grateful that you have come here to be such a helper, a valued facilitator. Your rewards are great, as they are received by realizing your intended results. We honor you always and provide you the fortitude to continue your focus on good and beneficial endings to all you do here on Earth.

TABITHA

Sometimes the dice just do not fall in place. Keep tossing the dice, anyway. Your lesson is to realize that risks are necessary in this particular world in which you find yourself. You simply cannot turn away just because some throws of the dice are scattered and do not yield the desired results. Your highest and best good is achieved through perseverance and the belief that, with effort and continued visualization, the dice will fall to serve your purpose. Life is not a game; it is a learning journey that has peaks and valleys. Behold all of it, for without both, it is simply monotone. Accomplishments are not realized through playing one note or rolling the same dice. Practice the whole scale and have scores of dice in your pocket. You will learn the excitement that comes from uncertainty combined with persistence.

TAMARA

Slow burn. Don't let this misconception alter your path. You are not a victim of a slow burn. You are not a victim at all. Your graciousness may, at times, result in unappreciative opportunists gravitating toward you. However, this is in no way a detriment to your pure and light-filled soul. Continue always on your path of service. You have the ability to discern how to veer away from the misled, and therefore you will not *be* misled. Teaching others the importance of discernment, and how to listen to their heart, is your purpose. We exalt you for your pure heart and your authentic desire to share your time and your gifts to benefit where they may.

TAMI / TAMMI / TAMMIE / TAMMY

Whether you are deemed right or whether you are deemed wrong in any circumstance at any time, you have the confidence and inner knowledge of the correct answers and courses of action. You, we call the personification of confidence. You were sent here to exemplify the expression of holding one's own—not in an obstinate manner, rather in an educational manner for those who *tend to* allow their own thoughts, beliefs, and actions to be influenced ... or worse ... to be *made* by others. We have given you owl energy to represent all knowing (when knowing is necessary), along with the humility to ask questions when needed, which will further your ability to make sound conclusions. Use it wisely, our confident one.

TANYA / TONIA

Slow burn. Don't let this misconception alter your path. You are not a victim of a slow burn. You are not a victim at all. Your graciousness may, at times, result in unappreciative opportunists gravitating toward you. However, this is in no way a detriment to your pure and light-filled soul. Continue always on your path of service. You have the ability to discern how to veer away from the misled, and therefore you will not *be* misled. Teaching others the importance of discernment, and how to listen to their heart, is your purpose. We exalt you for your pure heart and your authentic desire to share your time and your gifts to benefit where they may.

TARA

Slow burn. Don't let this misconception alter your path. You are not a victim of a slow burn. You are not a victim at all. Your graciousness may, at times, result in unappreciative opportunists gravitating toward you. However, this is in no way a detriment to your pure and light-filled soul. Continue always on your path of service. You have the ability to discern how to veer away from the misled, and therefore you will not *be* misled. Teaching others the importance of discernment, and how to listen to their heart, is your purpose. We exalt you for your pure heart and your authentic desire to share your time and your gifts to benefit where they may.

TASHA

Wind chimes and windmills, bringing forth music from seemingly nowhere, and energy from the same source. You are seen to be mysterious in the ways which you bring both melody and power. You do so in everyday, personal interactions as well as your profession. It is because you arrived here with this gift to share. At times we know you will feel lacking in the source of your melodic yet powerful mannerisms. We recognize this and allow you time to rest from your ultimate purpose of bringing your gift to the Earth plane. Never dwell on your ability to continue with your "personality," as it is called here.

You have an endless supply of the mysterious, unknown force behind the gentle, windchime-like song and the strong, windmill-like energy. We honor you for choosing this ability. We will always soothe you when needed. Lullabies from us are always only a prayer away for you.

TAYLOR

No matter how far you are stretched, your elasticity prevents you from breaking. Your resilience is your greatest strength, as you have endured immense "pulling" without changing the essence of your being. You arrived with an understanding that you will need to be bent and shaped throughout this lifetime in order to become the individual you chose to be on this plane. You also have an awareness that, despite the degree of tension, and despite the outward changes, you will always return to your core self. Transformation will occur, and you will serve your chosen role of demonstrating purposeful change while remaining true to your genuine, inner spirit.

TED

"Get a grip." This is a slogan for you, yet not *about* you, as you already are solid. You help others to realize they must 'get a grip' and you do so in such a way that it is firm yet not offensive ... nurturing, yet not too tender. Incarnates of this world need souls like yours to help them realize that they need not swim in their muddy water, rather they can create their own life jacket, grip their buoy, and swim rather than sink. Be careful not to become their buoy. They need their own.

TERESA / THERESA

Surely, you say, *"There must be something good for me."* Lassie, there *is* and always *has* been. You can build boulders larger than those that seem to block you. You can traverse rugged paths and clear the way toward progress, paving golden roads for easy ingress to fortunes of love, well-being, and peacefulness. Ah, yes, our road paver ... yes, there indeed is something good for you and for all with whom you share the secrets of clearing and paving a path of abundance at all levels. The *good* that comes to you is through your very purpose of clearing rubble and making room for enlightenment. The results manifest in the higher energetic frequencies that you came here to experience and to share. You arrived here having learned the lesson of *how to* fulfill this purpose. Continue to move as you feel directed by us, and we will, of course, direct you on every path.

TERI / TERRI / TERRY

You are able to speak your truth and you care not about the popularity of your truth. Although you enjoy attention and love to feel valued, you do not feel the need to grandstand. Others see you as highly self-assured whether you truly feel poised or not. Take this as a great step toward the lessons you chose to learn and abilities you chose to embrace this time on Earth.

Because of your lack of fear in expressing your thoughts and feelings, a major objective of your present journey has been met, and you are now finally able to check this particular lesson off your list. This major accomplishment will serve you in attaining your other goals this lifetime and those to come, one of which is to truly have self-love and sureness.

TESS / TESSA

You are stronger than you think. Your lesson is to eliminate self-degradation. We are sad that you hold back so much and find it difficult to show your feelings. We see your exterior strength masking your secret, inner feelings of weakness. We will help you embrace the authentic strength that you are. Just ask, and we will assist you to become what others already believe you to be. It will not be as difficult as you think. We are holding you up, always. You are destined to exude confident humility, which is seen in visionaries. Yes, it is your purpose and you are destined to set this example to others, who do not recognize their own value.

THOMAS / TOM

You function at a high vibration. You constantly are raising your vibration and show up to help others, which is your purpose. You are as an Earth angel placed where you are needed at the precise time when you can assist those needing rescue. We help elevate you to the energy vibrations you need in order to respond to those in distress, wherever they may be and whatever their need may be. We behold you for your willingness to serve through your energy, perceptions, and responses. Know that you are supported by us with your every endeavor and loved by us in every moment of time.

TIFFANY

Screaming is never necessary, and you know this truth more deeply than most. You were sent here, our soft-spoken one, to exemplify the positive outcomes brought forth from speaking without callousness or loudness. You are called upon to grace meetings of many sorts, difficult discussions, and yes, even disagreements. Your calm approach will bring an even temperament to whomever and whatever is necessary in order to achieve peaceful outcomes. Tarry not when you see or hear that your neutral and non-intimidating touch is needed. An entry will be made for you to interject peaceful contributions, and your lesson is to learn to recognize when to enter. Thank you for bringing diplomacy to gentle heights.

TIM / TIMMY / TIMOTHY

You are able to speak your truth and you care not about the popularity of your truth. Although you enjoy attention and love to feel valued, you do not feel the need to grandstand. Others see you as highly self-assured whether you truly feel poised or not. Take this as a great step toward the lessons you chose to learn and abilities you chose to embrace this time on Earth.

Because of your lack of fear in expressing your thoughts and feelings, a major objective of your present journey has been met, and you are now finally able to check this particular lesson off your list. This major accomplishment will serve you in attaining your other goals this lifetime and those to come, one of which is to truly have self-love and sureness.

TINA

Diamonds in the sand. Yes, your lesson during this lifetime is to not only realize that there are diamonds among the trillions of grains of sand ... you will learn to recognize those sparkling individuals who are precious, yet possess an indestructible spirit. Your purpose is to bring to attention their worth and help them to shine, as only they can. There are an endless number of diamonds in the sand, and most are unaware of their value. They are easily found. In fact, all grains are gleaming gems. However, some are just not ready to glisten with impenetrable endurance. They are here to learn different lessons. You are one such diamond who is aware of your value, and you will recognize those who are unaware or feel cracked. They are not marred, and you will know exactly how to transform their inferior self-image to that of gleaming intention for the benefit of the planet. We will help transport you to the many beaches where these dear jewels are waiting to be discovered.

TOBY

Outgoing people are needed; they are sought after; they are appreciated. You are one who brings these desired energies. You are depended upon to be the catalyst of optimism and the creator of positive atmospheres. More so, you enjoy this role and share your large personality freely. We do know that you cannot possibly be on key continuously. Therefore, we provide you with solace when you need to escape from this demanding role, even though you feel driven to be the joy bringer. At times you will feel the need for a weekend in the middle of the week. We understand the vast amount of energy used to create happy environments. We surround you with the color blue to remain calm and to restore your vitality. We also give you the energy of Celestite to reinforce you. Thank you for choosing such a role to uplift those around you.

TODD

Run, run, run. That's what you want to do and what it seems to you that you are usually doing. Please do not feel frustrated with this. You are made to run at all facets of your being and to withstand *running*. Of course, this is not in the literal sense of the word, rather it means that you are able to continue going, working, playing, thinking—DOING—more than most, and more than you think you want to or need to do. This strength will serve a purpose, as you are able to continue with what is necessary when the stamina of others has been depleted. Do not resist this; endurance is your greatest strength. Take care, however, to center. This is your life lesson. Enjoy the benefit—the strong suit—of endurance. We ask you to also take time to learn the lesson of becoming centered. This is your key. Seek out the teacher for this; we will guide you there.

There is another group of Todds, and the message is as follows:

"Have mercy!" Ah, our giver of kindness, our Todd, you are so generous with understanding and forgiveness. This is your purpose: To allow others to experience the freedom that "mercy" provides them. This is not to say that it is okay, or that you give the message that it's okay for wrongdoing. It is to say that poor choices happen, and one need not feel self-guilt or respond sadly to the criticism of others. You are here to help others realize that all do have human experiences and that this is all part of their individual lessons that they came to learn. In learning the lessons, they progress on their journey. Thank you for this enlightenment you bring to so many who may have felt guilty or discouraged along the way.

TOMMY

So be it. You have the ability to speak the final word, to be looked on as a person of authority. The buck often stops with you. Your gregariousness makes you stand out and helps others accept your role. Yes, you are often in charge, and you are chosen for this, as many roles are needed in this world. We have given you the friendliness and fortitude to carry out this role of an overseer without off-putting anyone you oversee or supervise. You are a benevolent delegator, and this role is not chosen by many. You will never fail to be a fair leader as long as you ask us to be your co-workers! We want you to know this holds true, too, for your family roles.

TONI

Shhh. Listen. You have so much to say, and others do listen to you. You provide counsel well, with valuable insight and information to many in need who may otherwise have gone without assistance. Although your destiny is being fulfilled in this manner, we need to remind you to listen. You can be your own counsel often ... if you take your wisdom within. We, of course, are always here to guide you if you ask.

Truths can fall silently. Within that silence is the depth of your lessons. Go within, with the shadows of the silence that follow you. It is there where your inner wisdom will mingle with the silence—and the answers you seek will be clear as they make their way to the light between the shadows. This light represents you and your helpfulness to others who turn to you. We thank you for being this welcomed light, and you will remain so as long as you take the time to listen.

TONY

So be it. You have the ability to speak the final word, to be looked on as a person of authority. The buck often stops with you. Your gregariousness makes you stand out and helps others accept your role. Yes, you are often in charge, and you are chosen for this, as many roles are needed in this world. We have given you the friendliness and fortitude to carry out this role of an overseer without off-putting anyone you oversee or supervise. You are a benevolent delegator, and this role is not chosen by many. You will never fail to be a fair leader as long as you ask us to be your co-workers! We want you to know this holds true, too, for your family roles.

TORI

Diamonds in the sand. Yes, your lesson during this lifetime is to not only realize that there are diamonds among the trillions of grains of sand ... you will learn to recognize those sparkling individuals who are precious, yet possess an indestructible spirit. Your purpose is to bring to attention their worth and help them to shine, as only they can. There are an endless number of diamonds in the sand, and most are unaware of their value. They are easily found. In fact, all grains are gleaming gems. However, some are just not ready to glisten with impenetrable endurance. They are here to learn different lessons. You are one such diamond who is aware of your value, and you will recognize those who are unaware or feel cracked. They are not marred, and you will know exactly how to transform their inferior self-image to that of gleaming intention for the benefit of the planet. We will help transport you to the many beaches where these dear jewels are waiting to be discovered.

TRACIE / TRACY

"Who goes there? Is it you?" Or is it a masquerade? We see that you do not like the necessity of donning masks to fit the occasion. This is a discomfort that you must experience in order to step into your purpose here as effectively as possible. You have known the discomfort of conforming at all costs, and because of this, you will now be able to achieve authenticity with the same level of comfort as the discomfort you have felt. This is your lesson: To be comfortable with who you are, with no apologies and no regrets. We are well aware of how difficult it is to maintain a genuine persona in the midst of all this worldly activity. Be assured that we will

reinforce you with the courage needed to follow your true nature. You will learn this lesson in order to fulfill your purpose, which is to be a mirror of authenticity to others. Thus, they will want to emanate a true reflection of themselves. We remind you: We give you the needed strength to accomplish this, and we celebrate with you the glorious freedom of its result.

TRAVIS

Scoop up the dessert, our giver of enjoyable delights! You are here for the purpose of adding sweetness and pleasure to all walks of life—at home, at work, at play, at social gatherings—and to those of all ages. Do not worry that your talent will wane or that you will tire from this role, as it is not something constant which you do. However, it is welcomed and remembered when you DO deliver. This Earth truly needs dessert-of-life servers such as you. We send you ribbons of orange light to sustain your own happiness and as a token of our thanks. Enjoy yourself, too!

TRENT

Sometimes the dice just do not fall in place. Keep tossing the dice, anyway. Your lesson is to realize that risks are necessary in this particular world in which you find yourself. You simply cannot turn away just because one throw of the dice is scattered and without the desired result. Your highest and best good is achieved through perseverance and the belief that, with effort and continued visualization, the dice will fall to serve your purpose. Life is not a game; it is a learning journey that has peaks and valleys. Behold all of it, for without both, it is simply monotone. Accomplishments are not realized through playing one note or rolling the same dice. Practice the whole scale and have scores of dice in your pocket. You will learn the excitement that comes from uncertainty combined with persistence.

TRINA

Chirp chirp. The challenge you feel is that you want to progress from chirping to singing. You sense a greater purpose, as you feel you may have arrived here to perform mundane tasks and to live an ordinary life. We say to you: Yes, you certainly can advance beyond your "lot in life" because you also came here to learn how to overcome any feelings of insignificance. Common tasks and a common life are merely relative, based on your own perception. Are you a laborer? Jesus was a carpenter of higher consciousness and a great teacher. Are you a servant? Think of all those who serve for a higher purpose, no matter what their label may be. Are you a white collar professional? Think of all the good you're in a position to manifest. You see, it does not matter what you do to earn provision. It is your perception of what your heart can create. We see and hear your song, and it is beautiful. Go forth and continue singing.

TRISH / TRISHA

You came to Earth to spread your sweetness, because you knew that this special type of kindness is so needed by its inhabitants. You have no expectations of others, and you generously provide a light, exultant touch to all. It is your nature; you don't even have to give it a thought to emanate sweetness. We also call you *Flower* because of the beauty of your presence everywhere you go. And unlike a flower, your essence does not fade away; it stays alive. You are a flower which does not wilt and brings serenity when needed. We will send increased energy to your heart center when an individual or situation is in need of this serenity. You will feel a deep tranquility sinking into and then springing from your heart ... that placidity will in turn soothe others' hearts. Thank you, our gracious flower.

TRISTA

Slow, rolling waves over motionless rocks create a contrast of strength ... strength of flow and power of stance. The waves learn that they can continue to move despite the resolute stones. The stones learn that when a position is required to maintain balance, the movement around and over them will not adversely affect them in the present moment, yet over time will create polished beauty. Your lesson is to learn how to be the wave and how to be the stone. Bring refreshing, cleansing beauty to the undaunted. Allow yourself to view threats to your convictions as an addition of peace to what must be unwavering in the now moment. You do have an understanding that, over time, the resolute may be altered or transformed by the beauty of a natural course of change. Embrace this understanding while you are being a mainstay of peaceful existence during this lifetime. We support you with the grace of Earth angels who we send to you throughout your time here.

TRISTAN / TRISTEN

Slow, rolling waves over motionless rocks create a contrast of strength ... strength of flow and power of stance. The waves learn that they can continue to move despite the resolute stones. The stones learn that when a position is required to maintain balance, the movement around and over them will not adversely affect them in the present moment, yet over time will create polished beauty. Your lesson is to learn how to be the wave and how to be the stone. Bring refreshing, cleansing beauty to the undaunted. Allow yourself to view threats to your convictions as an addition of peace to what must be unwavering in the now moment. You do have an understanding that, over time, the resolute may be altered or transformed by the beauty of a natural course of change. Embrace this understanding while you are being a mainstay of peaceful existence during this lifetime. We support you with the grace of Earth angels who we send to you throughout your time here.

TRIXIE

Bring on the confetti! You know how to celebrate. You are looked upon as the one who sees the rainbow in the storm, believes the pie in the sky can be reached, and focuses on the brilliance of stars rather than the darkness between them. You are the one who can turn what seems to be a dismal situation into a bright lesson that can have lasting, positive effects. Despite this, we know you experience doubt, and at times become weary of being the one looked to for a cheerful attitude. Of course you do. You are in human form. We have eternally surrounded you with a gleaming garland, and during these times we make it even brighter. Your role requires a great deal of energy; we assist you with this while you acknowledge the balance and move forward. Yes, we also give you space to rest so that you can regenerate. Thank you for having chosen to serve this life purpose repeatedly.

TROY

Imagine yourself in a dingy. It will carry you where you need to go without all the fancy things that others think they need to transport themselves where they want to go ... with yachts, limousines, or private jets. Shed yourself from weighty add-ons that only slow progress and place emphasis on the wrong things. In so doing you will serve as an example. You are aware that by simplifying, richness follows and values are prioritized. If you have not yet acted on this truth, do it now, for it is your lesson to understand—yes, simplify, embrace practicality and reap the rewards!

TRUDY

We liken you to a Ferris Wheel for viewing life. You bring attention to the panoramic view of the world and everyday life in general. On the seat you provide for others, they are able to see beyond the close detail. Detail is important, yes, and yet there are so many who do not look beyond their nose. The broad spectrum, the vast possibilities, the grand view is often missed. Not only do you assist in providing the big picture ... you assist in allowing others to view life at every level. As the Ferris Wheel rises to various heights, it also descends to various heights, and repeats. So it is with you and the viewing seats you provide. You allow a comprehensive exploration of life – of life's questions, of life's challenges, of life's solutions, and mostly of life's overall beauty. When looking at the grand scheme of things, the beauty and breathtaking views outweigh all else. Thank you for bringing attention to this; you are serving your purpose well.

TYLER

No matter how far you are stretched, your elasticity prevents you from breaking. Your resilience is your greatest strength, as you have endured immense "pulling" without changing the essence of your being. You arrived with an understanding that you will need to be bent and shaped throughout this lifetime in order to become the individual you chose to be on this plane. You also have an awareness that, despite the degree of tension, and despite the outward changes, you will always return to your core self. Transformation will occur, and you will serve your role of demonstrating purposeful change while remaining true to your genuine, inner spirit.

ULA

Sometimes the dice just do not fall in place. Keep tossing the dice, anyway. Your lesson is to realize that risks are necessary in this particular world in which you find yourself. You simply cannot turn away just because one throw of the dice is scattered and without the desired result. Your highest and best good is achieved through perseverance and the belief that, with effort and continued visualization, the dice will fall to serve your purpose. Life is not a game; it is a learning journey that has peaks and valleys. Behold all of it, for without both, it is simply monotone. Accomplishments are not realized through playing one note or rolling the same dice. Practice the whole scale and have scores of dice in your pocket. You will learn the excitement that comes from uncertainty combined with persistence.

ULYSSA

Slowly, we say to you ... slowly. You have a tendency to move a little too quickly through things that need more time in order to best perform the task at hand, and to more thoroughly derive joy from your work. Your lesson here is to learn to savor every action you take as though it is of importance to your soul's development of peace within yourself. This particular life lesson is learned through appreciation of your moments.

We also want you to know that "rattling the cage" gets you nowhere, plus it can agitate the very people who would love you most. Your other lesson is to find the ability to tame your restlessness, which leads to your purpose. Once achieved, you will be of great help to those who also need to be in touch with a milder approach. Call on us when you need respite from your head-on tendencies. We will bring you tolerance and comfort.

ULYSSES

Slowly, we say to you ... slowly. You have a tendency to move a little too quickly through things that need more time in order to best perform the task at hand, and to more thoroughly derive joy from your work. Your lesson here is to learn to savor every action you take as though it is of importance to your soul's development of peace within yourself. This particular life lesson is learned through appreciation of your moments.

We also want you to know that 'rattling the cage' gets you nowhere, plus it can agitate the very people who would love you most. Your other lesson is to find the ability to tame your restlessness, which leads to your purpose. Once achieved, you will be of great help to those who also need to be in touch with a milder approach. Call on us when you need respite from your head-on tendencies. We will bring you tolerance and comfort.

UMA

Striated hearts are drawn to you, as your heart is kindred to theirs. The striations have been formed throughout lifetimes of broken or interrupted relationships with loved ones. We do not speak solely of heartache from unhappy transitions. We do not speak of only romantic relationships, or betrayals, or perceived failures. We speak of scars upon the heart that have been carried forward to your kindred hearts from past lifetimes, as well as the new scars during this present time on the Earth plane. We say to you: It is your purpose, and it is vital, that you respond to those who have striated hearts. You have the healing energy to brush away the scars with your patience, unconditional love, and kindness. You can also set the example of Phoenix-like strength. These kindred hearts can only respond to one such as yours. You are their hearts' salvation as to healing from losses while understanding their loved ones can still be honored and kept sacred within. Here is the other critical part: In responding and assisting others, your own striated heart will be healed.

UMAR

Striated hearts are drawn to you, as your heart is kindred to theirs. The striations have been formed throughout lifetimes of broken or interrupted relationships with loved ones. We do not speak solely of heartache from unhappy transitions. We do not speak of only romantic relationships, or betrayals, or perceived failures. We speak of scars upon the heart that have been carried forward to your kindred hearts from past lifetimes, as well as the new scars during this present time on the Earth plane. We say to you: It is your purpose, and it is vital, that you respond to those who have striated hearts. You have the healing energy to brush away the scars with your patience, unconditional love, and kindness. You can also set the example of Phoenix-like strength. These kindred hearts can only respond to one such as yours. You are their hearts' salvation as to healing from losses while understanding their loved ones can still be honored and kept sacred within. Here is the other critical part: In responding and assisting others, your own striated heart will be healed.

UNICE / EUNICE

Like a loaf of freshly-baked bread, you draw family, friends, and other visitors to your welcoming, cozy home and remind them of the nurturing they crave through connection with the home base. Star light, star bright, all's well and good tonight … this is the peaceful countenance you exude. You will always be surrounded with people who gravitate toward and embrace the energy of a home with the welcome mat always available. This Earth on which you live is in grave need of wholesome connections. Thank you for serving this purpose.

URIAH

"Get a grip." This is a slogan for you, yet not *about* you, as you already are solid. You help others to realize they must "get a grip" and you do so in such a way that it is firm, yet not offensive ... nurturing, yet not too tender. Incarnates of this world need souls like yours to help them realize that they need not swim in their muddy water, rather they can create their own life jacket, grip their buoy, and swim rather than sink. Be careful not to become their buoy. They need their own.

URIEL

As an easy rain caresses the Earth, your gentle nature embraces all you encounter. You bring pure caring to your family, your friends, your associates, your pets, others' pets, and to the very essence of life ... to the vegetation, the animals, the sky and yes, to the Earth. Your deep appreciation and gratitude are reciprocal to the All That Is. You serve your purpose by reflecting this gratefulness. Hark, do not be dismayed when you are surrounded by what is seemingly much less than the beauty of the All That Is. Always remember that the universe will achieve balance— balance which you may not understand. And always remember that we will refresh and restore your thankfulness. We mostly want you to always remember that your special touch on all you do, say, and think will never change. You are eternally caring and will eternally bring comfort to all.

URSULA

We call you The Heart and the Moon. Both the heart and the moon emanate soft, subtle, calming energy. You are one such individual who strives to live from the heart, and you do put forth the soft energy of a peaceful evening, which brings about solace. When combined, the heart and the moon create a lullaby of nurturing, and a sense of harmony with the Earth, the stars ... the Universe itself ... the ease of harmony with the All. How precious this energy is, and it is your purpose to share it. We shower you with pastel rays so that you, too, can feel the blessing of the same energy others feel from you.

VALERIE

Do not take things personally, Valerie. Your lesson here is to accept and love yourself at a level so deep that nothing anyone can say to you will jolt your self-worth. The measure of success on this Earth is dependent on one's ability to not only dodge the swords, rather learn to remain apathetic toward them. Dismissal of any threat equates to strength. Continuing to work toward dreams heightens one's existence opposed to fighting in the trenches. This is accomplished to a large degree from the self-love of which we speak. Without self-love, there can be no complete inner peace. We wish to say to you that you will accomplish this goal, now that you understand its benefits. This is a difficult task for most, given the plague of ego-driven greed and power that is rampant on Earth. We repeat: You will achieve this state of being of self-love and inner peace. When you feel it is not possible, ask us. We will send you symbols of gold and pink. You will be free from the swords.

VANCE

Truly, truly, truly. We call you the honest one. The loyal one. You have learned that genuine commitment and truthfulness is the only way that anyone should possibly live this life. You chose to come here to withstand those who have no awareness of authenticity and to lift them above their misperceptions of how all interactions need to be approached. True passion, true work, true compassion, true love. All of these are you, and you exhibit it with all you do and all you represent. This is difficult to carry out within this society. For this reason, we lift you and your consciousness above the areas lacking light. We will always soothe you into the knowingness that you are genuine and derive joy from truth.

VANESSA

"Puttin' on the Ritz." Your role is to instill self-realization to those who have lost their self-worth, to those who never had an opportunity to develop their self-worth, and to yourself when you feel less than. By this phrase, we do not mean putting on the ritz of materialism and glamour. Rather, we mean to don your given spiritual gifts and allow those gifts to be seen ... to be admired as though they were diamonds of the soul ... and to teach those who are entrenched in materialism that the value—the gold—lies within each of us.

VICKY / VICKIE

Generosity becomes you. Together with the fun person you can be, you give free rides to many. By this, we mean that where there is a need, you approach it with an altruistic nature, with a smile, and offer a positive outlook. Some of your happy and generous actions may feel like a whirlwind ride, yet everything you do is appreciated. If you can recruit more like you, please do. Not many show up here with this purpose, however, some develop it because of the nature of their path. You, our giving one, arrived here as such. Your lesson is to learn to recognize, and accept, generosity that we send you through others.

VICTOR / VICTORIA

Imagination abounds wherever you go, because your imagination is contagious. And vivid it is ... vivid in a feasible way, and with sound possibilities. You are able to use your ideas to the fullest when and if you choose. You are equally adept at working on your endeavors alone, or sharing projects with those whom you inspire, and with those from whom you receive inspiration. Your gift is creativity from nothing. An exciting life you have through both original creativity and the promotion of others' aspirations.

VINCE / VINCENT

Truly, truly, truly. We call you the honest one. The loyal one. You have learned that genuine commitment and truthfulness is the only way that anyone should possibly live this life. You chose to come here to withstand those who have no awareness of authenticity and to lift them above their misperceptions of how all interactions need to be approached. True passion, true work, true compassion, true love. All of these are you, and you exhibit it with all you do and all you represent. This is difficult to carry out within this society. For this reason, we lift you and your consciousness above the areas lacking light. We will always soothe you into the knowingness that you are genuine and derive joy from truth.

VIRGINIA

Toe the line, Virginia. Contradictory to your seemingly rebellious nature, you are so good at this, and you are willing —unlike most. We give you the understanding of the great prophets and the strength of Samson to carry out your purpose, which is to be an example of the positive outcomes possible when following celestial guidance. We give you chariots with hundreds of horses and keen vision so that each of your quests are realized in divine order. You do what is needed at the exact time and in the precise manner needed because you listen to our guidance. Should you experience a disappointment, your depth of understanding will not allow you to falter—and you will always be able to toe the line. Your purpose is to be an example of divine result from adhering to divine guidance.

WADE

Stones will not break you—they will only help to build up your foundation and add to the solid fortress called your soul. Dismiss, then, all the rocks hurled at you as being damaging. Instead see them as building blocks to construct your true character of being the Guardian of both yourself and anyone along the way who has the need for armor to fend against the world's arrows. Your task is gallant. Your purpose is defined. You are guided and shielded as you continue to build your fortress and to house those in need of their own safe haven. Thank you for your willingness to bounce the stones away, to recognize the strength of your soul, and to share that strength when needed.

WALLACE / WALLY

Paying tribute is your forte. You see only the good in others, and if negative traits are pointed out, you simply reverse the perception by accentuating the positive. If you were a person to write reviews, all of your reports would be filled with resounding praise. There are too few of you who bring to attention the worth of others. Your purpose, then, is to light victory torches and teach the recipients to carry them proudly. They, in turn, will gift victory torches. Many will believe in themselves because of your efforts and those who you influence to do the same. Your lesson is to sacredly and silently pay tribute to *yourself* as well.

WALT / WALTER

Whatever it is, and whatever it will be that rocks your proverbial boat or upsets the proverbial apple cart, we will come to you and reassure you that all is well. We will ALWAYS speak to you … in ways you may not even notice, at times. You can, at times, be a little too vulnerable to those individuals who take advantage of your kindness and helpfulness. Although you have a tough exterior shell, your gentle inner nature is worn like a cloak, visible to everyone. You are deeply adored, respected, and appreciated by most of those who are fortunate enough to be in your energy field. We admire you, too, for continuing with this purpose of lifting others up in various ways despite those few "rotten apples" and those who would attempt to sink the boat. The most beautiful thing about your purpose, our dear altruistic one, is that those very wrongdoers learn about the blessing of giving and of honoring all. Your example teaches, without scolding or punishment, the true nature of the spirit's desire to love, give, and serve … and to do so in a non-competitive, cooperative manner. What a grand purpose you chose—to transform those who are unaware of universal love to an understanding of this deep truth. We thank you and we remind you of our eternal support.

WANDA

You have the driving force of a thousand stampeding buffalo. The excitement and charging energy you bring will surely lift the sanguine higher and the lackadaisical out of their resistance to tap in to the power you can bring to any life situation. Because of your gift, you never fear a stampede of any kind … you simply join in and divert to whatever direction needed. Not many, dear Wanda, possess this type of strength and determination. We honor you, because you perform in your stampeding manner with sincerity and with gentleness in your heart. Your objective is for the good of all. Your lesson is to know when to divert a stampeding herd, and when to let the herd run its course.

WAYNE

It's a tossup! That's what you find yourself often thinking. Should I choose this or that? Should I go here or there? Should I do this or that? You frequently feel, according the saying, "It's six of one and a half dozen of the other." Your lesson for this lifetime, then, is decisiveness. You have diverse interests, diverse abilities, and a zest for life. This is why you have such a difficult time deciding your direction. We want you to know that we will assist you when it is important to choose the path which will contribute to your purpose. You are here to not only be a contagious factor with your enjoyment of living; you are also here to help others discover their greatest gifts and to serve their own purpose with absolute joy. When others observe your activities with interests, leisure time, and following your calling, it will become apparent that a calling is ultimately blissful.

WENDY

Stirrings of the past need not haunt you. The wistfulness of your name need not dictate your outward personality. Your lesson in self-discovery is to abandon that which is perceived to be expected from you. You may often feel that you need to adopt a persona, or to take actions which rub against your grain. You may feel so driven to be present for others, that you lose yourself. We say to you: Authenticity can, and will be, achieved once you realize that your love is enough. Your love for yourself will accelerate your love toward all else. This will feel foreign to you, as you have sacrificed yourself so many times. You need not create certain behaviors, appearances, or actions. Love will direct your way and, in turn, will direct the manner in which all others perceive you. Once you attain self-love, knowing that you are indeed a spark of the divine, there will be no expectation from yourself or others. We adorn you with the energy of Rose Quartz to help maintain unalloyed gentleness with the all.

WES / WESLEY

Bombs are not necessary. This is, of course, not literal. You may be quick to anger and set in place bombs. We honor your assertiveness and we are here to quell your aggression, as this will only hamper your soul's growth. We ask that you heed our advice and pause when you feel anger set in. We ask you to wait, process, and choose a different approach. We ask you to pause and remember that we are helping you to be direct, yet not aggressive, and to be firm, yet not harmful in your actions. We are on constant call to help you choose the appropriate response, yet only if you choose to allow us to assist in calming your spirit and replacing it with an approach which will be most beneficial to all. Your soul yearns for our intervention; we are here to help you overcome what is necessary so that you can move forward with your self-actualization. Your gift of demonstrating peaceful means of resolution will surface, and this will fulfill your purpose.

WHITNEY

Clothe yourself with kindness, for that is what you are. Discard any garb which is unsuitable to your calling. Do not adorn yourself with worldly threads. Don yourself instead with the uniforms of service ... each costume unique ... to clothe the same freely-giving spirit. We treasure you for this unconditional and spontaneous, loving, giving spirit. You are the embodiment of all these, which you chose just before arriving here. You almost chose to come here as a taker ... a hedonist ... instead you made the decision to serve in this glorious way, which is your purpose.

We must add that there is another message for another set of Whitneys--those who are the can-doers. These Whitney's are never tiring, and others look to them for their confidence in "getting the job done." We ask you to heed our words of caution: Some will interpret you as a stubborn know-it-all, too independent and unrelenting in your stance. We advise you to ease up and allow others to *do it themselves*, as you could possibly thwart their own independence. Your purpose is to teach confidence through your own example.

WILL / WILLIAM

Startling you are at times, our bold one. When others fear taking a stand, you hesitate not. And you have the propensity to do so in unconventional ways ... breaking protocol and political correctness. You are needed for your startling mannerisms when the standard is being accepted, yet change is required for the good of all concerned. So, continue to be the one to upset the proverbial apple cart when it is necessary. We have your back. Your purpose, then, is to illustrate courage to speak one's truth, especially when it comes to recognizing the need for change. Your lesson is to *know* when the change is truly necessary to benefit the all.

WYATT

Do tell, our one who keeps so much close to the vest. Do tell. Among your purposes during this lifetime on the Earth plane is *to tell*. Tell about your experiences. Not all who hear will learn from the wisdom you have gleaned, or appreciate the energy you expended to that end. Tell about your feelings, with discretion of course. Strength comes from, and is exhibited by, the ability to share your thoughts and respond accordingly. You already possess the gift of discernment; therefore, you will know with whom to communicate, and when. By doing these things, you will rescue many from brutal lessons through circumstances that they would have not been able to withstand. Those who are meant to hear you *tell* will be sent; you will not need to seek them out. As we said, your discernment will complete the purpose. We say to you: Refrain from being reticent. When you know it is time to tell, move forward with no doubt. We do not want you to miss sharing with those who need to hear.

XAVIER

You are as a solid wooden house, giving shelter and warmth to all who enter your space. Those in your presence feel protected and secure. We call you our Great Oak, because you stand tall with stability, yet bend with winds of change without your strength being compromised. We strengthen you when needed and provide you with knowledge to share. Your purpose is met through your natural support for others as well as for yourself. And of course, you have support from us always.

XANDER

"Come 'round, everyone; hear what he has to tell." We see you as a great messenger of wisdom through parables, which is your purpose. You are humble enough as a student of life on Earth to also be a pillar among teachers. You are sought out when sound advice is deemed necessary; you are also a source of laughter, and insightful thinking to any age group. You are guided by Archangel Gabriel for this journey when you are commissioned to impart truth through allegories and analogies. We say to you: Do not doubt the wisdom and direction provided to you. Your lesson is to realize you arrived here with this calling, and to relax into it. Once you do, you will lose all doubt and easily, without effort, accomplish your mission.

XANDRA

"Come 'round, everyone; hear what she has to tell." We see you as a great messenger of wisdom through parables, which is your purpose. You are humble enough as a student of life on Earth to also be a pillar among teachers. You are sought out when sound advice is deemed necessary; you are also a source of laughter, and insightful thinking to any age group. You are guided by Archangel Gabriel for this journey when you are commissioned to impart truth through allegories and analogies. We say to you: Do not doubt the wisdom and direction provided to you. Your lesson is to realize you arrived here with this calling, and to relax into it. Once you do, you will lose all doubt and easily, without effort, accomplish your mission.

XANNA

Xanna, we call you our Willow because of your graceful resilience. You exude delicate strength, bending to compromise and to diplomatically meet with powerful forces. You have the wisdom to walk beside adversity with tolerance until it moves on. You weep not because of this wisdom. We hydrate you with the water from our angelic realm. Holy water? You could call it that. We stream a constant flow of cleansing, refreshing energy to nourish, nurture—and even rebuild—should powerful gales result in any damage. Your lesson is to acknowledge your delicate strength and resiliency while serving your purpose of being an example of the positive outcomes of flexibility.

XENA

Time after time. The wheels continue to turn despite the bumps, the nails, and potholes. Your lesson is to develop the knowing that, time after time, you will travel forward. You will fulfill your purpose time after time ... of teaching the art of acceptance blended with persistence. We stroke your forehead with comfort and pat your back with encouragement when you most need it. Your time is precious, and we will give you enough.

YANCY

Clear all the decks, Yancy. It gets too crowded. Too many interests dilute your richness. Clear the decks and give your attention to a few. You will know which one or which ones to devote your loyalty. They are the interests that are not merely interests; they are the ones that fire such a passion that you cannot clear them from any decks. Let the ones go that are intriguing, yet do not ignite a fire. This goes for people in your life as well. Your striking presence makes people gravitate toward you. Crowds do not serve you well. Limit the seating at your personal stadium. Allow all to visit, and allow only a limited number of back stage passes. Those with passes are those who will share with you mutually enriching experiences. Your life lesson is to achieve clarity. We say to you: Learn what is extraneous and what is pertinent to your life's purpose. You purpose is to pass along this ability.

YOLANDA

Tether ball is not your thing. Rather you are the type to go for the gusto and to take things to the limit. All things good and all things kind are what you seek, and you amplify these values in your daily life with strangers, friends, and loved ones. We caution you to be discreet, as your powerful ways can be misinterpreted. We will assist, if you ask, in guiding you to people and situations that are open to your grand personality. We do not mean your way is imposing, boastful or larger than life. Strength and enthusiasm can also be subtle. Continue to be the part in this movie of life as the doer and motivator. You will realize your purpose in so doing.

YVES / YVETTE

Slow, rolling waves over motionless rocks create a contrast of strength … strength of flow and power of stance. The waves learn that they can continue to move despite the resolute stones. The stones learn that when a position is required to maintain balance, the movement around and over them will not adversely affect them in the present moment, yet over time will create polished beauty. Your lesson is to learn how to be the wave and how to be the stone. Bring refreshing, cleansing beauty to the undaunted. Allow yourself to view threats to your convictions as an addition of peace to what must be unwavering in the now moment. You do have an understanding that, over time, the resolute may be altered or transformed by the beauty of a natural course of change. Embrace this understanding while you are being a mainstay of peaceful existence during this lifetime. We support you with the grace of Earth angels who we send to you throughout your time here.

YVONNE / IVONNE

Dolphin energy is what we send you, our unique communicator. By this, we mean that you communicate at a higher level. Without uttering a native language, and sometimes with only gestures and nods—even with silence— you have an unworldly ability to communicate. We ask that you tune in to this gift for the benefit of all. Your purpose is to open up the lines of communication between those who are at odds with one another. Some Yvonnes/Ivonnes also can communicate with animal friends. We urge you to heed this call. You have so incredibly much to offer.

ZACHARY / ZACK

Zachary, or Zack ... we call you The Phoenix. You are the reflection of Phoenix fire, with unrelenting strength to rise above each uncontrollable and raging, ominous fire. At least, that is what they appear to be for you. The fires of life will not scar you. They may singe you; however, they will not and cannot engulf you. You are among the strongest of incarnates, as it takes immense fortitude of mind, character, body, and spirit to rise above the many flames of life which you have encountered, and are yet to encounter. Yes, as with the Phoenix, you will yourself indeed create some of these uncomfortable and threatening fires. This is your lesson: To have an unwavering, inner knowing that you can and will conquer your demons.

ZANE

Your gifts may go unnoticed, especially by you, because you often become overly focused on external events and pursuits. Studies, work, family, friends, hobbies, and other interests fully occupy your being. It is normal in this world to divide time between all of the usual activities. However, we say to you: Once you have acknowledged and focused more time on discovering your passion, your gifts will be clear to you. Your lesson is to prioritize so that your focus will be keen. Once discovered, you will have the burning desire to create the time to follow your passion, which is also your calling. You will not need the validation of being noticed, as do so many. Recognition of your gifts will come despite your ego not craving it or seeking applause. Your reward will come in the form of complete self-fulfillment through meeting your calling, your burning desire. You will then be able to fulfill your purpose of demonstrating to others the focused attention that leads to the discovery of true passion.

ZELDA

A compromising soul you are. How does this work out for you? Your lesson is to learn that compromise can benefit all involved and create a spirit of cooperation, yet can cause you to resent some of your own decisions to compromise for convenience, or to simply avoid conflict. More than this, lack of personal fulfillment may result from too much compromise, too often.

If you are young and reading this, and wish to be a dancer, inventor, writer, pilot … any number of callings … do not allow your family, who may instead want you to become an attorney, an accountant, dentist, teacher, or any other profession, steer you away from your aspirations. Remember to always keep your eye on your golden prize. Yes, YOUR prize. If you are older and reading this, and find yourself reticent to dance, sing, play, or continue to follow your bliss – your calling – remember that society is not always understanding of individual consciousness. Enjoy this life and be fulfilled. Never, no matter what age you are, allow other opinions to dampen your true spirit.

You are the meaty fruit of your *own* dreams. Learn the lesson, and be the example of avoiding too much compromise in order to please others. Allow your growth to happen, and you will enjoy a plethora, a horn of plenty, of fulfillment.

ZOE / ZOEY

An umbrella of protection from sadness is what you bring to share. When there are unhappy feelings, where there may be a depression setting in, your positive umbrella of smiles and praise will not only protect from low frequencies—it will bring a shower of bright frequencies. You most often open your umbrella without conscious awareness, yet you will become aware of your role of alleviating mental anguish with your bright bursts of encouragement. You know exactly how and where to position yourself to shield with your special umbrella. Remember to shield yourself as well, by asking us to protect you from monsoons.

Contact Lahna

Visit spiritscribe.info for information about Lahna's services, as well as venues where she offers Spirit Scribe Messages and holistic services such as Energy Readings.

Please like her Facebook pages, **Spirit Scribe** and **Chakra Station – Lahna Harris**.

Learn more about Lahna's holistic offerings of Reiki, Hypnotherapy, Past Life Regression, Guided Meditation, and Handwriting Analysis at:

LahnaHarris.com

As always, you can contact Lahna directly for individual appointments, sign up for classes, or arrange workshops.

E-mail: lahnaharris@msn.com

Phone/Text: 502.377.9776.

Appointments Online: schedule at **LahnaHarris.com**

PURCHASE BOOK

Spirit Scopes is available from Amazon - after May 23, 2019. Search for book name and author name together:
i.e. Lahna Harris Spirit Scopes.

Spirit Scopes is also available at
spiritscribe.info or LahnaHarris.com
after May 23, 2019.

Keywords: Spirit Messages, Angel Messages, Life Purpose, Body Mind Spirit, first names, First Name, Spirit Blessing

Description of Book

BISAC Category: Body, Mind & Spirit/ Angels & Spirit Guides

About the Author

Lahna began her spiritual journey as a child. She was what many call a *reluctant intuitive*. By the time she was in her teens, her intuitive experiences had increased, and she found herself receiving messages through automatic writing. She eventually 'channeled' a way to use her intuition through energy work, handwriting analysis, and hypnotherapy.

While working with clients, she began to receive messages and felt the need to share the information. Once messages were being conveyed, her gift of channeled writing became elevated, which evolved into her current work as a spiritual messenger.

With her background as a medical social worker, Lahna's empathetic approach takes her to seminars, workshops, and spiritual / holistic festivals as a guest speaker and facilitator throughout Indiana, Kentucky, and Ohio.

Lahna currently resides in Southern Indiana, where she has a holistic practice.

Invitation

Now that you have finished this book, if you would like to learn about more names, or where Lahna will be presenting at holistic fairs, please visit her facebook page, **Spirit Scribe.** On this page you are welcome to share how the message for your name, or the names of your loved ones blessed you and gave you a higher understanding about life purpose, life lessons or how the messages caused an ah-ha.

If you enjoyed this book, your review at Amazon.com is greatly appreciated. Search for "*Spirit Scopes*" or for the author, <u>Lahna Harris</u>.

Reviews are the lifeblood of books and authors and we most sincerely appreciate yours. Thank you!

If you attend an event where Lahna is scheduled to present, please bring your book. She will be happy to autograph it for you.

Formatted by

Sybil Watts

and New Soft Publishing

Publishing, Cover Design, Interior Design, Formatting, Proofreading, Websites, graphics

Provider of print and digital publishing services

to Independent Authors

newsoftpublishing.com

newsoftpublishing@gmail.com

You have Word. Allow Sybil and her

NewSoft Publishing team to

get it on the Wind for you.

www.ingramcontent.com/pod-product-compliance
Lightning Source LLC
LaVergne TN
LVHW011217080426
835509LV00005B/171